D1249639

REBUILDING
BRAND
AMERICA

REBUILDING BRAND AMERICA

What We Must Do to Restore Our Reputation and
Safeguard the Future of American Business Abroad

DICK MARTIN

ΛMACOM

AMERICAN MANAGEMENT ASSOCIATION

New York ★ Atlanta ★ Brussels ★ Chicago ★ Mexico City ★ San Francisco
Shanghai ★ Tokyo ★ Toronto ★ Washington, D.C.

658.827
M379

LIBRARY
WITHDRAWN
MILWAUKEE AREA TECHNICAL COLLEGE
Milwaukee Campus

Special discounts on bulk quantities of AMACOM books are
available to corporations, professional associations, and other
organizations. For details, contact Special Sales Department,
AMACOM, a division of American Management Association,
1601 Broadway, New York, NY 10019.
Tel: 212-903-8316. Fax: 212-903-8083.
E-mail: specialsls@amanet.org
Website: www.amacombooks.org/go/specialsales
To view all AMACOM titles go to: www.amacombooks.org

This publication is designed to provide accurate and authoritative
information in regard to the subject matter covered. It is sold with
the understanding that the publisher is not engaged in rendering
legal, accounting, or other professional service. If legal advice or
other expert assistance is required, the services of a competent
professional person should be sought.

Library of Congress Cataloging-in-Publication Data

Martin, Dick, 1946–
    Rebuilding brand America : what we must do to restore our reputation and
safeguard the future of American business abroad / Dick Martin.
        p.   cm.
    Includes bibliographical references and index.
    ISBN-10: 0–8144–7333–4 (hardcover)
    ISBN-13: 978–0–8144–7333–7 (hardcover)
    1. Brand name products—United States.   2. International economic
relations.   3. Anti-Americanism.   4. Anti-Americanism—Arab countries.
5. United States—Relations—Foreign countries.   I. Title.

HD69.B7M375   2007
658.8'27—dc22

                                                                2006026851

© 2007 Dick Martin
All rights reserved.
Printed in the United States of America.

This publication may not be reproduced,
stored in a retrieval system,
or transmitted in whole or in part,
in any form or by any means, electronic,
mechanical, photocopying, recording, or otherwise,
without the prior written permission of AMACOM,
a division of American Management Association,
1601 Broadway, New York, NY 10019.

Printing number

10   9   8   7   6   5   4   3   2   1

For my parents and my brother,
who never had the opportunities I had.

Laura Brisette Martin (1919–2003)
Lucien Henri Martin (1916–1991)
David Martin (1952–2005)

CONTENTS

INTRODUCTION:
THE ANTI-AMERICAN CENTURY

"The terrorist attacks of 11 September 2001 sharply punctuated the end of the American century. Indeed, the era we are now entering may well come to be recalled as 'the anti-American century.' "[1]
— Ivan Krastev, research director, Remarque Institute, New York University

THE WORLD, WE'RE TOLD, IS FLAT. IT'S ALSO TIPPING, AND NOT in America's favor. Pollsters tell us that United States' foreign policy—especially in the Middle East—accounts for 35 percent of anti-American feelings around the world.[2] Whether the true proportion is 35 percent or 75 percent is small comfort for U.S.-headquartered businesses, which once happily rode on America's coattails but have grown tired of recent bumps. The question businesses should be asking is how much blame they share for the balance of the ill feeling and whether they are somehow contributing to the tilt.

Those are the issues explored in this book, along with best practices in dealing with them. But first, I should make it clear that I am neither a foreign policy expert nor an economist; I spent most of my career in the worlds of advertising, public relations, and brand management. This book starts from the premise that America is a "brand," not in the sense that the name itself has commercial value (though it does), but because the *notion* of America occupies a special place in the hearts and minds of people around the world. American businesses share that space and, if it has become a bit shabby and less welcoming lately, they share responsibility for restoring it. In fact, the deterioration of Brand America is due in no small part to foreign perceptions that U.S.-based companies are so obsessed with their stock price that they will mistreat employees, mislead customers, and bend the accounting rules to wring an extra penny a share out of their financial results. Executive compensation that verges on corporate looting reinforces perceptions of America as a materialistic, narcissistic society in which the powerful exploit the weak. The reputations of U.S. companies and the country itself are so intertwined that rebuilding Brand America must be a joint undertaking of government and business. Both have a lot to learn from each other and, in the end, they will only succeed if they share the burden because they already share the same brand.

DREAMS, DAYDREAMS, AND NIGHTMARES

The notion of America is both rational and emotional. Among some people, it is a sort of daydream constructed from bits and pieces of information, some of it relatively fanciful. So many people immigrated to the United States from Italy at the turn of the twentieth century, for example, that good wishes are sometimes expressed as *trovare l'America* (literally, "find America," i.e., "find happiness").[3] On the other hand, bits of information can also lead to less pleasant fantasies, akin to wakeful nightmares. These days, you need a multilingual scorecard to keep up with the varieties of anti-Americanism. To much of the Muslim world, America is the Great Satan, irreligious and immoral. To many Europeans, it practices "savage capitalism" and takes pleasure from cultural drivel. Many South Americans denounce it for "neocolonialism" and economic oppression. In Asia, it's a unilateralist, militarist bully. In Africa, as economist Julianne Malveaux put it so neatly, America is like "the preacher who came to Sunday dinner, ate all of the bird, save the wings and the back, and wondered why everyone is glaring at [him]."[4]

Of course, there are good explanations for some of the behavior behind these perceptions. For example, what many people see as America's unilateralism grew from the vulnerability and fear that followed the attacks of September 11, 2001. And while America's intentions may be pure, as Kishore Mahbubani, the former ambassador from Singapore, notes, "The rest of the world does not 'see' American intentions."[5] What people around the world personally experience is the turbulent wake of American actions reaching from the cornfields of Kansas and the halls of Congress to the shopping stalls of Kowloon, China, and the oil fields of Kuwait.

Furthermore, with 725 military bases outside the United States, troops in 70 percent of the world's countries,[6] nearly 200 military actions since the end of World War II,[7] and live TV transmitted from the battlefields of Iraq and Afghanistan, it is no wonder that for million of people around the world, Americans are people in uniform and the country is an outsize military base. As Princeton professor Bernard Chazelle put it, "Rambo's paternity rights are hardly Hollywood's alone."[8]

Finally, muscle—even unmatched military and economic muscle—does not automatically translate into leadership. "Before other countries accepted U.S. leadership," Francis Fukuyama reminds us, "they would have to be convinced not just that America was good but that it was also wise in its application of power, and, through that wisdom, successful in achieving the ends it set for itself."[9] Sadly, on that score, America's recent history in Iraq, and on its own storm-ravaged shores in the aftermath of Hurricane Katrina, leaves much of the world questioning not only America's sincerity, but its competence.

DEFINING ANTI-AMERICANISM

Google the word "anti-American" and you'll get at least 10 million results. But what is anti-Americanism? I like Tony Judt's description: "the principled distrust and dislike of American civilization and all its manifestations."[10] Judt is a scholar at New York University who specializes in European history, and his views on anti-Americanism are unavoidably colored by that perspective. But since most people agree that Europe was the birthplace of the phenomenon, his take seems apt to me.

Anti-Americanism is not the same thing as criticism of American actions, policies, or culture. Criticism—even when it is vehement and vitriolic—stems from an honest difference of opinion and can even be constructive. Anti-Americanism, on the other hand, does not seek to correct America's mistakes, but to condemn it as an inherently evil perpetrator. It interprets every American act in the worst possible light. To an anti-American, any apparently good act by the United States or its people is suspect, and all bad acts are the norm rather than exceptions. Author Lee Harris, whose book *Civilization and Its Enemies* earned him the sobriquet "the philosopher of 9/11," brings great insight to what others have termed the product of a "clash of civilizations."[11] "It is not that America went wrong here or there; it is that it is wrong root and branch,"[12] he writes.

CAUSES OF ANTI-AMERICANISM

There are numerous theories on the causes of anti-Americanism. One is the so-called structural theory; namely, that it is the natural reaction to America's economic and military preeminence. A second school of thought holds that it is an entirely rational response to America's foreign policies, especially in the Middle East. A third theory maintains that, whether America's policies are correct or misguided, its style in implementing them is arrogant and indifferent to the legitimate concerns of others. Closely related is the idea that Americans themselves are rude, loud, and overbearing. Their collective personality, it seems, grates on the world's nerves. Finally, some people believe that anti-Americanism is really part of a larger fear of modernization, with roots stretching as far back as the Luddites, who destroyed the textile machines that threatened their jobs at the beginning of the Industrial Revolution. Others say it's not modernization that people fear, but the soul-deadening effects of the coarse materialism that America typifies. Of course, it's also possible that people in other countries are just not that into America anymore.

Whatever its source, overt anti-Americanism may wax and wane with events, but the underlying resentment is palpable and enduring. Some people act on these feelings and ideas by shunning American fast-food restaurants; others, thankfully far fewer in number, are willing to kill or die for them. Such murderous anti-Americanism requires a proportionate response, and that's what governments are for. But a show of force is counterproductive in dealing with what I will call "expressive" anti-Americanism—boycotting American products, reflexively opposing "anything American," or joining the chorus of unrestrained rhetoric from the "Down with America" canon.

ANTI-AMERICANISMS

It may be more appropriate to speak of anti-Americanism in the plural, because it is a complex blend of emotions that condense in unpredictable ways. It can be in different measure, and simultaneously, envy of America's power and wealth, anger at its real and imagined faults and offenses, contempt for its ignorance and lack of sophistication, embarrassment at one's own dependency on America, fear of one's losses, and shame for one's own shortcomings. Different strains spring from both ends of the political spectrum. From the left, it is basically anticapitalist; from the right, it is nationalistic and culturally conservative, as in the original meaning of being "anti-change." In Germany, for example, the expression *Amerikanische Verhaltnisse*—"American conditions"—is a derisive term, referring to the inhumanity of American capitalism. In France, *Américain* is an insult that political opponents toss at each other.

A SPECIAL CASE

Anti-Americanism in the Muslim world seems to be in a category of its own. The French can be charmingly eccentric and irritating, but Muslim anti-Americanism comes off as a hatred that can be scary. Indeed, it exploded violently on American soil in the attacks on the World Trade Center and the Pentagon. Furthermore, Muslim anti-Americanism is not limited to a few fanatics. Attitudes toward the United States in the Middle East have consistently been the most negative in the world. That should not be too surprising: America is at war there; from an Arab perspective, the United States is on the wrong side of the Palestinian-Israeli conflict; and American values seem to be the antithesis of Islam's, the region's majority religion. To many, the situation seems practically hopeless.

For all these reasons, this book pays special attention to the Islamic world, particularly in the Arab states. But it is wrong to assume that anti-Americanism stems solely, or even primarily, from that region. Nor is it the result of a unique set of religious and political circumstances, unlikely to be repeated elsewhere. As we shall see, it has taken root practically worldwide. And American businesses play a role both in its causes and possible solution.

RESPONSE TO ANTI-AMERICANISM

Popular debate in the United States has focused on whether the appropriate solution to what has been termed "America's image problem" is one of better information dissemination or the more substantive challenge of adjusting policies. The Bush administration's view is that it is the former. Its answer is to do a better job of explaining what America stands for. In practical terms, that has resulted in an approach not unlike the one most Americans use when confronted with someone who speaks no English: Speak more slowly and loudly, use lots of broad gestures, and add a vowel to the end of important words.

But the challenge for America, and American business, isn't pumping out more information, packaging it more seductively, or changing policy to win a hypothetical popularity contest. The real issue is understanding. Not primarily *others'* understanding of America, but America's understanding of them.

No country can afford to sacrifice the safety and security of its people to quiet its critics. But it can't achieve true security either, unless it understands how its actions are perceived by others and how others perceive their own interest. America will not be truly secure until the people of other nations believe it is using its power to serve their interests as well as its own, or at least taking their interests into account. Every poll suggests that is far from the case. But it doesn't have to be that way. Joseph Nye, former diplomat and dean of the Kennedy School of Government at Harvard University, reminds us: "The United States was even more preeminent at the end of World War II than it is today, but we pursued policies that were acclaimed by Allied countries. It matters if the big kid on the block is seen by the others as a friend or as a bully."[13] There is still plenty America can do, even while ensuring its own security, to demonstrate that it is a friend to the rest of the world.

America's response to the 2005 East Asian tsunami, for example, improved its standing in the region. According to a poll commissioned by an organization called Terror Free Tomorrow thirty days following the tsunami, 65 percent of Indonesians had a positive opinion of the United States because of the American response. And the highest percentage was among people under age 30. In fact, their opinion of America's efforts to fight terrorism was about evenly split (40 percent in favor to 36 percent opposed). "In a stunning turnaround of public opinion, support for Osama bin Laden and terrorism in Indonesia has dropped significantly," according to the group, "while favorable views of the United States have increased." For the first time ever in a Muslim nation since 9/11, support for Osama bin Laden dropped significantly, from 58 percent favorable to just 23 percent.[14] The images of U.S. military helicopters delivering relief from American businesses to refugees did more to improve America's reputation than any number of feel-good TV commercials could.

SURVEY CENTRAL

In studying anti-Americanism, I was reminded at every turn how exceedingly complex the issue is, how full of contradictions and prone to easy generalizations. I also discovered that anti-Americanism has become a publicity boon for numerous polling firms and other commercial interests. Fielding a poll designed to generate provocative results is a tried-and-true formula for generating publicity. The introduction of online polling makes the exercise relatively quick and inexpensive, if of sometimes dubious validity. I was struck by how many newspaper articles quoted breathless survey results from firms I had never heard of before and have not heard of since.

As a general rule, most surveys should be taken with a grain of salt. Finding a truly random sample of sufficient size to be statistically valid is increasingly difficult in an era of "do not call" lists and telemarketing wearout. Even the most statistically rigorous surveys are only a rough approximation of what is on people's minds. The way a question is asked, the order in which it's asked, and the general news of the day all influence the way people answer surveys. Multicountry surveys raise questions of language and interpretation. Further, there is usually a significant lag between fielding a survey and publishing its results. Time moves on and attitudes move with it. Surveys only accrue real validity if they produce consistent results over long periods of time.

Survey results can also be colored by factors beyond anyone's control. Often, people don't have a well-formed opinion on a survey's specific questions until the moment they're asked, so the opinion they manufacture in that instance may simply "average" their feelings about a related subject that is more salient to them. For example, a citizen of Yemen may have very few opinions about American consumer products. But when asked if he would buy them given the chance, he develops an instant answer based on his feelings and thoughts regarding the most closely related topic on which he does have strong feelings, say the Israeli-Palestinian conflict. Unconsciously, his mind ticks off a succession of thoughts: "American consumer products . . . America . . . America's friend, Israel . . . Israel, enemy of Palestine . . . Palestine, my fellow Arab country, abused by Israel, America's friend . . ." And as a result, he concludes, "No, I wouldn't buy American consumer products if they were free."

Other people have very strong opinions on many subjects, but these opinions aren't necessarily the result of their own careful analysis and deliberation. Many people regularly bathe in streams of elite opinion—whether political, religious, or cultural—that were selected in the first place because they generally conform to their own basic predispositions. While they don't consciously ask, "What would Bill O'Reilly think about this?" or "What would Maureen Dowd say?" their survey responses often reflect what the elite of their camp are saying.

None of this is meant to undermine the validity of surveys, but to inject an element of caution into their interpretation. Because surveys produce numbers bracketed by a "statistical margin of error," many people give them the same weight as a trusted thermometer. But the touted "margin of error" itself is not 100 percent accurate; in fact, the pollster's confidence in its accuracy is usually qualified somewhere in the footnotes (e.g., "subject to a margin of error of plus or minus three points at a confidence level of 95 percent"). And the margin of error itself can change when applied to subsets of the total survey sample.

I raise these issues because this book necessarily builds on the results of some fairly extensive surveys. For the most part, I have used data from reputable organizations with no obvious axe to grind, long years of research experience, and several waves of generally consistent results. The Pew Research Center and the World Values Survey not only have considerable experience in global markets, but they are generally open about their methods, making their questionnaires available, for example. Zogby International, which does extensive polling in the Middle East, is a special case described in Chapter Four. Most of the other data, including the statistic used at the start of this book—that "U.S. foreign policy accounts for 35 percent of anti-Americanism"—should be considered directionally correct at best.

Whenever possible, I have tried to use data that seem to be confirmed across two or more sources and are consistent with long-term trends. Even then, a sharp-eyed reader will undoubtedly find some apparent inconsistencies or an aberrant statistic or two. And in dealing with polling data, trends and relative positions are usually more telling than a specific numerical score read in isolation. With all that said, the rise of anti-Americanism around the world is nonetheless undeniable and troubling. On that assertion, at least, our statistical data pass the most rigorous red-face test.

RECOVERING AMERICA'S MOJO

When *The Economist* magazine polled its readers at the end of 2005 for its special edition on what to expect in 2006, more than half (53 percent) said that America's reputation abroad would deteriorate further. That was an even higher percentage than when the question was asked previously in October 2004, just before the U.S. presidential elections. And a Pew Research Center survey in mid-2006 confirmed *The Economist*'s pessimism. Clearly, America has lost its mojo.[15] But recovering it doesn't depend on extinguishing the last vestiges of anti-Americanism.

As Walter Russell Mean of the Council on Foreign Relations cautions: "The challenge is not to end anti-Americanism; only the collapse of American power could accomplish that task. Today, the task is to manage pragmatically the resentments, irritations, and real grievances that inevitably accompany the rise to power of one nation, one culture, and one social model in a complex, divided, and passionate world."[16] This book hopes to help American business people understand the basis of those resentments and ill-feelings and, at minimum, avoid exacerbating them.

This book is not primarily a prescription for government action, though much is needed, and American businesses acting in concert can probably do more to move Washington along than all the earnest think-tanks that have addressed the issue. At last count, more than twenty-nine different organizations of all political persuasions have weighed in. While some of their recommendations tend to cancel each other out, there is general consensus that the government has to greatly expand its efforts to win the hearts and minds of the world's people, communicating with them directly rather than solely through their governments.

In government circles, such an effort is called "public diplomacy," a term coined in the 1960s by Edmund Gullion, a career diplomat and subsequently dean of the Fletcher School of Law and Diplomacy at Tufts University.[17]

THE ROLE OF BUSINESS

This book is directed to business people, but it is not a twelve-step program for unreconstructed imperialists. It's not an etiquette guide, either—although I have plenty of material on the subject of business etiquette. I've traveled with many American business people who spent most of their time in the most exotic settings complaining that every-thing wasn't the same as "back home." I once stood in line at a duty-free shop in Quito, Ecuador, cringing as the American woman ahead of me loudly complained that the clerk had given her change in "for-eign coins." On the way into the country, she had probably asked how much the taxi ride to her hotel would cost in "real money." And I once spent an uncomfortable evening trying to keep a British CEO, who had arranged a private tour of a world-class porcelain collection, from hearing the disparaging comments my boss was making about "all the crockery."

There are excellent guides to doing business in other countries with-out offending people. An organization called Business for Diplomatic Action has published a guide full of useful advice and cautions for business people traveling abroad. For instance, in Japan, it's consid-ered rude to look directly into someone's eyes for more than a few seconds, and in some countries casual dress is interpreted as showing a lack of respect. It also pinpoints American mannerisms—a loud voice and hurried movements or gestures—that can be perceived as boast-fulness or arrogance. (More information is available online at www .worldcitizenguide.org/index2.html.) Anyone interested in delving even further into the cultural differences that can influence global busi-ness—ranging from manners and mannerisms to different concepts of time—should get a copy of Michael Goodman's *Work with Anyone Anywhere*, a practical guide to navigating cultural borders.

But something more than Miss Manners on steroids seems called for here. Americans hardly have a monopoly on rudeness, and, even if they bend the curves on that score, those transgressions can't solely account for the depth of antipathy toward the United States around the world. Anti-Americanism may be one of the most serious challenges facing U.S. businesses in the twenty-first century, all the more so because its effects have been so insidious. I don't pretend to have laid out all the answers in this book. Rather, I have tried to identify the key questions that thoughtful business people should ask themselves. Every business will come up with its own answers appropriate to its history and current circumstances. My goal in this book has been to lay bare both the roots and the fruits of anti-Americanism to stimulate a dialogue on how to halt its growth and ultimately eradicate it. I have no illusions that this mission will be easy. One of my neighbors allowed a stand of knotweed to take seed in his yard. Every summer it invades my patio. I have doused it liberally with herbicides and pulled it out by hand, following its roots into adjoining yards. Nothing has worked. Anti-Americanism may be the knotweed of global commerce. Cutting it back only encourages more growth. There's no magic potion for stopping it. But it's neither invincible nor inevitable.

NOT A "PR" PROBLEM

While anti-Americanism is orders of magnitude more complicated and intractable than typical business problems, it will yield to analysis and concerted action. This book offers thoughts on both and is roughly structured in three parts. The first section of the book reviews the now-familiar, if eye-glazing, numbers that describe the sad condition of America's reputation on the world stage. While only a few of the survey results will be new to anyone who regularly reads a daily newspaper, seeing them all in one place can still be jarring. The next section dives under the numbers to explore some of the historical, sociological, and even psychological factors that account for their depressingly low levels. The final section builds on this analysis by drawing some recommendations from the best practices of leading global companies, as well as from the collective wisdom of the foreign affairs specialists who have studied the issue.

Among my foundation beliefs, however, is a rejection of the position taken by some very smart people that the answer to the problem of anti-Americanism lies not in the realm of public relations. If by "public relations" they mean "publicity" or a hectoring rebuttal of criticism, I am in absolute agreement, just as I believe advertising is the wrong lever to pull in the early days of repairing a reputation. But, to me, public relations involves more than generating ink. PR has less to do with what an organization says than with what it *does*. PR's core role is to bring an organization's policies and practices into harmony with the needs and expectations of its "publics." Sometimes that means trying to convince those publics that an organization is acting in their interests. Often, it means modifying the organization's actions to reflect the public's needs and reasonable expectations.

AMERICA'S PUBLICS

In the nineteenth century, America could afford to ignore the public outside its borders. But in the twenty-first century, it has lost that luxury. America's greatest challenges are global in nature and require coordinated global responses. For the moment, America is powerful enough to go its own way if it can't jolly or bully others into line. But the list of problems that will yield to unilateral action is getting shorter even more rapidly than the cost of going it alone is rising. The idea that America has "publics" outside its own borders, whose needs, interests, and expectations it should take into account, may be too novel for some, but it is at the heart of this book.

I don't believe I have any other preconceptions or biases, though I am admittedly a white, practicing Roman Catholic who usually votes for Democrats and is in his sixth decade. My parents were children of the Great Depression and never finished eighth grade. For most of their lives they were what we call "the working poor." I was the first member of my family to graduate from college. And I spent more than half my life working for a company—AT&T—that was the pride of the capitalist system for more than a century. My personal success within that economic system undoubtedly colored my perceptions of its strengths, weaknesses, and ultimate fairness. But most of all, I love America.

In many ways, I have realized the American Dream. This book is written with the conviction that people around the world share the same dream of personal opportunity. I believe the secret of rebuilding Brand America is to reconnect to that dream in a way that is meaningful to all Americans as well as to the people of the world. That dream is the real source of America's fabled mojo. And that's what this book is about.

PART ONE

CHAPTER 1

TILTING AT WINDMILLS

"If the United States doesn't act forcefully and intelligently to define itself in the post-9/11 world, our enemies and detractors across the globe will gladly do it for us. U.S. corporations have a responsibility to leverage their enormous reach and influence to improve the overall reputation of our country."[1]

—Keith Reinhard, president,
Business for Diplomatic Action, and chairman emeritus,
DDB Worldwide Communications

DESPITE HIS FASHIONABLY CLOSE-CROPPED HAIRCUT, DESIGNER eyeglass frames, and black-on-black tailored clothing, Keith Reinhard's pulse beats to the easy rhythms of the Midwestern states where he was brought up and lived until the mid-1980s. Those homely sensibilities have made him a wealthy man.

Reinhard is an ad man, a legendary creative director and chairman emeritus of one of the world's leading agency networks, but he learned his craft on Madison Avenue side streets that pass through the small farm communities of Indiana and Illinois. That's where he began his career, albeit on the edges of advertising. His story is uniquely American.

For Reinhard, the attacks of September 11, 2001, were personal. Much of the destruction occurred less than five miles from his office on Madison Avenue behind Saint Patrick's cathedral. When he went into the street he could smell the smoke and feel the ash from the collapsed World Trade Center buildings. He could hear the sirens of emergency vehicles screaming south, and he saw the stream of blackened survivors moving north through the heart of midtown Manhattan.

Like everyone else in New York and the country, Reinhard was shaken by the attacks. But what scared him most—what made him angry—was knowing that the terrorists weren't trying to bring down some buildings. They were attacking a way of life that had been very good to him and to millions of people like him. It was personal.

ONLY IN AMERICA

Reinhard's father died when he was four years old, and he was raised by his young mother in a tight-knit Mennonite community in Indiana. When he was a teenager, she got him a part-time job as a stock boy in the grocery store where she was a clerk. One of the job's perks was that he got to take home all the posters and displays that wouldn't fit into the store's cramped aisles. He says Betty Crocker was his first pinup. For a kid brought up without movies, which the Mennonites frowned on, those posters were like being plugged into a new world. He was captivated by their energy and excitement and imagined himself designing his own displays.

After high school, Reinhard didn't have the money to attend college, but he convinced his mother to let him take an art correspondence course he had seen in the back pages of *Popular Mechanics* magazine. "Can You Draw Me?" the ad asked, next to the profile of a young woman, and Reinhard—who had studied every line in Betty Crocker's face—knew he could. The correspondence school quickly agreed and accepted his $600.

When he read Book Four, on advertising layouts, everything fell into place. He convinced some buddies to drive to New York City in a 1929 Model A pickup nicknamed "Asthma," because its engine wheezed so much. A state trooper pulled the truck over on the New Jersey Turnpike for failing to maintain the minimum speed. Kicked off the highway, Reinhard and his friends wound their way through the gritty industrial belt between the turnpike and the Hudson River. By the time they had surfaced on the other side of the Lincoln Tunnel in New York City, Reinhard's friends were ready to go home, but he knew that his future was somewhere in those tall buildings.

New York was the advertising center of the country at that time, but for someone without a college degree and no relevant experience, it might as well have been the surface of the moon. Reinhard returned to Indiana, but he couldn't get an advertising job back home either, so he spent ten years on the fringes of the industry, working for photographers, designers, and film production companies. He finally landed a job at a small promotional agency in Bloomington, Illinois, whose main client was State Farm Insurance, which was headquartered there. Reinhard designed brochures and staged the insurance company's sales meetings. A slide show he produced for an agent convention attracted the attention of the far bigger Chicago agency that handled State Farm's national advertising, and in 1964 he was invited to move to the Windy City.

Ignoring his correspondence school art diploma, the agency made him a copywriter. By then he was nearly thirty years old, Reinhard says, and "the oldest beginning copywriter in the agency's history."[2] But his big break didn't come until another Midwestern company, McDonald's, started shopping for an ad agency in 1970. While others dreamed up new ways to pitch burgers, Reinhard realized that what was between the buns didn't matter nearly as much as what eating at McDonald's implied about the mom who brought her kids there.

In those days, good moms put fast food in the same category as frozen TV dinners. Reinhard realized they needed "permission" to pass under the Golden Arches. The result was an iconic ad campaign— "You deserve a break today"—that fueled McDonald's expansion for nearly a decade.

It wasn't a fluke. *The Economist* magazine once noted that "Reinhard's talent has been to find and promote the hitherto unknown virtues of products."[3] For example, he also realized that having a friendly insurance agent nearby was more important to people than saving a few dollars on their policy. Then he teamed with a young composer named Barry Manilow to remind people that "like a good neighbor, State Farm is there." Manilow has had bigger hits, but few have been as long-running. Reinhard's career was built on a talent for sensing what really motivates people, even before they realize it themselves.

Reinhard's success was more than the magic touch of a copywriting muse. He's also a doggedly tenacious man. For example, he never really accepted it when McDonald's abruptly switched agencies a decade later (as most big advertisers eventually do). But instead of complaining, he bombarded McDonald's advertising department with unsolicited campaign ideas, ads, and promotions, some in Spanish. It took fifteen years, but Reinhard ultimately won back the business.

By 1984, Reinhard was the ad agency's CEO, and within two years he merged it with two New York–based agencies to create Omnicom, one of the world's largest ad groups. The kid from Indiana who couldn't get past the receptionists on Madison Avenue moved to Manhattan to take over the agency founded by the legendary Bill Bernbach, acknowledged as the single most influential creative force in the history of advertising.

That someone with that background could become CEO of one of the world's biggest ad agency networks could only happen in America. No one cared about his family pedigree. Talent and stubborn persistence got him in the door; a succession of good bosses gave him room to take risks and helped him pick up the pieces when they didn't work out. He ended up running the company. Where else could that happen?

SEPTEMBER 11, 2001

When Reinhard settled in to his den to watch President George W. Bush's first news conference, thirty days following the September 11 attacks on the World Trade Center and the Pentagon, he had lived in Manhattan for fifteen years. He had not lost his feel for the wants and worries of ordinary people. He prided himself on keeping up with popular culture and could sometimes even recognize the hip-hop/rap leaking out of the office messenger's iPod earbuds. As a business leader in one of the world's leading economic centers and as an employer with hundreds of foreign offices in ninety-six countries, his passport was well worn. He kept up with international affairs and was on dozens of business and charitable committees. But the attacks baffled him, almost as much as they horrified him.

So when President Bush posed a question near the end of the news conference, Reinhard's ears perked up.

"I'll ask myself a question," the president said. "How do I respond when I see that in some Islamic countries there is vitriolic hatred for America?"

"I'll tell you how I respond," he said. "I'm amazed. I just can't believe it, because I know how good we are. And we've got to do a better job of making our case."[4]

A BRIEF BY ROBERT BURNS

Reinhard was sixty-six years old at that point, rich, successful, and famous. But if he had learned anything in advertising, it was that the product isn't king, the customer is. What he thought of America didn't matter nearly as much as how others perceived it. So when he got into his office the next morning, he asked his strategic planning vice president to send an e-mail off to the agency's offices in seventeen countries, asking them to poll their own employees for their attitudes toward American businesses. "Their brief was a quote from Robert Burns," he later said. "O would that God the gift might give us, to see ourselves as others see us."[5]

It wasn't exactly a scientific survey, and to be honest, Reinhard didn't think he was polling a very tough audience. These were advertising people like himself. Many of them had already sent heartfelt e-mail messages to him immediately following September 11. Their spontaneous outpouring expressed the same overwhelming sadness and outrage he and his colleagues in New York had felt. But it was a place to start while he read everything he could find on anti-Americanism.

The first replies suggested his employees outside the United States shared some common gripes about America that had never bubbled to the surface in any of his foreign office visits. It was as if they were all saying, "Well, now that you ask, we really aren't keen that Americans' ignorance of other cultures is exceeded only by arrogance about their own."

The French, for example, viewed Americans as obsessed with money, ignorant of history, and uninterested in the finer things in life such as art and culture. Germans detected an American tendency to tackle problems head-on in a narrow, single-minded way that didn't allow for alternatives. Employees in Central Europe considered Americans fairly provincial compared to the standard in their own countries, where foreign language study and travel are the norm.

Australians were bemused that Americans seemed to think they all lived in the outback and wrestled crocodiles. Chinese employees resented the bullying, overt aggressiveness, and insensitivity that characterized America's government, people, and companies. The Japanese were particularly offended by Americans' tendency to assume that, physical appearances aside, the two countries' people are identical. Worse, Americans assume that in those few areas where Asians do differ from Americans, they're all like each other.

Employees in the Middle East liked the quality and style of American brands, but they were simultaneously repelled by the materialism and loose morals associated with them. Inanimate American objects were more welcome, they said, than American businesses, tourists, or culture. Send us your iPods, but leave the country-western music at home.

Even the British, who share a common heritage and language with many Americans, felt a mixture of resentment, contempt, and snobbery toward the United States. They saw U.S. culture as materially excessive, unsophisticated, and even braggadocio. To them, Americans are overpaid, overfed, and oversexed.

There were local nuances in the responses, of course, and they were not uniformly negative. The respondents admired American creativity, diversity, can-do spirit (even if it is a bit naïve), and wealth (even if it sometimes comes off as benevolence). But what ran through the comments overall was an image of American businesses as bullies—big, boorish, arrogant, clumsy, and destructive. Reinhard remembers thinking, "Just when American brands have an expanding presence in the everyday lives of people outside the United States, they give off ominous vibes just by showing up." What particularly struck him was that few of the comments had anything to do with the government of the United States. (The survey was done before the invasion of Afghanistan and long before the Iraq War.) The comments in this first survey primarily reflected a reaction to the international expansion of American businesses.

CULTURAL IMPERIALISM

The picture that had emerged showed U.S. businesses behaving like "the worst cliché of the American tourist," Reinhard later said. "They arrive, complain about the food and accommodations, park their RV in the middle of a revered site, and then decide to redecorate it to look just like home."

Of course, Reinhard and his team knew that no successful American company would consciously rub its customers the wrong way. And for every inadvertent offense, they probably committed dozens of quiet acts of neighborliness. The problem is that American brands carry more symbolic power than those of practically any other country, so every act is magnified. And every positive American brand attribute has a darker side. For example, American "modernity" can be seen as disrespectful of older, more mature cultures and heritages. Individualism and opportunity can be interpreted as selfishness and opportunism.

For a while, Reinhard summed up the problem as "cultural imperialism," and he thought companies could deal with it through a careful and candid examination of conscience. Might potential customers consider you exploitive? Figure out how the local community benefits from your company's presence. Worried about being seen as a corrupting influence? Examine your brands and actions as seen through a screen of different cultural values—for instance, local religious doctrine, gender roles, family structure, child-rearing practices, social class distinctions, and modes of dress. Concerned about appearing arrogant? Make sure everyone involved in your global expansion understands how your local customers differ from those in the United States with respect to your product category and brand.

Borrowing from the tenets of psychology, Reinhard's team suggested the task for U.S. companies was to unbalance the positive and negative attributes associated with Brand America. Instead of arguing with the negatives, emphasize the positives and make them relevant to your customers' local situation. Most important, U.S. companies need to demonstrate through concrete actions that they are not just passing through to peddle their wares, but are committed to the local markets.

TAKING HIS CASE ON THE ROAD

By January 2002, Reinhard had the results of his informal survey and his deep dive into the literature on anti-Americanism reduced to a "thought paper" entitled "America and Cultural Imperialism: A Small Step Toward Understanding." He took it to the World Economic Forum being held in New York that year. He gave copies to the CEOs he met there and mailed it to clients. He even produced a two-and-a-half minute video of the most incendiary comments and screened it for 100 average citizens in each of nine U.S. cities.

The video stimulated an angry reaction, as he expected, but not much else. One in four viewers said "Who cares?" or worse. "These other countries are chicken crap," one annoyed respondent offered. "Let them say what they want. Who needs them?"

Surely, American business leaders would not be so naïve. "This has deep implications for any American company's global expansion plans," he argued to the CEOs who would see him. "Shouldn't business people be mobilized to address the problem?" He later said, "I thought if I presented [anti-Americanism] as a business problem, it wouldn't be shunted to the vice president of being nice." He was wrong.

Half the business leaders he briefed agreed it was a problem, but not theirs. They were doing just fine thanks. The other half agreed it was a problem, but it was an old story going back as far as the nineteenth century and the writings of Alexis de Tocqueville. It came with the territory. The Bush administration had already anointed its own advertising and brand guru and was approaching the problem with its characteristic message focus and impatience with outside distractions. The Council on Foreign Relations was pulling together its own plan to address anti-Americanism through a program of reinvigorated public diplomacy and didn't want anything competing with it.

Then came the Iraq War, which stimulated an even more rabid strain of anti-Americanism, and even then most business leaders simply adjusted their blinders. The problem is "situational" they said. It will go away when the Iraq War (which, after all, had been advertised as a walk in the park) goes away. Besides, no one wanted to risk being perceived as anti-Bush in the middle of a war and on the cusp of an election.

A MIDWESTERN DON QUIXOTE

Showing the same determination that eventually opened the door to his first job in advertising, Reinhard persisted. He testified before Congress. He traveled indefatigably, armed with PowerPoint slides and focus group videotapes. Visitors to his office received a presentation punctuated with slides showing America's favorability ratings on a timescale and sliding downward. Everyone who came to discuss the subject with him left with a thick folder of press clippings and speech reprints.

Perhaps surprisingly, considering his background, Reinhard doesn't believe advertising can correct the problem. A World Citizen Guide he created to clue college students into the etiquette of foreign travel is the closest he's come to producing advertising on this issue. "Our strong feeling is that while communications can play an important part in sensitizing U.S. citizens to the worsening problem of anti-Americanism," he said, "it is actions, not ads, that will provide the answer in the end."

Reinhard's consistent (some would say persistent) focus on substance has even won over some of the skeptics who initially thought he was muddying the waters. Leading thought leaders, including the Council on Foreign Relations, the National Committee on American Foreign Policy, the United Nations Business Council, and the Public Diplomacy Council, have embraced his efforts. In January 2004, he formed a nonpartisan, not-for-profit organization—Business for Diplomatic Action—to further study the issue and to mobilize business leaders to do something about it. The board of directors included leading academic and marketing people, including the head of communications for McDonald's. But at the end of 2005, he still had not persuaded a single sitting CEO of a major U.S. corporation to join the board.

Companies with no significant presence outside the United States don't see a problem. Those that have international interests don't consider themselves "American," but "global."

And frankly, to some, Reinhard seemed like a Midwestern Don Quixote, tilting at windmills. Unfortunately, those windmills really are turning. And the currents flowing from them threaten to muss more than a few salon-styled haircuts.

CHAPTER 2

THE QUEEN OF BRANDING

"How can a man in a cave outcommunicate the world's leading communications society?"[1]
—Richard Holbrooke, U.N. ambassador during the Clinton administration

"How is it that the country that invented Hollywood and Madison Avenue has such trouble promoting a positive image of itself overseas?"[2]
—Henry Hyde, congressman (R-IL)

KEITH REINHARD, IN FACT, HAD BEEN A LITTLE SLOW ON THE UP-take. President George W. Bush had asked the same question—why do they hate us?—several weeks earlier when he addressed Congress in the immediate aftermath of 9/11. It also came up in even blunter terms at numerous White House meetings. The answer was always the same, too: We have to do a better job of telling our story.

In any large organization, once the guy at the top makes his wishes known, people two or three levels down fall all over themselves finding ways to show that they "get it." Often, their advice has the practical effect of settling scores, expanding their turf, or funding their favorite project. And so it was in the Bush administration in the days following 9/11. The bureaucracy churned with new initiatives. And political appointees went into campaign mode, hewing to the message of the day, which in the run-up to the war in Afghanistan and through the first months of the war in Iraq, was that "we are not at war with Islam." Unfortunately, by declaring "war" on terrorism, the Bush administration positioned the struggle with Al Qaeda as a military conflict, best managed by the Pentagon. The purpose of public diplomacy from that point forward was to legitimize whatever action the military would take on the ground. But fighting terrorism—and rebuilding Brand America—is primarily a political and ethical challenge, not one of arms and rhetoric. The task at hand was to isolate the terrorists within their own community by claiming the high moral ground and addressing their supporters' legitimate grievances.

THE INFORMATION WAR

To its credit, the Bush administration learned from earlier conflicts. For example, in the early days of NATO operations in Kosovo in 1999, the Clinton administration was frequently caught flat-footed when time zone differences made it nearly impossible to respond quickly to developments on the ground. So, the White House created Coalition Information Centers in Washington, D.C., London, and Islamabad, Pakistan. The Washington center was set up in grand style in the Indian Treaty Room of the Old Executive Office Building. Complete with flat-screen monitors and clocks showing the time in every war zone, it looked like mission control for the information war. But the real action was in the other two centers, which were staffed with Arabic-speaking public affairs officers who could respond to events as they happened rather than waiting for business hours in Washington.

The Department of Defense created an Office of Strategic Influence to serve as the focal point for the Pentagon's "strategic information campaign in support of the war on terrorism." It "was to develop a full-spectrum influence strategy that would result in greater foreign support of U.S. goals and repudiation of terrorists and their methods."[3]

When word leaked that the new office would even plant "disinformation" (i.e., "lies") in foreign media, career government public affairs officials expressed alarm that it would undermine their credibility. Negative stories about the effort, both in the United States and abroad, convinced Secretary of Defense Donald Rumsfeld to cut his losses. As the often-cantankerous Rumsfeld later recalled, "I went down [to the press briefing] and said, 'Fine, if you want to savage this thing, fine— I'll give you the corpse. There's the name. You can have the name, but

I'm gonna keep doing every single thing that needs to be done.' And I have."[4]

One of the things that "needed to be done" was to significantly increase the Defense Department's psychological warfare capabilities. The Defense Department retained political communications consultants and assigned them to tasks ranging from translating Arab media reports and analyzing their content to setting up media centers in war zones and placing stories in Arab media.

But some of the work on the ground was amateurish at best. For example, according to *Foreign Affairs* magazine, "U.S. psy-ops (psychological operations) radio messages to Afghans—broadcast over Afghan airwaves from transmitters on converted ec-130 aircraft—sounded like the Cold War rhetoric of a 1950s-era comic book."[5] The Pentagon did not pretend that it was bound by the same standards as the Voice of America. "We have no requirements to adhere to journalistic principles of objectivity," an Army psychological operations specialist told *The New York Times*. "We tell the U.S. side of the story to approved targeted audiences" using truthful information.[6] But while the information might be "truthful," it was clearly one-sided, decidedly upbeat, and didn't necessarily reflect all the relevant facts.

Bad news and setbacks, for example, were seldom mentioned. And if a story's literal facts were true, its actual author was well-hidden. Most of the psy-ops unit's stories were told in the voice of the local "man on the street" (in this case, Muslim on the street). If the stories did not go out through media secretly owned by the United States, legitimate Arab journalists and editors were paid to run them. According to *The New York Times* and other publications, the Pentagon paid newspapers from $40 to $2,000 to run more than 1,000 articles in twelve to fifteen Iraqi and Arab newspapers. One of the Pentagon's contractors was a regular fixture at the Baghdad convention center, where the Iraqi press corps hung out. Most people knew they could earn $400 to $500 a month writing pro-American pieces.

Accustomed to state-controlled media, Muslims viewed it all with a skeptical eye. When the full dimensions of the Pentagon's clandestine propaganda effort became known (as any realist would have known it would), the man on the street's natural skepticism turned to cynicism that even undermined some of the administration's real accomplishments. Edward R. Murrow, who had a very pragmatic attitude toward the issue of America's strategic communications to the rest of the world, once said: "To be persuasive we must be believable; to be believable we must be credible; to be credible we must be truthful. It is as simple as that."[7]

ENTER THE QUEEN

This is the environment into which Charlotte Beers parachuted in September 2001. Beers is a tall, stylish woman given to wearing long, flowing scarves. She lost her Texas accent years ago, but none of her girlish flirtatiousness. In meetings, she has been known to call male clients "darlin'" and "honey." On the other hand, she had no aversion to getting her hands dirty, figuratively and literally. Once, while pitching the Sears advertising account, she famously gave her entire presentation while taking apart and reassembling a power drill, pointing out such workings as the ball bearings and the armature field as she went along.

Beers graduated from Baylor University, where she studied physics and math, in 1957. After a short stint teaching, she found a job as a research supervisor at Uncle Ben's Rice in Houston, a division of Mars, Inc. By 1966, while still in her twenties, she became the company's first female product manager, although she still had to deal with clueless male executives who assumed she was a secretary and asked her to get them coffee. Her ability to find elegant solutions to complex problems so impressed the brand's ad agency that it hired her away. "I went in as a mathematician," she later said, "but I left as a marketer and a lover of the consumer dialogue."[8]

Although she's thin to the point of appearing frail, she was tough enough to rise to the top of not one, but two of the world's iconic ad agencies, Ogilvy & Mather and J. Walter Thompson. For years, she was the most prominent woman in advertising, an industry with a notorious ceiling of shatterproof glass. The only other women to achieve and keep similar positions of influence either started their own agency (Mary Wells Lawrence of Wells, Rich, Greene) or followed Beers at one (Shelly Lazarus of Ogilvy & Mather). Famous for cultivating chief executives at prospective and current client companies, Beers was known in the advertising trade press variously as "The Queen of Branding," "The Queen of Advertising," or "The Queen of Schmoozing." But there was no doubt that, in the worlds of advertising and marketing, Beers was royalty.

Upon retiring from the ad agency world at age 66, Beers succumbed to the entreaties of Secretary of State Colin Powell, who sought her help in doing something about America's deteriorating image around the world. Powell had gotten to know her when they both served on the board of Gulfstream Aerospace Corporation during the 1990s, and he thought Beers was uniquely qualified to lead an effort to win the hearts and minds of people around the world on behalf of the United States. When she was officially nominated as undersecretary of state for public diplomacy, on March 29, 2001, months before the September attacks, no one in official Washington took particular notice. By the time she was confirmed on October 2, the assignment had not only grown in complexity and importance, but all eyes were now on her.

Five days before the September 11 attacks, Secretary Powell explained why he believed Beers was the right person for the job. "I wanted one of the world's greatest advertising experts," he said, "because what are we doing? We're selling. We're selling a product. That product we are selling is democracy. It's the free enterprise system, the American value system."[9]

Others weren't so sure. William J. Drake of the Carnegie Endowment for International Peace sniffed, "I just find the notion that you can sell Uncle Sam like Uncle Ben's highly problematic."[10] Frank Rich of *The New York Times* noted that Beers was chosen not for her expertise in foreign policy, but for "her salesmanship on behalf of products like Head&Shoulders shampoo." He wrote that if we can't win the war on terrorism, "it's reassuring to know we can always win the war on dandruff."[11]

BEERS AT WORK

Undaunted by such criticism and seemingly oblivious to the skepticism within the entrenched federal bureaucracy, Beers went quickly to work and put in the eighty-hour workweeks for which she had been famous in the advertising world. One of her first steps was to plug a glaring hole in the State Department's capabilities: It didn't have a single spokesperson fluent in Arabic who could go on Qatar-based Al Jazeera, the widely watched satellite TV network, and speak with authority. Beers asked former ambassador Chris Ross, a fluent speaker of Arabic who had lived in the Middle East, to be her senior adviser.

The next time Osama bin Laden released a tape to Al Jazeera, Ross went on the air to rebut its allegations point by point.

RESEARCH

Not surprisingly for someone who had begun her career as a data analyst, Beers is a great believer in research. She was flabbergasted at how little the State Department knew about America's reputation around the world. It had reams of top-line data of the same sort that had appeared in magazines and newspapers ever since the September 11 attacks. But there was little of the deep analytical data that could shed light on people's motivations, unexpressed fears, and latent desires.

Later she would tell a radio interviewer that the State Department's principal source of knowledge about foreign publics was foreign governments themselves. It was "anathema," she said, "to talk to the peoples of these countries." Unfortunately, in some cases, foreign regimes are part of the problem, not the solution. As Beers discovered:

> The governments don't actually know very much about what their people are thinking and feeling. They went to school in the United States, and they [and] all their friends are sophisticated about the United States, and they don't understand [the seriousness of] the myths, the biases, the misinformation that exists and travels throughout these countries.[12]

Beers immediately commissioned more research, hired a consultant to assess the State Department's ongoing needs, and began meeting personally with prominent Muslim Americans in search of the insight that could drive an effective communications strategy. In January 2002, she even spent several days in Cairo, Egypt, meeting with Muslims as part of her "listening" campaign.

Meanwhile, expectations were high, and Beers didn't have the luxury of waiting until all the data were in.

COMMUNICATING INTANGIBLES

Ever since her confirmation hearing, Beers had been raising awareness about her mission. "We need to become better at communicating the intangible, the behavior, the emotions that reside in lofty words like *democracy,*" she told Congress. "So the burden is now on us to act as though no one has ever understood the identity of the United States, and redefine it for audiences who are at best cynical."[13]

Her approach would be nontraditional and decidedly more evocative than the typical government information program. For example, a brochure issued within thirty days of Beers's confirmation was titled "Network of Terrorism." It featured graphic photographs of the destruction at Ground Zero, including its ash-covered, bloodied victims. Still more photographs depicted the human cost of Al Qaeda's previous attacks in Nairobi, Kenya, and Dar es Salaam, Tanzania, and a world map showed all the countries in which Al Qaeda operated. Bin Laden's own words were used to condemn him, and no fewer than four Muslim clerics were quoted denouncing the attacks (their remarks featured in typeface that filled half a page each), while a Muslim American woman was shown in prayer for the victims. The leaders of countries from China to Uzbekistan were presented as part of a solemn coalition committed to stamping out terrorism. The brochure ended by showing how the people of Afghanistan were betrayed by the Taliban and rescued by America.

Released on November 6, 2001, the brochure quickly became the most widely distributed document ever produced by the State Department. Produced in thirty-six different languages, copies were sent to audiences ranging from members of the Japanese Diet to guards at the Beirut airport and students at boarding schools in Jakarta. It even ran as an insert in publications such as Italy's *Panorama,* Kuwait's *al-Watan,* and the Arabic edition of *Newsweek*—all firsts for the State Department.

A new multilingual website headlined "Response to Terrorism" followed in December. It featured dramatic visuals, including a map showing the eighty-one countries that lost citizens in the World Trade Center attack and a photo essay documenting life in New York City three months after the attacks. Unabashedly emotional, it interspersed heart-wrenching photos of the devastation at Ground Zero with images of the many handmade memorials to the victims and the personal stories of witnesses and first responders to the attacks. The photos told the story of the city's indomitable spirit through the faces of its children and multiethnic community.

Beers also commissioned a series of photographs of American mosques. Beautiful, poster-size images of domes and minarets were distributed in the Islamic world. The "Mosques in America" posters graphically demonstrated the religious diversity of the United States and complemented a website photo gallery that showed Muslim family life in America.

Finally, in addition to churning out websites, brochures, videos, and even "Wanted Dead or Alive" posters for bin Laden and his henchmen, Beers expanded programs that would not pay off for many years. She expanded the "American Corners" program, installing shelves of books and magazines about the United States in borrowed space outside embassies, in order to foster an understanding of American life and culture. She refocused educational exchange programs in the Muslim world, reaching out especially to nonelite, often female, and non-English-speaking youth. She even put Secretary of State Colin Powell on MTV, interacting with young people around the world[14] via satellite.

SHARED VALUES CAMPAIGN

One relatively small, $15 million campaign came to define Beers's tenure. "Shared Values" was built on commercial research showing that, while Americans and Muslims were far apart on values such as "modesty," "obedience," and "duty," they placed similarly high importance on such values as "family," "faith," and education.[15] Beers designed a multimedia campaign focused on religious tolerance. The centerpiece was five brief videos showing the daily life of American Muslims, so their coreligionists around the world would see that Islam flourished in a tolerant United States. The State Department called the videos "mini-documentaries" and scheduled them to run on Muslim television channels during Ramadan, a month-long period of both heightened religious sensitivity and soaring television viewership.

The plan was to supplement the TV spots with a media tour by the American Muslims featured in the videos. To this day, Beers considers the program a success. She says:

> Where [countries] got the whole program, with the follow-up research, with the visit from the Muslim families who were in the documentaries going to these countries and speaking [with people there]—we had exceptionally positive response. I mean, the women would say, one after

another, "I had no idea you could wear your scarf in the United States."[16]

Copy tests conducted among 500 students in London, Singapore, and Cairo have confirmed Beers's confidence. After viewing the mini-documentaries, the students were more likely to agree that "Muslims are treated fairly in the United States." In fact, Muslim students showed the greatest improvement in attitudes on that dimension as well as in their attitudes toward the United States's government and its people.[17]

But the firestorm of criticism began even before the first video had been aired. *The New York Times* called the videos "as Muslim as apple pie" and said unnamed U.S. diplomats thought they were "patronizing and too simplistic."[18] Some critics questioned the very basis for the campaign. "America's record on tolerance is not a central issue for the vast majority of Middle Easterners," wrote Dr. Robert Satloff of the Washington Institute for Near East Policy. "Indeed, if anything, most would say that Americans are *too* tolerant—too promiscuous, too libertine, too open to various lifestyles and competing views of the world. In other words, the U.S. government is spending much of its time fighting the wrong war."[19]

As'ad AbuKhalil, a research fellow at the Center for Middle Eastern Studies at the University of California at Berkeley and the author of *Bin Laden, Islam, and America's New "War on Terrorism,"* charged that the videos, which didn't address the substantive policy issues that affect America's relations with the Arab world, especially the Israeli-Palestinian conflict, demonstrated the U.S. view that "Muslims and Arabs are idiots—simple-minded, feeble-minded idiots. . . . Even if they send dancing monkeys, even if they send Britney Spears to live for five years in the Middle East, it's not going to change how people feel," he said.[20]

LEFT AND RIGHT WEIGH IN

If Beers considered the Arab-Israeli conflict too loaded a subject, liberal media analysts Sheldon Rampton and John Stauber suggested she should at least have attempted to persuade Muslims that the war in Afghanistan was justified. "Most Muslims found the war in Afghanistan more disturbing than anything that handshakes or posters could address," they wrote. But, "of all the military activities in which the United States has engaged during the last fifty years, the war in Afghanistan was certainly one of the easiest to defend on its merits."[21]

At the other end of the political spectrum, neoconservatives David Frum and Richard Perle accused Beers of being too soft on the "evil" Muslims. According to Frum and Perle, "active propitiation of Muslim opinion at home and abroad was not merely undignified, but dangerous."[22] Why should the United States have to explain to anybody why it's doing what it's doing? Beers's campaigns, they said, made them "cringe."

Still others were skeptical that the video series would even be aired in countries where the media is state-controlled and largely hostile toward the United States. In fact, Egyptian and Jordanian stations refused to run the series and, after saying it would be "honored" to run it, Al Jazeera was unable to come to financial terms with the U.S. State Department. But television stations in Pakistan, Indonesia, Malaysia, and Kuwait ran the videos, and some spillover even reached viewers in Egypt, Saudi Arabia, and the United Arab Emirates.

Government insiders seized on the so-called "distribution difficulties" as an indication that Beers was having problems with the professional foreign officer corps around the world. A Republican aide in Congress said there was a "cultural problem"[23] between her office and the bureaucracy she tried to influence. Then, in January 2003, someone at the State Department leaked that the "Shared Values" series had been shelved. Beers was reduced to the unusual position of going on CNN to explain that the videos were always scheduled to be pulled following their initial airings to remove mentions of Ramadan. But within two months, Beers had resigned for "health reasons" and official Washington distanced itself from "her advertising campaign." The Queen of Branding had been on her State Department throne for eighteen months.

CHAPTER 3

CHARLOTTE IN WONDERLAND

"It would be so nice if something made sense for a change."[1]
—*Alice in Wonderland*

CHARLOTTE BEERS MADE THE CLASSIC ADVERTISING ROOKIE mistake of giving her client what he wanted rather than what he needed. And despite her illustrious Madison Avenue career, she *was* a rookie inside the Beltway, trying to reconcile the mandate Secretary of State Colin Powell had given her with the intricate web of overlapping "communications offices" that existed not only within the State Department, but across the administration. For example, early every morning she sat in on conference calls where the president's communications director, Karen Hughes, led State and Defense Department staffers in hammering out the "message of the day" and plotting political strategy. Instead of setting strategic direction, Beers found herself running to jump on a train that was already chugging away from the station.

Her second major shock was that, even assuming she knew what she wanted to say—and she was working day and night toward that goal—she didn't have the necessary human or media channels to deliver it. "It was simply shocking how little equipment we had, had we agreed on a message to get the word out," she later observed, "and there was a complete dearth of training."[2]

None of that would have come as a surprise to old foreign service hands. "At the end of the Cold War, we unilaterally disarmed our public diplomacy apparatus," former ambassador Edward P. Djerejian told the Council on Foreign Relations. "We thought the ideological struggles were over."[3]

THE GOLDEN AGE OF THE USIA

For nearly fifty years, the engine of America's outreach to foreign publics was the United States Information Agency. The agency's director reported directly to the president and, by law, served as his principal adviser on matters of strategic communications. In practice, though, the USIA director's relationship with the president depended on the personal chemistry they had before they assumed their respective offices. Some of these relationships were remarkably close. Charles Wick, for example, had been President Ronald Reagan's friend in his Hollywood days, and the president joked that he knew Wick could handle the Washington scene based solely on his successful production of the film classic *Snow White and the Three Stooges*. Reagan's instincts were right; Wick held the post longer than any of his predecessors and greatly increased its budget. Under President John F. Kennedy famed broadcaster Edward R. Murrow became one of the USIA's most influential directors and set journalistic standards that gave it unquestioned credibility around the world.

But whether the agency director had a seat at the president's decision-making table or only knew what he read in the papers, the agency he led in those days had unparalleled capabilities to disseminate information around the world and to foster understanding through educational and cultural exchanges. The agency was flexible and responsive. It had the human and technical resources to reach into every corner of the world as required. Agency staff members were assigned to every embassy; they were full members of the country teams and served as senior advisers to their ambassadors. But they also reported back to the USIA director in Washington, who controlled their salaries and careers. Among the local staffs' most important responsibilities were to recruit, train, and supervise foreign nationals with public relations or journalism backgrounds so they could represent the United States to the local media in their own language. They opened libraries to give foreign nationals access to U.S. media. They hosted lectures by prominent Americans, mounted concerts by American performers, even drove jeeps into the African bush to screen 16-millimeter films against the cleanest whitewashed walls they could find.

The Voice of America, which was the agency's broadcast outlet, beamed shortwave English-language programming around the world and broadcast in more than fifty other languages to individual countries. Its newscasts and jazz concerts tore a hole in the Iron Curtain. For more than four decades, for example, Willis Conover's jazz program was the living incarnation of freedom and racial equality. In a contest between *Pravda* and Dizzy Gillespie, the man with the horn would win every time.

USIA RIP

When the Soviet Union collapsed in 1991 and the West declared victory, the United States Information Agency was an easy target for budget cuts. The number of public diplomacy officers overseas—as high as 2,500 in 1991—was cut in half almost immediately and allowed to wither even further over the following years. Key programs were eliminated and the foreign broadcasting budgets were slashed, all without critically rethinking the agency's mission. For example, the agency's budget for Indonesia, the world's largest Muslim country, was cut in half. From 1995 to 2001, academic and cultural exchanges dropped from 45,000 to 29,000 participants annually, while many storefront libraries and cultural centers were either abandoned or moved into spare rooms at fortress-like embassies.[4]

In 1998, Congress passed the Foreign Affairs Reform and Restructuring Act to cement the cost cuts. After a half-century of independence, the USIA was absorbed into the State Department and essentially shut down. Most of the agency's staff, including those responsible for media and public opinion research, was reassigned to other State Department bureaus. Agency field directors found themselves reporting to regional assistant secretaries below the undersecretary for political affairs. Local initiatives now had to navigate lengthy embassy and ambassadorial reviews. A new undersecretary for public diplomacy and public affairs inherited the remnants of the Bureau of Educational and Cultural Affairs and a greatly diminished information bureau.

VOICE OF AMERICA

The Voice of America was stripped away completely and transferred to an autonomous Broadcasting Board of Governors (BBG) to figure out.

Convinced that the Voice of America was failing to connect with the masses, the BBG redirected budgets to programming with more commercial appeal. For example, in 2002, the shortwave Arabic Voice of America service was replaced by the MTV-like Radio Sawa, which programs a mix of Western and Arab pop music, interrupted every half-hour by brief news reports.[5]

Meanwhile, the classic Voice of America service was struggling both to keep its budget from being cut further and to maintain its journalistic standards of "fair treatment for all points of view." For example, the head of its Pashto-language service was reassigned after running excerpts from a telephone interview she conducted with Taliban leader Mullah Muhammad Omar just after the September 11 attacks. Agency staffers cited it as just another example of political interference with their news judgment. Agency editors complained of pressure to report more favorably on the Bush administration's actions in the Middle East and of repeated requests from political appointees that they develop "positive stories" emphasizing U.S. successes, rather than report car bombings and terrorist attacks.

BEERS'S BRIEF

But if Beers had neither the mandate nor all the tools necessary to restore America's reputation, she was hampered most by serious misconceptions of the task at hand. Beers would never have attempted to launch a brand campaign for Sears, let alone the U.S. State Department, based on a brief as thin as that available to her. And the issue at hand was a lot more complicated—and more important—than a power drill.

Nevertheless, Beers's efforts responded to a widely held belief within the Bush administration that the principal need was to correct deep misunderstandings about America in the Islamic world. But their underlying assumption—that Muslims were "disinformed" (i.e., actively misled by America's enemies)—was wrong. Some Muslims did worry that America's actions in Afghanistan and Iraq were approaching an implicit attack on Islam, but it wasn't because of the war on terror. It was because they saw America consistently siding with Israel against the Palestinians and actively propping up what they consider impious, or even apostate, regimes in places such as Egypt, Jordan, Saudi Arabia, and the Gulf States. Many even remembered a day when the United States sent money and weapons to the now hated Taliban and even to bin Laden.

Furthermore, the notion that the Islamic world is homogeneous was naïve in itself. The reality on the ground is much more nuanced and complicated. Islam is a cacophony of quarrelsome groups and a single Muslim may be balancing up to five identities: as a religious Muslim, as a sectarian Muslim (Sunni, Shia, Ismaili, etc.), as a citizen of a particular nation, as a person of particular ethnicity (Arab, Kurd, Turkmen, etc.), and as member of a tribe or clan.[6] Muslims vary as much in their interpretations of Islam as followers of other faiths with theirs.[7] And their visions of Islamic Renewal—what some call the return of the caliphate—are just as varied.

Finally, Beers's message strategy completely ignored the reality of increasingly unfavorable attitudes toward America in the rest of the non-Muslim world.

HIJACKED BY THE WAR ON TERROR

The war on terror contributed to America's declining reputation, but the world had been falling out of love with the United States even before September 11, 2001. Restoring America's reputation must address broader issues, and it must go beyond the tried and true practices of earlier conflicts. A Defense Department task force put its finger on the underlying problem in 2004[8]—the Cold War paradigm that shaped United States foreign policy is not relevant to the war on terror. If you think of the war on terror as replacing the Cold War, it makes perfect sense to focus on Muslims as your target audience. That, in fact, is exactly how the Bush administration sees it. But that analogy is seriously flawed.

First, as the task force pointed out, the Cold War was as bipolar as conflicts get. The driving ideologies of the two sides—communism and capitalism—were well defined. It wasn't hard to figure out who was on which side because states proudly professed their allegiance. Most nations aligned themselves either with the Soviet Union or with the United States. The conflict played out in actions between sovereign states. And it was truly global in character, giving U.S. foreign policy an overarching goal.

Beyond the defeat of the Taliban in Afghanistan, the war on terror is not being waged between states, but against loosely affiliated groups who don't so much share the same ideology as common tactics of political conflict. These groups even draw support from a shifting set of patrons. Finally, while the United States has characterized the war on terror as "global," there is little doubt that its center of gravity is in the Middle East, where groups have used such methods since the twelfth-century Crusades. Furthermore, the war on terror cannot influence U.S. foreign policy as decisively as the Cold War did because other concerns loom larger in America's relations with some countries. And while the war on terror may color the world's perceptions of the United States, other factors clearly play a large role.

But even if the problem of anti-Americanism were solely rooted in the Middle East and tightly intertwined with the war on terror, the analogy with the Cold War fails on other grounds. During the Cold War, the Soviet Union and its allies kept their people under a hermetic seal that defined their reality to a very great extent. The Voice of America and cultural exchanges were often able to slip in credible, nonpartisan information about the outside world, but it was the rise of new global media and communications technology that ultimately contributed to the decline of communism.

The Islamic world, however, has easy access to global media. The Arab Advisors Group, an Amman, Jordon-based media and telecommunications consulting company, estimates that there are currently 130 Arab satellite television channels.[9] Furthermore, the Arab media bears a much closer resemblance to the media in America than old Soviet-style TV ever did. For example, about 20 percent of satellite TV fare available in all Arab countries except Iran, which bans satellite receivers, consists of music videos that would not look out of place on MTV.[10]

Unlike in the Soviet Union, the problem is not that Arabs and Muslims lack information, the problem is that they object to American foreign policy and to what they consider America's irreligious culture. One intrepid reporter had raised this possibility in the first State Department news briefing following Beers's confirmation. "This all stems from what you say is a misunderstanding of what America is about," he asked innocently enough. "But are you prepared for the possibility that people *do* understand what America is about, and just don't like it?"[11]

His question evoked laughter from the assembled press and was taken no more seriously by the State Department spokesman. "I think it is quite clear, from what we are seeing," he said, "that they don't get the message."

After studying the matter, Rand Corporation analysts came to a different conclusion. "Misunderstanding of American values is not the principal source of anti-Americanism," they wrote. Foreigners understand us just fine. They just don't like what they see. "Some U.S. policies have been, are, and will continue to be major sources of anti-Americanism."[12]

Some Muslims consider American rhetoric about bringing democracy to Islamic societies patronizing and hypocritical. It implies that Muslims are like the enslaved people of the old communist world, and they don't necessarily feel that way.

Furthermore, the "America" that many Muslims experience does not match its marketing. Many thousands of people in the Middle East experience America as an occupier, a supporter of dictatorial regimes, and a strangely narcissistic nation intent on remaking them in its own image.

America's deteriorating reputation complicates achieving its foreign policy goals in the region, which were neatly summarized by Ambassador Edward Djerejian: "First of all, conflict resolution: Arab-Israeli, Kashmir, Western Sahara. Two: broadening political participation with the goal of democratization. Three: private-sector economic reforms, anticorruption, human rights, et cetera."[13] The United States can take a leading role in many of these areas, but as history has demonstrated, it won't get very far as a Lone Ranger whose motives are suspect. And Beers's message strategy ignored deteriorating attitudes toward America in the rest of the non-Muslim world.

Ironically, it was the opportunity to reposition the United States in the minds of the world's people that had attracted Beers to the State Department in the first place. But between the time of her nomination and confirmation, the September 11 attacks had understandably redirected everyone's attention to a very specific, and somewhat mysterious, part of the world. Rebuilding Brand America was hijacked by the war on terror.

TYPECASTING

Complicating things even further was a widespread perception that Beers was essentially a glorified ad manager who was going to fix America's image with a few well-produced thirty-second spots. Beers was typecast that way from the start until long after she was gone. In a 2005 issue of the web magazine *Slate,* Fred Kaplan wrote that Beers's credentials were based on the "assumption that a clever ad can sell America in pretty much the same way a clever ad can sell Coca-Cola, Nike, or Britney Spears."[14] No one honestly believed advertising could work that way, certainly not Beers, so no one thought she could pull it off. In hindsight, her use of marketing terms in her congressional testimony, speeches, and daily meetings was perceived as "superficial" by the diplomatic establishment that didn't know what she was talking about, and she didn't make much of an effort to translate the principles of marketing and branding into a language foreign affairs specialists could understand. When she eventually produced something that looked like an ad, it confirmed every preconception the bureaucracy had and defined her tenure.

Beers herself continues to believe the Shared Values mini-documentary campaign was a success. Years later, she can still rattle off research data from Indonesia where its message recall was even higher than that for a typical U.S. soft drink ad. But when asked if, with the benefit of hindsight, she would do anything differently, she readily admits to certain "obstacles."

First, a cumbersome government approval process delayed the campaign for four critical months, during which the invasion of Afghanistan was launched. By the time the program began, the issues it was designed to address were not only less topical, they had been supplanted by more pressing concerns. Further, Beers readily admits that she should have done more to win the support of the Middle East embassies. The embassies didn't embrace the program, she says, because they didn't really believe the United States should talk to foreign publics directly and "it just made their daily diet with their government officials more difficult."[15] Finally, Beers concedes that she never won over the "elites" who flit in and out of the State Department and onto network television. One of the campaign's most vociferous Muslim-American critics, she remembers ruefully, told her the campaign was "wonderful." Then he slammed it in media interviews. "The [foreign] elites—the people who know everything about the United States," she has said, "don't know what their own people think. They have no idea."[16] Beers's research showed her that the most important issues for the Muslim in the Arab street were not matters of foreign policy, but faith, family, and education. Foreign policy "was not even number six on their list . . . regardless of what . . . the highly sophisticated elites know about the subject,"[17] she has said.

When Beers resigned for unspecified "health reasons," some speculated she had been frustrated by the bureaucracy, and she was tired of competing with the White House Office of Global Communications for message control. Whatever the facts, this was not simply another bureaucratic turf battle. Nothing is more strategic than branding. The 9/11 Commission concluded that "coordination" was not sufficient in the realm of intelligence, and it is inadequate for the Herculean task of rebuilding Brand America as well. Without control over communications strategy, Beers could do little more than respond tactically to the crisis of the day. She allowed herself to become hostage to the idea that disinformation in the Islamic world was the root cause of Brand America's decline. It was certainly a significant factor, but America's brand problems are much broader and deeper.

CHAPTER 4

THE PRINCE OF POLLSTERS

"I want to be the Gallup of my generation, the household word, the generic."[1]
—John Zogby, CEO and president, Zogby International

"Many of these surveys—by Pew, John Zogby, and others—that tell us what is being said about America in foreign lands, in my opinion, are really just a way for a segment of the American elite to talk about America and put it in the words of foreigners."[2]
—Fouad Ajami, director of the Middle East Studies Program, Johns Hopkins University

THE WAY JOHN ZOGBY TELLS IT, HE RAN INTO AN OLD HIGH school friend he hadn't seen for years during the Friday evening happy hour at a bar in his hometown of Utica, New York. "I told him I was a pollster, spread the word," Zogby says. "Lo and behold, first thing Monday I got a call from his aunt, and she said, 'You're a pollster?' and I said yes, and she said, 'Well, I have a sofa and a chair.' "[3]

His friend's aunt clearly didn't wear out her upholstery watching much television news or she would have recognized Zogby as the man Bill O'Reilly of Fox News and Chris Matthews of *Hardball* on MSNBC both introduced as "the nation's most accurate pollster." In the weeks and months since the September 11 attacks, Zogby was a frequent guest on the *Today* show, *Good Morning America*, and all the network news programs. As an Arab American himself, no one seemed to be better positioned to answer the question on every pundit's lips: Why do they hate us? Indeed, in the last few years, with the help of a voracious media, he has set himself up as the "go to" guy for insight into the Arab mind.

JOHN ZOGBY

Zogby is an unusual name, at least in the United States. It's Lebanese and so common a name in the village where Zogby's parents grew up that both his father and mother were Zogbys, though unrelated. In fact, their village northeast of Beirut is still largely populated with Zogbys. Shortly after marrying, his parents immigrated to Utica in upstate New York, where his father started a small grocery store and his mother landed a teaching job. Zogby attended Le Moyne College, a small Jesuit school in Syracuse, where he majored in history. After graduating in 1970, he took a job teaching at Catholic schools around Utica, largely to avoid the draft.

In those days, Zogby was a budding socialist who helped found a "free university" to teach civil rights and peace activism. From there, he started a consumer advocacy group, the Utica Citizens' Lobby, and that in turn led to a run for mayor of Utica in 1981. When the surveys he and his students fielded showed that he was going to lose the election by 14–15 percent of the vote, Zogby decided that he enjoyed polling more than campaigning. He started his own firm in 1984 but didn't attract much attention until he called the 1996 presidential race more accurately than any other pollster. While nearly everyone else had Bill Clinton beating Bob Dole by double-digit margins, Zogby predicted a margin of just 8 percent. When Clinton's actual margin of victory was 8.5 percent, politicians on both the right and the left took notice. TV producers love his genial personality and the fact that he speaks in words more than numbers.

Described by *The New Yorker* as "mild, overcaffeinated, inquisitive, watchful, cautiously friendly, somewhat anxious, yet fundamentally optimistic,"[4] Zogby has carved out a reputation for insightful analysis of public opinion on a wide range of issues. In fact, he's quick to admit that statistics are hardly his first love. What gives him the greatest satisfaction is divining the meaning behind the numbers. Some critics maintain that his real strength is in knowing how to design a questionnaire and mine the numbers to arrive at whatever meaning has been previously determined by his client.

CONTROVERSY

A Zogby poll sponsored by the Doris Day Animal League purported to show that 51 percent of Americans believe that "primates are entitled to the same rights as human children."[5] But when Chris Mooney, a writer for the liberal *American Prospect,* looked behind the numbers, he discovered that respondents to the survey had only been given four choices to the question of how "chimpanzees" (not the larger species of "primates") should be treated: "like property," "similar to children," "the same as adults," or "don't know."[6] Given those choices, it's not surprising the second one came out on top. But how "similar to children" became "the same rights as children" in the news release announcing the results is a bit of a mystery.

Even more controversial is Zogby's practice of weighting poll results according to his feel for what is happening on the ground. While pollsters often weight their results to correct for under- or oversampling of different demographic groups, most look askance at the practice of adjusting for more subjective factors. Zogby merely points out that his projections of election results have been accurate and asks if that isn't the real goal. "There's artwork involved," says Zogby. "I'm not a statistician, I'm a historian. I'm used to using soft methods."[7]

Any suspicion that Zogby is working a standard political agenda is dampened by his practice of accepting work from both sides of the aisle. "I can't think of any pollster other than Zogby who regularly works for people on both sides and is touted by people on both sides,"[8] notes University of Virginia political analyst Larry Sabato. Furthermore, Zogby's bread and butter is corporate work, which accounts for about two-thirds of his company's revenue. If anything, Zogby is considered a "hired gun" who has toiled for companies such as Coca-Cola, Microsoft, and Philip Morris, as well as for antibusiness groups such as WakeUpWalMart.com.

But at least two groups believe some of Zogby's recent polling is also working an agenda near to his heart. The Militant Islam Monitor has called him a "shyster pollster" whose "sound bytes and polling statistics often go unchallenged despite the evidence of their Islamist and pro-Saudi bias."[9] Similarly, the Zionist Organization of America has called Zogby's Middle East research "suspect" because of what it calls his "anti-Israel extremism." The organization's president said, "A Zogby poll concerning Israel may be no more trustworthy than David Duke taking a poll on attitudes toward blacks in America."[10]

THE ZOGBY FAMILY

The Zogby family, in fact, is Lebanese-Catholic, but John and his older brother, James, were turned on to Arab causes as young men. For James, the turning point came during the days he spent working with Palestinian refugees as a young college student headed toward a doctorate in religion at Temple University. John's awakening came during antiwar protests in the late 1960s. "I saw how some of the Jewish kids could be antiwar and pacifists," he later recalled, "and at the same time just relish the idea of kicking the hell out of the Arabs."[11]

On leaving Temple University, James Zogby cofounded and became chairman of the Palestine Human Rights Campaign. He later cofounded and served as the executive director of the American-Arab Anti-Discrimination Committee, for which his brother John was the national field representative. In 1985, the two brothers set up the Arab American Institute, a Washington, D.C.-based organization that promotes the political interests of Arab Americans and works to improve American understanding of Arab interests in the Middle East.

Today, although John works out of converted factory space in the gritty industrial town of Utica and James's offices are on Washington, D.C.'s fashionable K Street, the two brothers still talk by telephone several times a day. Professionally, they have a mutually beneficial relationship. John serves on the board of the Arab American Institute while his brother James is a "senior analyst" for the Zogby International polling firm. John's polling company does work for the institute, and the institute has been helpful in giving the polling company access to the Arab world—not an incidental advantage in a part of the world where governments control the media, telephones are sometimes rare, and many homes don't even have street addresses.

As a result, Zogby International has many contacts in the Middle East and was one of the first companies to publish survey results from post-invasion Iraq. But even with these contacts, polling Iraqis wasn't easy. In August 2003, John Zogby sent four Lebanese pollsters into Iraq to supervise seventeen Iraqi men and women as they interviewed 600 people in four cities. Despite selecting cities they considered safer than Baghdad, the interviewers had to navigate checkpoints everywhere. Some of them were caught in the crossfire in Al Ramadi during an attack on a military convoy. One of Zogby's supervisors was seized by Kurdish forces in Kirkuk and held for ransom. The team in southern Iraq, in Basra, was summoned by religious leaders and questioned about the purpose of the study. And one group was chased by an unidentified car.

MIDDLE EAST POLLS

Polling public opinion elsewhere in the Middle East can be just as difficult, if less dangerous. Nevertheless, it's a growth business as the West tries to plumb the Arab mind. For example, Zogby's affiliate in Lebanon, Information International, fielded a survey in and around Beirut the week after the September 11 attacks. It showed that the Lebanese were just as likely to think the attacks had been staged by Israel as by Osama bin Laden—31 percent versus 28 percent, respectively. Just as many people described the attacks as "the result of U.S. foreign policy" as "an act of terrorism." And two out of three of those polled believed the U.S. had no right to attack countries "harboring terrorists" if it would involve civilian casualties. A follow-up poll in October and November 2001 revealed deep antipathy toward the United States, which at that point had invaded Afghanistan.[12]

The Gallup Organization greatly expanded on Information International's polling in a multicountry study of the Islamic world in early 2002. The results were just as negative with half (53 percent) of those polled claiming an "unfavorable view" of the United States, and three-fourths (77 percent) saying that U.S. military action in Afghanistan could not be justified morally. Another three-quarters (74 percent) even denied that Arabs carried out the attacks of September 11.[13] Clearly, something was going on. So with financial support from Shibley Telhami, the Anwar Sadat Professor for Peace and Development at the University of Maryland, Zogby International launched its own poll of the region as American troops amassed on the Iraqi border in late February and early March of 2003.[14]

The results were striking in several respects. The long-assumed Islamic antipathy to American values of freedom and democracy, science and technology, movies and television, and even U.S. products failed to surface in any significant way. But very few people in the survey countries had a favorable opinion of the United States itself: only 4 percent in Saudi Arabia, 6 percent in Morocco and Jordan, 13 percent in Egypt, and 32 percent in Lebanon. Most interestingly, what did show up was a striking linkage between unfavorable attitudes toward America and its policies on the Israeli-Palestinian conflict.

For example, the poll showed that three-quarters of Arabs believed Washington's real motive in threatening to invade Iraq was, first, to control Mideast oil and, second, to support Israel.[15] Only the Kuwaitis expressed support for war, but even they expressed similar frustration with American policies regarding "the Israeli occupation of Palestine." As if to drive the point home, the Zogby poll asked respondents how they would react "if the U.S. were to apply pressure to ensure the creation of a Palestinian state." Apparently that's all it would take for large majorities in every country except Iran "to react more favorably" toward America. That included 69 percent of people polled in Egypt, 79 percent in Saudi Arabia, 87 percent in Kuwait (91 percent of Kuwaiti nationals), 59 percent in Lebanon, 67 percent in the United Arab Emirates (76 percent of Emirati nationals), 73 percent in Pakistan, and 66 percent in Indonesia.

Zogby conceded that the poll results may have been colored somewhat by an Israeli incursion into the West Bank while the surveys were being conducted. Nevertheless, he said, "There is an overwhelming sense that the U.S. is not an honest broker when it comes to Middle East peace, and that shows itself in every single poll we do."[16] Most troubling, while Zogby's poll found that only 6 percent of respondents sympathized with Al Qaeda's goal of seeking an Islamic state, more than 30 percent said they sympathized with Al Qaeda itself, because the group stood up to America.

In July 2003, after the invasion of Iraq had begun, Zogby could only poll in Saudi Arabia, where large majorities now said they no longer even liked American movies, much less its notions of freedom and democracy. But the kicker was once again the Palestinian question. More than 93 percent of Saudi respondents said they had an "unfavorable impression of U.S. government policy toward the Palestinians."[17] That was even greater than the 83 percent who had an "unfavorable impression of U.S. government policy toward Iraq," a country the United States was actively bombing and invading.

THE ROOT ISSUE?

Zogby was convinced he had unearthed the root cause of America's declining favorability in the Islamic world—the Palestinian issue. "Our polling shows that it is among the top-three issues for at least 70 percent of Arabs surveyed in all countries," he wrote, "including Kuwaitis, who threw the Palestinians out in 1991." But Zogby believed that Arab concerns for the Palestinian cause were far more personal than political. "It is self-identifying, emblematic, and defining for Arabs," he wrote. "It represents to Arabs—young and old, Shia and Sunni, rich and poor—the betrayal and humiliation that they have felt in the past century. In that sense, the Palestine issue is in the bloodstream of Arabs."[18]

Zogby may be on to something. He is hands-down the most credible pollster in the Middle East, despite the protests of skeptics who point to the way his polling on animal rights was used and to the obvious political agenda of Jawad Adra, who runs Zogby's Beirut affiliate, Information International. When Adra came up with similar results in an earlier poll limited to Lebanon, he told a local reporter, "We hope the results of the poll would send a message to policymakers in the United States."[19]

In Zogby's worldview, the United States has two choices: Do a better job of explaining the U.S. position on the Israeli-Palestinian issue, or change it.

At least one academic review of Zogby's methodology confirmed the principal thrust of his pre-invasion surveys—that Arab attitudes toward America are much more closely tied to U.S. policies in the Middle East than to differences over "values."[20] However, as we will see, values do matter, though pinning down their precise meaning is often a hard slog up Semantic Hill.

It is worth noting, too, that by including the Palestinian issue among the policy areas respondents were asked to assess, and at a time when it featured so prominently in the news, Zogby's questionnaire may have helped highlight the issue. In all, respondents were asked to give their general impression of U.S. policy in six areas: 1) policy toward the Arab nations; 2) policy toward the Palestinians; 3) the American-led effort to stop ethnic cleansing in the Balkans; 4) the American-led effort to free Kuwait; 5) the American-led effort to fight terrorism; and 6) U.S. policy toward Iraq. When responses were coded on a four-point scale ranging from "Very favorable" (1) to "Very unfavorable" (4), U.S. policy toward the Palestinians received the lowest "favorable" scores and by far the fewest "Don't knows."

When all six issues were considered together, however, around 90 percent of respondents expressed an unfavorable opinion of American policies toward the Arab nations, the Palestinians, and Iraq. While American policies in the Balkan conflicts, in Kuwait, and on the war on terror received slightly higher levels of approval, they also generated substantially larger percentages of "Don't know" responses, which could reflect mixed feelings about the policies or unspoken support as much as a genuine lack of opinion.

A similar picture emerges from the Global Attitudes Survey of fifty nations commissioned by the Pew Research Center in 2002 and 2003. It found that America was less popular in the Middle East than in any other part of the world. However, the Pew study offered a more nuanced view of the sources of this disfavor. As in the Zogby studies, "U.S. foreign policy" was the driver of what Pew began to term "anti-Americanism," but it found four policies especially relevant to countries in the Middle East.

First, the U.S. invasion of Iraq fueled anti-American sentiments. "America's global popularity plummeted at the start of military action in Iraq," the Pew study noted, "and the U.S. presence there remains widely unpopular."[21] Second, the 2002 survey found that the U.S. war on terror drew more opposition from Arab and other Muslim-majority countries than from any other part of the globe. Third, majorities or pluralities in the Middle East said that the United States acts unilaterally in making foreign policy decisions, paying little or no attention to the interests of other countries. Finally, the 2003 survey found that "enormous majorities in Arab and Muslim countries (at least 90 percent in Jordan, the Palestinian Authority, Morocco, and Lebanon) believed the U.S. favors Israel too much."[22]

Commenting on these results in front of the Senate Foreign Relations Committee, Andrew Kohut, president of the Pew Research Center, reached a gloomy conclusion: "True dislike, if not hatred, of America is concentrated in the Muslim nations of the Middle East and in Central Asia, today's areas of greatest conflict."[23] Others have noted that by casting the war on terror as a global conflict with radical Islamists, then following up by invading two Arab countries—one of which later proved to be only marginally involved in terror acts outside its borders—the United States put all Muslims on edge.[24]

But there was a great deal of evidence in Pew's own surveys that America's declining reputation was not confined to the Islamic world, nor did it necessarily spring from there. Indeed, Zogby may not have uncovered a root cause of anti-Americanism, but merely one of the tendrils of a deeper, more invasive scourge.

CHAPTER 5

MEASURING DISTANCE
IN KILOGRAMS

*"Trying to understand hatred with logic is like trying to measure
distance in kilograms."*[1]
—Ali Salem, Egyptian playwright and author

IF DISTANCE GIVES YOU PERSPECTIVE, BRUCE BAWER HAS AN
excellent perch from which to figure out what has happened to America's image abroad. He lives in Oslo, Norway, where he writes literary
criticism as well as carefully crafted essays on religion, history, politics,
and culture for publications ranging from *The New York Times* and
The Nation to *The Wall Street Journal* and *The New Republic.*

A conservative, gay Episcopalian who once wrote for the right-wing *American Spectator,* but voted for Bill Clinton, Bawer is hard to
pigeonhole sociopolitically. He moved to Oslo in 1999 so he could
legally marry his Norwegian partner who had exhausted his American
visa. And he says he's been making comparisons between Europe and
the United States ever since. Initially, Europe came out on top.

"I was tempted at one point to write a book lamenting Americans'
anti-intellectualism," he once wrote, "their indifference to foreign languages, ignorance of history, indifference to academic achievement,
susceptibility to vulgar religion and trash TV, and so forth."[2] But as
time passed, he came to better appreciate his homeland's qualities, as
well as its faults. Lots of words that begin with "i" found their way
onto his list of American virtues: individualism, imagination, initiative,
inventiveness. "Americans," he wrote, "were more likely to think for

themselves and trust their own judgments, and less easily cowed by authorities or bossed around by 'experts.' "[3]

The statistics seem to bear him out. "Malice towards America," he notes by example, "is inversely proportional to the amount of time people have spent there."[4] Bawer says this helps explain the gap between theory and practice in Norway, "where the press sneers about Americans' devotion to McDonald's and Coca-Cola, but both corporations have bigger market shares than in the U.S."[5]

Most significantly, Bawer points out that none of this is a recent phenomenon. He notes that the famous editorial in *Le Monde* following the September 11 attacks (*Nous sommes tous américains*—"We are all Americans") was, in fact, a tiny nub of sympathy in an unbroken strand of hostility stretching back to the eighteenth century.

Today, every thread in that strand has been weighed and measured within a statistically certain margin of error. Nevertheless, its most frequent use is to tie ourselves in knots.

PEW RESEARCH

Between the events of 2001 and mid-2006, the Pew Research Center has surveyed one hundred thousand people in more than forty countries in seven separate polls. Every survey showed the United States to be "broadly disliked." When Pew reported the results of its fifth survey in March 2004, it tried to put them in context by starting with this gloomy assessment: "[J]ust a quarter of the French approve of U.S. policies, and the situation is only slightly better in Japan and Germany . . . majorities in many countries say America's strong military presence actually increases the chances for war." Then, before anyone got too worked up, it threw in the kicker—"those results are from a poll conducted by *Newsweek* . . . in 1983."[6]

If that dose of "there's nothing new under the sun" was supposed to reassure readers, the pages that followed gave them plenty to think about. A year after the start of the Iraq War, hostility toward America in the Islamic world was pretty much a given. It comes with the territory when you invade a couple of Muslim countries and chase terrorists through mosques and madrasahs, not to mention blow up countless civilians in the process. It also wasn't news that the French were in a snit. After all, they're . . . well, they're French.

But if America had been down the "Ugly American" road before, the Pew research demonstrated that it now was on a twisted path in countries once thought to be friendly. "Anti-Americanism," the March 2004 Pew study reported, "is deeper and broader now than at any time in modern history. . . . It spans the globe—from Europe to Asia, from South America to Africa."[7] Most alarmingly for those who were betting on a change of administration in the 2004 elections, the Pew research suggested that the hardening of attitudes toward the United States amounted to more than a thumbs-down on the current occupant of the Oval Office. America's global reputation hadn't just slipped in the period following the invasion of Iraq, it had plummeted, but it was declining even before.

No one was surprised by the decline in France, which had long engaged in recreational anti-Americanism. But, in fact, at the end of 2000, more than six out of ten of the French had a favorable opinion of the United States; by mid-2006, barely four out of ten did. Whereas eight out of ten people in Britain, Germany, and Indonesia had a favorable opinion of America in 2000, by mid-2006, only about half the Britons and about one-third of the Germans and Indonesians did.[8]

At the heart of the decline in world opinion (see Figure 5-1) was a strong perception that the United States acts internationally without taking other nations' interests into account. Two out of three Britons,

Percent (%) Favorable		
	1999/2000	2006
Japan	77	63
Britain	83	56
France	62	39
Germany	78	37
Indonesia	75	30
Pakistan	23	27
Spain	50	23
Turkey	52	12

Figure 5-1. World opinion of the United States.

Source: 1999/2000 data from the Office of Research, U.S. Department of State. 2006 data by Pew Research Center.

Germans, and Russians felt that way. More than half the people surveyed in France, Russia, Germany, Morocco, Turkey, Jordan, and Pakistan said they thought America's real motive in invading Iraq was "to control Mideast oil."[9] Large majorities of Europeans, Latin Americans, and many Asians believe the United States backs policies that increase the gap between rich and poor.[10] Chillingly, more than half of non-Americans believed U.S. foreign policies "caused" the September 11, 2001, attacks; nearly three out of four believed it was "good for the U.S. to feel vulnerable" following the attacks.[11]

CULTURE GAP

While much of the world expressed hostility toward U.S. foreign policy, America's democratic ideals were still popular in much of the world. Even where the United States was held in low regard, there was broad admiration for its technology. And most people around the world even admitted that they liked American movies, television, and music. But at the same time they viewed the export of American ideas and customs "a bad thing." More than half of Canadians, British, and Italians disliked it, as did two-thirds of Germans and more than 70 percent of the French. The same pattern held in Eastern Europe, Latin America, and much of Asia and Africa.

There was also a cultural gap on matters of religion. "As much as any single issue," the Pew Research Center reported, "religion has come to define the transatlantic values gap." In its 2002 survey, Pew found that 58 percent of Americans considered "belief in God" as necessary to morality. Just a third of Germans and even fewer Italians, British, and French agreed. Of course, American politicians had taken their constituents' lead long before, and their pious religiosity cemented the stereotype in foreign minds. "Professing religion is practically a political necessity, whether one believes or not," Catholic writer Garry Wills noted. "There is now an inverse proportion between religiosity and sincerity."[12]

In March 2004, ten daily foreign newspapers joined in an unprecedented effort to coordinate their polling on America's image. In eight of the nine countries where the question was asked, more than half said their view of America had worsened in the past two or three years, including two-thirds of the Japanese, French, Korean, Canadian, and

Spanish respondents. Overall, only two out of ten said it had improved. Only in Israel did the majority of respondents say their opinion had improved. (The question was not asked in the tenth country, Russia.)[13]

ATTITUDES TOWARD AMERICANS

A Harris Interactive poll in seven nations compared attitudes toward the United States held by Europeans, Canadians, and, yes, Americans.[14] About a third of Canadians and Europeans "felt positively" about the United States, while an equal percentage was negative. Perhaps not surprisingly, Americans are far more positive about the United States than others on everything from its food to its values and system of government.

But Canadians and Europeans liked U.S. films and TV programs even more than Americans themselves (see Figure 5-2). In fact, Americans were divided about the wisdom of spreading American culture around the world. In August 2002, an *Investor's Business Daily/Christian Science Monitor* poll found that only 47 percent of Americans surveyed felt that "American movies and popular culture" had a positive impact on "the rest of the world." Forty-four percent thought the impact was negative.[15] But if Americans, Europeans, and Canadians were divided about American popular culture, they all had the same

Percent (%) Positive			
	Europeans	Canadians	Americans
American food	17	53	76
American values	30	36	54
American system of government	26	31	59
American film and TV	48	60	44
The way Americans do business	37	31	46
American multinational companies	28	21	27

Figure 5-2. Rating the United States on cultural issues.

Source: Harris Interactive, February and March 2004.

low opinion of U.S. multinational companies—less than a third, regardless of country, had a positive opinion of them.

When Pew went back into the field in mid-2006 for a seventh time, favorable opinion of the United States had continued to decline after showing signs of leveling off in the year before.[16] Worse, according to the report, worldwide opinion about the American *people* was beginning to decline. Not liking whoever happened to be president at the time was one thing. After all, it had been a long time since a solid majority of the U.S. electorate itself was in love with whoever happened to be in the White House. But turning sour on the lovable American people suggested something was seriously amiss.

The 2006 data was consistent with ambivalent feelings the 2005 survey had revealed. In that survey, large majorities of Western Europeans, for example, characterized the American people as "honest," "hardworking," and "inventive." But equally large majorities considered them "greedy" and "violent." Muslims, not surprisingly, were more likely than others to consider Americans "immoral." But the Chinese were also critical of Americans. Although some 70 percent considered Americans "inventive," they were also least likely to consider Americans hardworking (44 percent) and just over a third (35 percent) saw Americans as honest. On the contrary, a majority of Chinese thought of Americans as violent (61 percent) and greedy (57 percent).[17] And while a 1988 survey of the French rated *power, dynamism, wealth,* and *liberty* as the words most often associated with American society, by 1996 the top choices were *violence, power, inequalities,* and *racism.*[18]

A 2004 survey by Research International found that Latin Americans considered their neighbors to the north fat, ignorant, suspicious, and self-centered. Eight out of ten people in ten Latin American countries believed Americans eat too much, only care about themselves, and mistrust people from other countries. Just 13 percent believed Americans respect other cultures.[19]

ATTITUDES TOWARD U.S. GOVERNMENT

Not even broadly popular U.S. policies have done much to repair America's image. The Bush administration had taken concrete steps toward elections in Afghanistan, Iraq, and the Palestinian territories.

After a tentative start, U.S. aid for tsunami victims in Asia had been well received in many countries. But since the last survey overall opinions of the United States improved significantly only in Pakistan and China. Part of the problem is simply a personality conflict—many Europeans don't like President Bush. The left-leaning French newspaper *Libération* reported Bush's reelection with a witty little headline: *L'Empire s'empire* ("The Empire gets worse").[20] As *The New Yorker*'s Adam Gopnik put it: "What the French, from left to right, see as Bush's shallow belligerence, his incuriosity, his contempt for culture or even the idea of difference . . . make him a heavy burden even for the most wholeheartedly pro-American thinker."[21] For example, few French, Gopnik notes, ever forgave the president for ridiculing an American reporter in Paris for speaking to the French president in French. But even the British, whose government followed Bush into Iraq, look down their noses at the man. The London *Daily Mirror* announced Bush's 2004 reelection with a front-page headline that asked, "How can 59,054,087 people be so dumb?"[22] And a poll taken in the summer of 2006 by the U.K. consumer research organization YouGov showed that 77 percent of Brits considered Bush a "pretty poor" or "terrible" world leader.[23]

Most worrisome, significant support has begun to develop across every country surveyed for some other country or group of countries to rival the United States militarily. Eighty-five percent of the French, for example, thought it would be *merveilleux* if the European Union or some other country emerged as a military rival to the United States.[24] A BBC poll taken in eleven countries in 2003 found that 65 percent of the population—and a majority in every country—considered the United States an arrogant superpower that posed a greater danger to world peace than North Korea.[25]

Finally, America's core image as a "land of opportunity" showed signs of deterioration. When Pew Research asked respondents where they would "advise a young person to move in order to lead a good life," Australia, Canada, Great Britain, and Germany were all more frequently recommended as first choices than was the United States.[26]

The European Union's own soundings in 2003 revealed surprising rancor toward the United States. For example, only 15 percent of the French believed the United States "plays a positive role regarding peace in the world," and only 11 percent thought America is contributing to the fight against global poverty.[27] And sour feelings are not limited to the perennially dyspeptic French. For example, according to

Australia's Lowy Institute for International Policy, the United States didn't even make the top-ten list of most-favored nations down under. In its 2005 poll, eight out of ten Aussies felt fine about Japan, nearly seven out of ten liked China, more than six out of ten had warm feelings for the French. But barely half had "positive feelings" toward the United States.[28]

The 2005 Transatlantic Trends poll of public opinion in nine European Union member states must have been disturbing reading for the State Department: Despite acknowledging the Bush administration's diplomatic efforts to court European public opinion, it noted that there had been little change in attitudes toward the United States. Some 70 percent of those surveyed disapproved of President Bush's international policies and about 50 percent of European respondents believed that strong U.S. leadership in the world is "undesirable."[29]

After years of ranking global threats similarly, Americans and Europeans even seem to have developed differing views about the world's most pressing problems (see Figure 5-3). Notably, Americans feel significantly more likely to be personally affected by terrorism, while Europeans feel more likely to be affected by the effects of global warming. The 2006 Pew research confirmed a wide gap in concern over global warming. Two-thirds of Japanese and Indians and roughly half of Spaniards and French respondents said they "personally worry a great deal" about global warming. But just 19 percent of Americans did, the lowest percentage in the fifteen countries surveyed.[30]

In the next ten years, are you likely to be personally affected by the following threats?		
	Americans	Europeans
Terrorism	71%	53%
Spread of nuclear weapons	67%	55%
Islamic fundamentalism	50%	40%
Immigration/refugees	61%	51%
Global warming	64%	73%

Figure 5-3. Differing attitudes toward threats.

Source: 2005 Transatlantic Trends Survey.

ATTITUDES TOWARD U.S. BRANDS

Many believe global attitudes toward American brands have become intertwined with those toward the U.S. government. For example, when General Motors announced in 2004 that it would eliminate 12,000 jobs in its European operations, the German magazine *Stern* ran a cover showing workers at the Opel plant in Russelsheim cowering under a cowboy boot with the stars and stripes on its side. The headline? "The Way of the Wild West."[31] Many global consumers believe American business and government are both run by ruthless cowboys.

Edelman, the public relations firm, released a study at the Davos World Economic Conference in January 2006 showing that U.S.

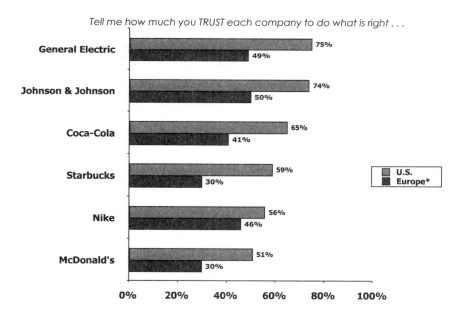

Tell me how much you TRUST each company to do what is right . . .

* France, Germany, and the United Kingdom

Figure 5-4. Companies have a trust deficit in Europe.

Source: Edelman Trust Barometer, January 2006.

brands suffer a "trust deficit" in Europe, Latin America, and Canada when compared to non-U.S. brands (see Figure 5-4 on the previous page). The Edelman survey found that more than 40 percent of "opinion leaders" in Europe, Canada, and Brazil said they would avoid buying American products because of the Bush administration.[32] This finding seemed to confirm a survey released by Global Market Insite the year before, which showed that almost 80 percent of consumers surveyed abroad distrusted the U.S. government, 50 percent distrusted U.S. companies, and 20 percent said they "consciously avoid American brands" as a result.[33] Research International's survey of Latin American consumers showed that about a quarter said they wouldn't wear Levi's because of U.S. policies.[34]

Whether reflecting attitudes about a country or a country's products, the data from each survey have been depressingly consistent. Former U.S. National Security Advisor Zbigniew Brzezinski reminds us that what the world thinks of the United States may have never mattered more. "In this age of worldwide political awakening and shared international vulnerability," he wrote, "security depends not only on military power but also on the prevailing climate of opinion."[35] Sadly, in our entire history as a nation, world opinion has never been as hostile to the United States as it is today. The unanswered question, of course, is why?

PART TWO

CHAPTER 6

WHY DO THEY HATE US?

"There are two schools of thought about the famous question: Why do they hate us? One school of thought says: 'They hate us—what's wrong with us?' The second school says, 'They hate us—what's wrong with them?' "[1]

—Fouad Ajami, Johns Hopkins University

THE KEY TO THE MOST BURNING QUESTION OF OUR TIME—*WHY DO they hate us?*—may have been unlocked more than eighty years ago by a journalist known for Olympian detachment.

Walter Lippmann was one of the most influential journalists in America, from the time he wrote his first book in 1913, just five years after graduating from Harvard, until he published his last newspaper column in 1971, just three years before his death. The son of second-generation German-Jewish parents, Lippmann flirted with socialism, cofounded *The New Republic* magazine, and was an adviser to President Woodrow Wilson, writing eight of the "fourteen principles" the president took to the Paris Peace Conference ending the First World War—all before he turned thirty. By 1935, James Thurber was confident enough in Lippmann's celebrity to make him the punch line of a *New Yorker* cartoon: A wife looks up from her newspaper and tells her husband, "Walter Lippmann scares me this morning."[2]

By modern standards, Lippmann was not a media bomb thrower. His stock in trade was not facile solutions, but deep ruminating analysis. His copy was sonorous and filled with phrases one might expect to hear echoing off marble walls. He was a rare commodity in journalism—a genuine intellectual who interpreted current events within the wide sweep of history. Yet he was first to recognize that, in most political debates, ideas take a back seat to feelings. And that most of what passes for "ideas" in society are really hairballs of accepted wisdom caught in the lint traps of our own brains.

For example, back in the 1920s, Lippmann observed that most of us know the world as "pictures in our heads" rather than through personal experience. The pictures in our heads, of course, are seldom perfect representations of reality. Our attention spans are too short, our vocabulary too inadequate, and our storage capacity too limited for that. Furthermore, the constant stream of incoming pictures is colored by images we have already stored—the stereotypes, prejudices, and preconceptions through which we interpret the world and which direct the play of our attention. Over time, the pictures in our heads fade or sharpen, condense and combine until we have made them our own. At that point, we have such an emotional stake in those "pictures," they form part of our identity.

PUBLIC OPINION

"Those pictures which are acted upon by groups of people," Lippmann wrote, "are Public Opinion with capital letters."[3] To Lippmann's mind, public opinion doesn't arise from the careful consideration of a group of facts. On the contrary, it is the screen through which we *see* the facts. So when the late Democratic Senator Daniel Patrick Moynihan quipped that everyone is entitled to his own opinions but not his own facts, he may have underestimated the power of the former over the latter.

Public opinion is not coolly rational and analytic. It is highly emotional. "Opinions are not in continual and pungent contact with the facts they profess to treat," Lippmann wrote. "But the feelings attached to those opinions can be even more intense than the original ideas that provoked them."[4] In other words, over time people know what they feel without being entirely sure why they feel it. And of all the pictures in our head, the most loaded are those dealing with home, country, and flag.

So answering the now famous question—*Why do they hate us?*—requires more than number crunching. Like all the other "isms" of our age—sexism, ageism, racism, etc.—anti-Americanism is not the product of careful analysis; it is a predisposition. As the Italian political scientist Robert Toscano pointed out, anti-Americans hate America "for what it is, rather than what it does."[5] But people aren't born that way. Their predisposition must be based on something.

Paul Hollander, who has been studying and writing about anti-Americanism since at least the early 1990s, says it can have only two possible foundations. Either it's based on a clear-eyed view of reality, in which case there really isn't a lot to discuss, or it's the product of some "deeply rooted scapegoating impulse."[6] In the first case, America is a "morally repugnant entity, an aggressive global power . . . riddled with domestic injustices."[7] In the second case, anti-Americanism springs more from the circumstances of those who express it than from America's foreign policy, society, or culture. While Hollander concedes that America has many faults, he rejects the sweeping generalizations that anti-Americans draw from them, saying they "spring from the needs of human beings to explain and reduce the responsibility for the pain and misfortune in their lives."[8] Others, of course, maintain that anti-Americanism is the only rational reaction to the pain and misfortune America is inflicting on them, its own people, and all the other people of the world.

The truth is probably somewhere in between those opposing views. Just as some paranoids really do have enemies, some anti-Americans really do have a point. But true or not, all those individual points can draw a compelling, if inaccurate, "picture" of America.

THE ROOTS OF ANTI-AMERICANISM

Anti-Americanism has deep roots, deeper even than the country itself. Some writers trace it all the way back to the "degeneracy thesis" of colonial days, which held that because the biblical flood had reached America later than the rest of the world, the land was still soggy and the climate, excessively humid. As a result, the growth of plants and animals was stunted. Dogs did not bark. Birds sang off-key. All of nature deteriorated in disgusting sogginess, and people who came from Europe were bound to degenerate as well.[9]

Only slightly more rational was the quasi-Darwinian notion that people who wanted to immigrate to America must be slightly "off" and all their interbreeding couldn't produce anything but genetically inferior brutes. The theory of degeneracy was considered cutting-edge science in the eighteenth century and was so popularly held that Founding Fathers Alexander Hamilton, Benjamin Franklin, and Thomas Jefferson devoted considerable energy to debunking it.

The intervening years, of course, proved the degeneracy thesis wrong. But the upstart new country provided fertile ground for European philosophers whose studied poses of intellectual skepticism had degenerated into cynicism toward modernization and societal change. Political scientist James W. Ceaser traced the genealogy of anti-Americanism from eighteenth-century French scientists to later German thinkers such as Hegel, Nietzsche, Spengler, and Heidegger, who viewed America as a culturally inferior, soulless wasteland.[10] Latin America's elites, who were always more culturally and intellectually European than "American," adopted these notions as readily as they did the latest Parisian fashions. In nineteenth- and early-twentieth-century Latin America, anti-Americanism was the perfect foil to the stirrings of nationalism ignited by the Monroe Doctrine. Of course, all that was put on hold during the Second World War.

POSTWAR ANTI-AMERICANISM

In postwar Europe, anti-Americanism was principally confined to the French and British intelligentsia whose gratitude for liberating them from the Nazi yoke did not quite outweigh their resentment for being displaced as colonial powers. As Tony Judt notes in his masterful history of the period, their influence made anti-American sentiment appear more widespread than it actually was. Over time, British and French cultural conservatives and radicals shared a common caricature of America. To them, "America was a land of hysterical puritans," Judt wrote, "given over to technology, standardizations, and conformism, bereft of originality of thought."[11] Elsewhere in the world, anti-Americanism became the natural byproduct of embracing communism, socialism, nationalism, or "Third Worldism."

By the last quarter of the twentieth century, Britain had resolved any remaining nostalgia for its old empire, forgiven the Americans' success, and begun rebuilding its own economy along the lines of the U.S. model, with a safety net to protect workers. But anti-American sentiment had moved out of the salons and cafés of France into the town squares of Continental Europe. America, which had seemed so familiar and friendly during the Cold War, now appeared alien and threatening.

Part of it was social and economic. Caught between the economic models of communism and free market capitalism during the Cold War, most European countries had adopted a middle path of relatively free, though heavily regulated, markets in which the state owned key industries, taxes were heavy, and workers were protected by thick safety nets. Part of it was cultural. Even though many Europeans embraced U.S. popular culture, they couldn't understand Americans' earnest religious fundamentalism, fondness for personal firearms (including semiautomatic assault rifles), and frequent resort to the death penalty. Part of it was political. Europeans couldn't understand why Washington was so hesitant to approve international treaties on issues such as banning land mines or creating an International Criminal Court. But all of it was palpable to anyone paying attention.

All this intellectual posturing and grumbling produced what Robert Hughes called a "culture of complaint" in his 1994 book of the same name. America became a symbol of modernity, as it has lately become a symbol of globalization, and with the same schizophrenic ambivalence. As Paul Berman pointed out in *The New Republic,* one puzzling aspect of this cultural tradition is its capacity to condemn America for entirely contradictory reasons. America is "a country without values," Berman noted, "and appallingly moralistic." It is "repulsive for being racist; and for mixing its races." America is simultaneously "governed by a dictatorship of millionaires" and "by a rabble of corner grocers." The contradictions continue. America is "hopelessly Christian" and "dominated by Jews." "Coldly calculating" and "religiously insane." But the greatest danger that the United States poses to the world is a culture that "despite its lack of appeal" is "dangerously appealing, and going to crush all other cultures."[12]

It was within these contradictory feelings that Europe forged its own identity, becoming a "pole of opposition" to America.

VIRTUOSO ANTI-AMERICANISM

The depth of that opposition is sometimes hard to fathom. For example, one year after the September 11 attacks, a French intellectual named Emmanuel Todd published a screed, *After the Empire,* that accused the United States of pretending that terrorism was a worldwide threat so it could shore up its reputation as a superpower by attacking insignificant adversaries. Todd explained the "myth of universal terrorism" as a "transitional crisis" the Muslim world could work out in due time without outside intervention. According to Todd, America manufactured its "war on terrorism" to remain "at least symbolically at the center" of a world that no longer needed it. It was all part of U.S. efforts to "maintain the illusory fiction of the world as a dangerous place in need of America's protection." In this way, America can stay in the middle of things to further its real strategic objective— "political control of the world's resources."[13]

This would all be outrageous and strangely amusing except that Todd is a French demographer whose 1976 book *The Final Fall* predicted the demise of the Soviet Union before it became popular wisdom. Given his track record as a prognosticator, his book on America was taken very seriously. It spent several months on best-seller lists in France and Germany and is said to have influenced French policy on the war in Iraq.

As bizarre as it was, Todd's book did not represent the nadir of anti-American virtuosity. That was reached with the March 2002 publication of *L'Effroyable Imposture* ("The Appalling Deception") by Thierry Meyssan, which claimed that no airplane slammed into the Pentagon on September 11, 2001. There was an explosion all right, but it was a truck bomb set off by shadowy elements in the U.S. government itself to justify gigantic increases in the defense budget. Meyssan's book was also a best-seller in France.

In fact, at least three more anti-American books rolled off French printing presses in 2003.[14] But anti-Americanism is not the exclusive province of Gauloise-sucking French eggheads. The culture of complaint and conspiracy may have been born in France and Germany, but it has since spread across the globe to groups that have not yet given up on Marxism or feel threatened by globalization (which they consider a new form of American colonialism). For example, just days after the September 11 attacks, the respected Brazilian economist Celso Furtado opined that the destruction of the World Trade Center was most likely part of a plot by the American extreme right to justify a government takeover. Argentine activist Hebe de Bonafini told interviewers in the days following the attacks that "in the Twin Towers died the powerful. And the powerful are my enemy . . . I am happy and celebrate the fact that this savage capitalism which destroys us for once has been hit."[15] Nobel Prize–winning Italian playwright Dario Fo asked, "What is 20,000 [sic] dead in New York when the great [Wall Street] speculators wallow in an economy that every year kills tens of millions of people with poverty?"[16] And after the initial expressions of sympathy, pundits around the world opined that the terrorism unleashed on America could be explained—maybe even justified—on the grounds that the American-driven wave of globalization was leaving nothing but poverty and exploitation in its wake.

ANTI-ANTI-AMERICANS

The late French writer Jean-François Revel was impatient with this pious intellectualizing. For one thing, he pointed out, globalization has not spread poverty but prosperity. "In the last fifty years," he noted, "in what used to be called the Third World, a threefold increase has occurred: in average income, in population, and in life expectancy."[17] The few exceptions—especially in Africa—were due to a combination of political corruption, socialism, and civil war rather than global capitalism. Furthermore, Revel was certain that this long, nearly unbroken plaint about America had deeper motives.

Revel saw sinister motives at work—America as global scapegoat. By blaming America for all the world's real and imagined problems, he notes, Europeans can avoid responsibility for their own actions.[18] "Here we see how the Americans are useful to us," he writes. "To console us for our own failures, serving the myth that they do worse than we do, and that what goes badly with us is their fault."[19] A Mexican intellectual, José Antonio Aguilar Rivera, traced the roots of anti-Americanism within Latin America to the same phenomenon. "Victimization has always been a part of nationalist sentiment," he wrote. "Anti-Americanism is an emotionally satisfying explanation of our faults."[20] And writing in *Foreign Affairs,* Barry Rubin suggested that promoting anti-Americanism is simply the best means various Arab leaders have found to distract their people from their real problems.[21] In their own "wag the dog" fashion, they have made anti-Americanism a weapon of mass distraction.[22]

According to Revel, anti-Americanism constitutes the ruling archetype of the world's economic, cultural, and political leadership. "Anti-

Americanism is becoming the way people think about the world and position themselves within it," wrote *Newsweek International*'s editor Fareed Zakaria. "It is a mindset that extends beyond politics to economic and cultural realms."[23]

Some people are fairly sanguine about this turn of events. The most celebrated postwar French historian, Fernand Braudel, took a fairly long view. "At the center of the world-economy," he wrote, "one always finds an exceptional state, strong, aggressive and privileged, dynamic, simultaneously feared and admired. In the fifteenth century it was Venice; in the seventeenth, Holland; in the eighteenth and still in the nineteenth it was Britain; today it is the United States."[24]

ISLAMIC ANTI-AMERICANISM

So does anti-Americanism simply boil down to scapegoating, jealousy, and resentment? In part. But like influenza, it comes in various strains, each a particularized mutation responding to local fears, insecurities, and grudges. To paraphrase Tolstoy, friends of the United States are all alike; anti-Americans are all anti-American in their own way. For example, while many Europeans are put off by the ostentatious religiosity of prominent American leaders, most Muslims consider Americans materialistic and irreligious.

Adherents of the fundamentalist Wahhabi/Salafi ideology carry a particularly virulent strain of anti-Americanism. They follow a strict and rigid interpretation of Islam and see the United States not only as a nation of "infidels," but as the principal obstacle to establishing a utopian caliphate from Morocco to Indonesia and the Philippines and eventually around the world.

Financed by oil-rich patrons who consider this fundamentalist brand of Islamic politics a useful counterweight to stirrings of democracy, the Wahhabi have made substantial inroads throughout the Muslim world. *Newsweek*'s Zakaria estimates that in the past thirty years, "Saudi-funded schools have churned out tens of thousands of half-educated, fanatical Muslims who view the modern world and non-Muslims with great suspicion."[25] According to the former president of Indonesia, Abdurrahman Wahid, "Islamic fundamentalism has become a well-financed, multifaceted global movement that operates like a juggernaut in much of the developing world, and even among immigrant Muslim communities in the West."[26] Even Muslims who don't buy into this puritanical strain of Islam resonate to its proud refusal to submit to American economic and military dominance. And when the Pew Research Center surveyed residents of the Middle East in 2005, majorities or pluralities in every country except Jordan considered Islam's growing role in politics a positive development. In stark contrast, solid majorities in all five predominantly Muslim countries, when surveyed, expressed unfavorable views of the United States.[27]

CLASH OF CIVILIZATIONS

Harvard political scientist Samuel Huntington predicted as much in 1993. Following the end of the Cold War, Huntington famously predicted that future conflicts would not be between nation-states, but between civilizations. Huntington believed the processes of globalization would increase contact between people of different civilizations, highlighting their fundamental differences on such core issues as the relations between God and man, between the individual and the group, between husband and wife, and between parent and child.

Such contacts have multiplied, not only because of modern communications media, but also because of increasingly free travel and immigration. Muslims now represent 5 percent of the population of Western Europe, three times what it was thirty years ago, and it is projected to double again by 2025. That Muslims have not been fully assimilated into European society became painfully obvious when gangs of Islamic young people torched cars and clashed with police in the housing projects surrounding Paris during October and November of 2005. Muslim mass protests across Europe when a Danish newspaper printed cartoons depicting the prophet Muhammad demonstrated their alienation. And bombings in Madrid and London showed that the threat of violence is real.

"These differences," Huntington wrote, ". . . will not soon disappear. They are far more fundamental than differences among political ideologies and political regimes . . . and over the centuries they have generated the longest and most violent conflicts." One of the most obvious flash points, he said, would be along the fault line between Western and Islamic civilizations, "where conflict has been going on for 1,300 years."[28] In that clash, America is simultaneously a stunt double for the West and a scapegoat for the failings of Islamic civil society. All because of the pictures in their heads.

CHAPTER 7

THE PICTURES IN THEIR HEADS

"The United States lost the public relations war in the Muslim world a long time ago. They could have the prophet Muhammad doing public relations and it wouldn't help."[1]
—Osama Siblani, publisher, *The Arab American News*

DARK, SLENDER, AND HANDSOME, AS WELL AS A CERTIFIED foreign policy wonk, Fareed Zakaria has been called everything from an "intellectual heartthrob"[2] to a "junior Kissinger."[3] When he isn't on the road, he oversees the international editions of *Newsweek* magazine from a spacious corner office in a midtown Manhattan skyscraper. Although he carries the title of "editor," he seldom actually edits anything in the sense of marking up copy. His job is to come up with story ideas for *Newsweek*'s ten international editions, in addition to writing a biweekly column that is also syndicated by *The Washington Post*. That's his day job. He is also a very popular public speaker; writes books; hosts a half-hour weekly program on PBS, *Foreign Exchange*; and is a regular guest on both ABC's *This Week with George Stephanopoulos* and Comedy Central's *Daily Show with Jon Stewart*. He even used to write a wine column for the online magazine *Slate*. Straddling such dissimilar worlds seems to have been his destiny.

FAREED ZAKARIA

Zakaria was born and raised in Bombay (now Mumbai), India, to a father who was a popular political figure and a mother who was an editor at *The Times of India*. The country's best architects, poets, and political figures were often guests in his home when he was growing up. And although his parents were practicing Muslims, they also celebrated Hindu holidays and sent Fareed to an Anglican primary school where every day began with the singing of Christian hymns. From that ecumenical childhood, Zakaria attended Yale and then Harvard, where he received his Ph.D. in political science.

At twenty-eight, he became the youngest managing editor in the history of *Foreign Affairs* magazine, the official journal of wannabe and wannabe-again secretaries of state, foreign ministers, and ambassadors. Then in 2000, he made the leap to a general interest newsweekly just in time to explain the events of September 11, 2001, to a frightened and confused readership. The cover story he wrote for *Newsweek*—"The Politics of Rage: Why Do They Hate Us?"—catapulted him from a rising star of the foreign policy apparatchik to a mainstream member of the commentariat who could explain the other 95 percent of the world to Americans. His upper-class, Indian accent and Muslim upbringing only added credibility to the package, just as the brilliantine jet-black hair, deep set eyes, and sharply tailored suits added sex appeal.

Zakaria is generally regarded as a neoconservative. He confesses that Ronald Reagan was a hero, and although he supported the Bush administration's invasion of Iraq, he has been highly critical of its actions since. As a cultural interpreter of the Middle East, he may be without peer. To those who see terrorism as an angry reaction to America's wealth, he points out that there are billions of poor people in the world who have never used airplanes as guided missiles. To those who see a "clash of civilizations" between Islam and the West, he points out that Indonesia, the largest Muslim country, has been relatively free of anti-Americanism and that the second, third, and fourth largest Muslim countries—Pakistan, Bangladesh, and India— have successfully mixed Islam and modernity. In fact, all three elected women as prime ministers before many countries in the West.

NOT ISLAM, OIL

The rabid anti-Americanism of the Middle East, in Zakaria's view, is a byproduct of its oil riches. Because they could fund their regimes with petrodollars, the monarchs and dictators of the Middle East had no incentive to liberalize their economies and societies. And since they could stifle dissent by controlling the universities, media, and local political groups, there wasn't much downside, either. In the Middle East, sitting on oceans of oil created both economic and political retardation.

Two developments made this situation particularly unstable. First, Arab societies are undergoing the same demographic phenomenon that dislocated much of the West in the late 1960s—a huge youth bulge. More than half of the Middle East's population is under age 25. Millions of young people have come of age with absolutely no economic opportunity and no political voice. Second, this demographic change has coincided with a wave of globalization that is washing over the Middle East through satellite television, the Internet, and the DVDs sold in local market stalls. According to a 2003 study of Middle East media for the Conference of International Broadcasters' Audience Research Services, satellite television "is the most popular entertainment and information medium" in the Middle East.[4] With satellite dishes selling for the equivalent of about $100, penetration exceeds 75 percent in most countries.

Thus, Arab young people know what is going on in the world outside. "[Arab] societies are open enough to be disrupted by modernity," according to Zakaria, "but not so open that they can ride the wave."[5] In other words, young Arabs can watch the West's television shows, eat its fast foods, and drink its soft drinks, but they have no opportunity to participate beyond the level of consumer.

Thomas Friedman, columnist for *The New York Times,* blames much of Arab hostility toward the U.S. on "the failure of many Muslim countries to build economies that prepare young people for modernity."[6] In fact, according to the World Bank, unemployment in the Middle East and North Africa is more than 13 percent overall and nearly twice that rate among young people. In many countries of the region, unemployment rates are *higher* among the better educated than among the illiterate.[7]

The only significant institutions free of state control in the Arab world are the mosques, which had long ago turned into places to vent feelings of frustration, discontent, and opposition to the status quo. Religion became the language of politics. Fundamentalist groups such as the Muslim Brotherhood, Hamas, and Hezbollah didn't hesitate to mine a "purer" form of Islam from the Quran, which proved malleable enough to serve their political purposes, and they built a following by providing social services to the poor.

Determined to erase the line between politics and religion, the fundamentalist groups rejected the corrupting effects of modern culture. "Modernization is now taken to mean, inevitably, uncontrollably, Westernization," wrote Zakaria, "and, even worse, Americanization."[8]

And it all started with the pictures in their heads.

HOW THE PICTURES GET IN THEIR HEADS

One of the multifarious committees tasked with evaluating U.S. efforts to repair its lousy image abroad noted that "effective public diplomacy requires respectful dialogue and vigorous engagement at the level of ideas, not images."[9] Who could argue with that? But the dialogue will never be fruitful if one of the participants harbors false images of the other side.

Most of what the world knows of America is filtered through the media, and, in many parts of the world, the media's normal angle of repose is almost by charter counter to American politics, society, and culture, if not abjectly anti-American. In many Western minds, exhibit A is probably Al Jazeera, the most popular television news network in the Middle East. Arabic for "The Island" or "The (Arabian) Peninsula," Al Jazeera is based in Qatar and claims to be the only politically independent TV station in the Middle East. Broadcasting via satellite since 1996, it has an audience of 50 million viewers, including a whopping 57 percent of viewers seeking news. In fact, 61 percent of viewers rated Al Jazeera the most credible source for news.[10] Fareed Zakaria calls the network a major lane of "the new Arab Street in the Middle East."[11]

Al Jazeera has also become must-see TV for U.S. officials trying to gauge public opinion in the Arab world, and they have not always been happy with what they see. The TV network provided the only footage coming out of Taliban-controlled Afghanistan, showing the killing and maiming of Afghan civilians during the U.S. air strikes. Similarly, during the war in Iraq, Al Jazeera's cameramen documented the effects of American bombing on Iraqi citizens. The network also broadcast videotapes of blindfolded hostages kidnapped by the Iraqi insurgents pleading for their lives.

All of these actions moved the Bush administration to accuse the network of engaging in propaganda for the enemy. Things came to a head during the April 2004 assault on Fallujah by U.S. Marines and Iraqi security forces. During one week of the assault, the Coalition Provisional Authority in Baghdad detailed thirty-four instances of alleged distortion by Al Jazeera, including stories about American soldiers killing and mutilating Iraqi citizens.

U.S. Defense Secretary Donald Rumsfeld described Al Jazeera's coverage as "vicious, inaccurate, and inexcusable."[12] According to a leaked memo from Number 10 Downing Street, President Bush suggested shutting up Al Jazeera by bombing its headquarters in Qatar. As the London *Sunday Times* later reported in typical British understatement, "[I]t is not known whether he was joking."[13] For its part, the White House labeled the accusation "outlandish."

While being attacked from both ends of the political spectrum is hardly proof of objectivity, it's worth noting that, as of 2002, Arab governments had filed more than 450 official complaints against Al Jazeera for "bruising Arab sensibilities, breaching the Arab code of ethics, [and] having inappropriate coverage of certain news events."[14]

The only country in the region that hasn't yet banned Al Jazeera's reporters is Israel, despite the network's brutally anti-Semitic programming. And some of the Western criticism leveled against it turns out to be spurious on closer examination. For example, although figures as prominent as Secretary Rumsfeld have accused the network of broadcasting videos of hostages being beheaded, Al Jazeera has never actually done so.

In the end, Al Jazeera may be the single most significant exception to Fareed Zakaria's thesis that Middle Eastern regimes have successfully stifled all secular paths of dissent. The network's coverage of events in Arab countries hews to no official line, and by giving airtime to opposition leaders, it may even help raise standards for the official state media. The frequent inclusion of Israelis on the network's panel discussions at least brings their point of view to a broad Arab audience. And it makes no friends among fundamentalists by giving airtime to dissident, even revolutionary views of Islam. Its programming may occasionally fan flames of populism and even anti-Americanism, but in the long-run Al Jazeera is also laying the foundation for pluralism and modernization in the Arab world.

In fact, Al Jazeera may have already succeeded on that score. In 2003, the Saudi-controlled Middle East Broadcasting Center pulled together a group of Arab investors to launch Al Arabiya television, a Dubai-based all-news channel that claims to be a more moderate alternative to Al Jazeera. The network's Saudi backing caused some to suspect that its programming would be heavily censored, but like its principal competitor, Al Arabiya has drawn fire from both sides—literally. Eleven of its employees have been killed in three separate incidents in Iraq, three by U.S. troops and eight by insurgents.

CONTEXTUAL OBJECTIVITY?

Are Al Jazeera and Al Arabiya biased against the United States, or do they simply cover the news from an Arab point of view, or is there a difference? Two Muslim journalists turned academics, Mohammed El-Nawawy and Adel Iskandar, borrowed a term from quantum physics to explain Arab TV networks' journalistic standards, which they suggest also apply to CNN, the BBC, and Fox News.

All news organizations, they suggest, practice "contextual objectivity." That is, they strive to "reflect all sides of any story while retaining the values, beliefs, and sentiments of the target audience."[15] In other words, Al Jazeera and Al Arabiya approach every story—including the decision of whether or not to cover it, and if so, how—from the perspective of the typical Arab, while CNN and the BBC reflect the point of view of Westerners. *The Economist* dismissed the concept as a clumsy effort "to defend the network [Al Jazeera] from its detractors" and "at best a muddle, at worst, an evasion."[16]

But is it such a leap to presume that news media do their reporting from the same perspective as their target audience? At minimum, every news outlet tries to appeal to potential viewers' interests.

Consider the February 2, 2005, *Newsweek* edition distributed in Japan. The cover showed an American flag, dirtied and tossed in a trash can, its staff snapped in two. The Japanese headline read: THE DAY AMERICA DIED. In the rest of the world, the international edition of *Newsweek* had a photograph of President Bush on the cover with the caption, "America Leads . . . But Is Anyone Following?" Both editions featured the same cover story by Andrew Moravcsik, entitled "Dream on, America," which described how the rest of the world was rejecting the "American way of life." (In Japanese, the story title read: "America, the dream country, is rotting away.") Moravcsik's article didn't run in the American edition of that same issue, which had three Hollywood movie stars on the cover.

The *Newsweek International* cover story was an example of contextual objectivity from an American publication serving up news that would appeal to its foreign audiences.

El-Nawawy and Iskandar see nothing incompatible between reporting the news from a particular point of view and simultaneously reflecting all sides of the story. Within that context, they say, such news coverage would be "objective." So, in the early days of the Iraq War, coverage by Al Jazeera and Al Arabiya focused on civilian casualties, playing to the feelings of their Arab viewers. Meanwhile, the American networks focused on the performance and well-being of U.S. troops, which was of obvious interest to their viewers at home. None of the networks ignored the rest of the story—the Arab networks covered U.S. casualties and the American networks reported on civilian deaths—but the thrust of their reporting was diametrically different.

STEREOTYPES

None of this would have surprised Walter Lippmann. After a long newspaper career, he concluded that the commonsense assumption that we first see and then define has it backward. He wrote:

> For the most part, we define first and then see. In the great blooming, buzzing confusion of the outer world we pick out what our culture has already defined for us, and we tend to perceive that which we have picked out in the form stereotyped for us by our culture.[17]

Nor did Lippmann consider journalists immune from this phenomenon. Consider an editor sitting at the end of a long conveyor belt of reports on the day's events, trivial and significant, recent and yet to occur. As Lippmann observed:

> [The editor] sits in his office, reads [reports, but] rarely does he see any large portion of the events themselves. He must woo at least a section of his readers every day, because they will leave him without mercy if

a rival paper happens to hit their fancy. He works under enormous pressure, for the competition of newspapers is often a matter of minutes. Every bulletin requires a swift but complicated judgment. It must be understood, put in relation to other bulletins also understood, and played up or played down according to its probable interest for the public, as the editor conceives it. Without standardization, without stereotypes, without routine judgments, without a fairly ruthless disregard of subtlety, the editor would soon die of excitement.[18]

Lippmann could not have foreseen an age of twenty-four-hour television news and peripatetic Internet blogs, but his observations on the nature of news and newspeople are timeless.

But "contextual objectivity" may not give Arab (or American) viewers the "best available version of the truth," which is how Carl Bernstein famously defined what journalists should report. That, one supposes, would require Arab viewers to watch CNN or the BBC as well as Al Jazeera or Al Arabiya. And Americans would have to watch Al Jazeera as well as the U.S. networks. Neither is likely, even though Al Jazeera is starting an English-language service that will be available in the United States. So most Arab viewers—and French, Brazilian, Japanese, and, yes, American—are left with their own version of the truth, which in some instances may be only second- or third-best, in an endlessly reinforcing loop.

HOMEGROWN ANTI-AMERICANISM

Foreign media are not the only source of distorted portrayals of America and arguably not the most the most troubling.

The 2003 report of the House Advisory Group on Public Diplomacy for the Arab and Muslim World observed that "Arabs and Muslims are . . . bombarded with American sitcoms, violent films, and other entertainment, much of which distorts the perceptions of viewers."[19] What seems innocuous to Americans can cause problems abroad: "A Syrian teacher of English asked us plaintively for help in explaining American family life to her students," the report noted. "She asked, 'Does *Friends* show a typical family?'"

If all you knew about the United States was what you saw or heard on prime-time television, at the movies, or through the stereo, you might be afraid to leave your home. To you, the United States would be a violent place of marauding gangs and a few privileged, gun-toting rich people riding between gated communities in limousines with darkened windows. Ironically, that image—the pictures we put in people's heads—constitutes one of America's largest exports. According to a report by the U.S. Intellectual Property Industries, a Washington, D.C.-based lobbying group, the motion picture, video, recorded music, and publishing industries accounted for $13 billion in exports in 2003,[20] not as much as the auto or aerospace industries, but growing at a much faster pace.

For years, U.S. movie studios were virtually shut out of many foreign markets by a variety of barriers. But in the mid- and late-1990s, these restrictions were lifted as a result of free trade agreements enforced by the World Trade Organization. In recent years, foreign box-office revenue has grown much faster than the domestic market by nearly a two-to-one ratio. At the end of 2005, of the 100 top-grossing films of all time outside the United States, all but four were American.[21] In fact, in France, the top-grossing film of 2005 was *Star Wars: Episode III* and the top-grossing film of all time was 1997's *Titanic*. According to *Variety*, even in an otherwise poor year at the box office, U.S. movie production companies accounted for more than 70 percent of total worldwide ticket sales of $12 billion in 2004.[22]

Exports are just as important for music and TV. Foreign sales represent 50 percent of the U.S. recording industry's revenue. The United States has historically exported more than three times the total television programming as the next three leading exporting nations combined. And while American television programs no longer dominate prime-time schedules in foreign countries, series such as *Desperate Housewives, Law and Order,* and *The Sopranos* are popular from Oslo to Beijing. The programs are dubbed or subtitled, of course, and even sometimes edited for local mores. For example, *Desperate Housewives* runs several minutes shorter in China than in the States because trysts are shortened to satisfy censors. Nevertheless, U.S. popular entertainment provides the most sustained and consistent view many people have of America.

INCIDENTAL ANTI-AMERICANISM

The popularity of American entertainment around the world may be good for the U.S. trade imbalance, and it's certainly welcome in Hollywood and on Wall Street. But what's good for show business may not be great for America's image. Psychological studies since the advent of the first television sets have pretty much established that no single TV program can rewire a viewer's head, even with extremely heavy viewing. In the short run, the effects of any particular TV program or movie are selected and limited. However, over an extended period, small effects occurring a few at a time can eventually add up to significant long-term influences. And when the media—television, movies, and recorded music—corroborate and reinforce each other, people's opinions, attitudes, and beliefs can be subtly affected and even changed.

Viewers acquire what is known as "incidental knowledge," which refers to the learning that people unconsciously acquire in the course of doing something else. Most psychologists agree that in learning a second language, after the first few thousand most common words, vocabulary is predominantly acquired incidentally.[23] Very young children watch television for entertainment, but in the course of watching (and rewatching) *Sesame Street*, they not only learn their letters and numbers when Cookie Monster eats the letter H or when Count Von Count enumerates the bats in his castle, they also learn a lot about the world outside—what it looks like, how it works, and how they fit into it. Little of that learning is explicit, a lot of it is somewhat fuzzy, but it will inform and sometimes even dominate most of their everyday decision making and thought processes for the rest of their lives.

Researchers in England, for example, found that teenagers who watched movies in which a lot of the characters puffed on cigarettes were significantly more likely to start smoking, even if their parents didn't smoke.[24] A similar study in the United States suggests that exposure to such movies accounts for more than a third of all the adolescents who start smoking.[25]

HOLLYWOOD'S AMERICA

When two researchers at Boston University set out to examine the "incidental learning" teenagers around the world have acquired about American life from exposure to U.S. entertainment media, they were shocked to discover that "the majority of young people around the world . . . learned that [Americans] are violent, criminally inclined, and that American women are sexually immoral."[26] They found such a strong correlation between these attitudes and exposure to American media that it would have taken seventeen decimal places to express the probability that it was a statistical fluke.[27]

On reflection, the Boston University researchers were not completely surprised since "media entertainment provides subtle but abundant lessons to the youth in societies around the world as to what ordinary American people are really like." And thanks to an explosion in satellite television and DVDs, as well as Hollywood's freer access to export markets, American entertainment programs are pouring into societies that have little other direct contact with the United States.

And what kind of movies sell best outside the United States? The Internet Movie Database lists twelve genres of films, from Romance to Horror. When researchers at New York University's Stern School of Business correlated foreign box-office sales to these genres, they discovered that "seven of the genres had a significant impact on how films performed in foreign countries. Action, Fantasy, Adventure, Animated, Mystery, and Horror all performed significantly better in foreign countries, while Family performed significantly worse." For the other five genres, the differences were not significant.[28]

The Boston University researchers would not have been surprised. In their view, teenagers are the biggest audience for entertainment media and "above all, young people the world over want to see *exciting action*."[29] If kids enjoy fistfights, car chases, explosions, and shootouts, then that's what Hollywood will give them. If young males want to see nude women, bring them on. "Exactly this kind of exciting content has been increasingly incorporated into the motion pictures, TV dramas, music videos, and other forms of popular culture that are produced by media corporations (mostly in the United States) and shipped to other countries," the BU researchers wrote, because "competition for audiences is *fierce*."[30]

When U.S. adman Keith Reinhard saw this study, he took the results with a grain of salt. He had seen his own work put through the research grinder and watched helplessly while commercials he had sweated over were vivisected by number crunchers. But one chart, in particular, troubled him, and he seldom failed to include it in his roadshow presentation on anti-Americanism. It was a depiction of age distributions in developed and developing countries (see Figure 7-1). In developed countries, the chart showed a fairly even distribution of age

Population Structures by Age and Sex, 2005
Millions

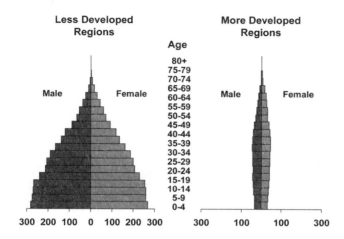

Figure 7-1. Age distribution of the world's population.

Source: United Nations, *World Population Prospects: The 2004 Revision,* 2005. © 2006 Population Reference Bureau. Reprinted courtesy of the Population Reference Bureau.

groups—nearly a straight column from birth to four years old, all the way up to age 70 plus. But in developing countries, it was a pyramid with a very broad base in the ages below 30, including 600 million teenagers, nearly three times as many as in the developed world. "What pictures of America are forming in their heads?" he wondered.

CHAPTER 8

THE BUSINESS OF AMERICA

*"Japanese and American management is 95 percent the same, and
differs in all important respects."*[1]
—Takeo Fujisawa, cofounder of Honda Motor Company

BY 2004, KEITH REINHARD HAD BEEN AN AD AGENCY CEO FOR
twenty years, but he had never been more than a tourist on Capitol
Hill. And if he had planned a family excursion with his grandchildren
to the nation's capital, it would not have been in the sticky days of
August. But he had more than the weather on his mind. Reinhard was
about to testify before a congressional committee. And not just any
committee, but the House subcommittee considering the 9/11 Commission's recommendations on public diplomacy. Three years after
surveying his own foreign employees about their attitudes toward
America, and just a few months after incorporating Business for Diplomatic Action, Reinhard had accumulated enough credibility to testify
alongside the former and present undersecretaries of state for public
affairs.

That, of course, was part of his problem. He didn't want to be
identified with either of them—neither with Charlotte Beers, who
fairly or not, had been typecast as an "ad gal," nor with Patricia
Harrison, a political appointee and former cochair of the Republican
National Committee. Over three years, Reinhard had pored over everything he could find on the issue of anti-Americanism, analyzed
every survey, met with every expert who would make room on his
calendar. After all that, he was pretty sure there was no "silver bullet,"

and he was absolutely convinced advertising wasn't the answer. In fact, he thought it could make the problem worse, because after a long series of missteps, the United States had no credibility left where it needed it most around the world.

Reinhard had refined his theory of "cultural imperialism" significantly since 2002. "Much resentment of America results from the misunderstanding of, or disagreement with, U.S. foreign policy," he said. "But much does not." Reinhard identified three other root causes: the effects of globalization, the pervasiveness of American popular culture, and the American people's "collective personality." All three were squarely within the scope of U.S. businesses. "People feel we have been exploitative in our global expansion," Reinhard said. "Many feel that our culture promotes values that are in conflict with local mores or social norms. And Americans are broadly seen as arrogant, insensitive, ignorant, and loud." If American values of freedom and democracy were not at the root of anti-Americanism, the country's cultural values were.

Reinhard's testimony was not intended as an indictment of U.S. businesses but as an attempt to engage them in the fight. He believes American businesses have greater credibility than the U.S. government, more feet on the street outside the United States, and just as much at stake. "The message that CEOs need to hear," he later said, "is that the alarming rise in anti-Americanism around the world simply cannot be good for business long term, and that beyond business concerns, they have a responsibility to use their influence to help win back friends for America."[2]

He suggested anyone who didn't think American business and government were linked in people's minds should review the political cartoons that ran overseas the day after Saddam Hussein's statue was toppled in Baghdad. "In at least half a dozen [of them]," he said, "we saw Saddam had been replaced by Ronald McDonald."[3]

THE TRIUMPH OF CAPITALISM

With the collapse of communism, many in the American business community naturally assumed that American-style free-market capitalism had become the reigning ideology and U.S. corporations, its principal delivery vehicle. *The Wall Street Journal* was even moved to declare in an editorial, "We are all capitalists now."[4] But much of the world has a sharply different conception of capitalism than the American model and, consequently, of a corporation's role in society.

A 2003 survey by the Pew Research Center showed broad support for the "free-market model" almost everywhere, whether in Eastern Europe, sub-Saharan Africa, the Middle East, or Asia.[5] Majorities in thirty-three of forty-four nations surveyed felt that people are better off in a free-market economy, even if that leads to disparities in wealth and income. But this endorsement of free markets went hand in hand with equally broad support for a government safety net. Nearly two-thirds of Americans believed success is within their personal control. Except for Canadians, most of the world disagreed.

And when the possible impacts of free-market capitalism get specific—such as closing inefficient factories or laying off large numbers of people—a great deal of resistance surfaces. Surveys show that majorities in most countries would not agree to close inefficient factories because it would cause too much hardship on people. For example, 53 percent of the people of India say they favor free markets, but 78 percent oppose closing inefficient factories. The contrast between principle and reality could not be starker.

None of this should be a surprise. We tend to forget that business corporations are relatively new institutions. For centuries, most business was conducted by individuals or partnerships, tapping their own assets or borrowing from others to finance their activities. Throughout most of history it took an act of the legislature or the monarch to create a company, and even then its charter was limited to well-defined activities, usually of a charitable or semipublic nature, such as building roads. Occasionally, the legislature would also charter companies to undertake projects considered too risky or expensive for individuals or the government itself. Many of the early trade routes between Europe and India, for example, were developed by royally chartered companies such as the British East India Company. It wasn't until the second half of the nineteenth century that British Parliament passed a series of laws making it far easier to form profit-seeking, jointly owned corporations and, most important, limiting their shareholders' liability to the investment they had made in the firm.

CORPORATE AMERICA

Nowhere was the concept embraced more enthusiastically than in the United States, where many of the original thirteen colonies were actually corporations chartered by the King of England to extract timber, furs, and minerals from the American continent and ship it all back to England. When the U.S. Constitution was drafted, it gave the individual states the authority to grant corporate charters. By 1860, most of the thirty-three states then in existence had adopted laws allowing the creation of "limited liability joint-stock companies." The new form was perfectly suited to raising capital for the railroads that were snaking their way across the continent at the time. Retailing and manufacturing were next in line at the capital trough as they rode the rails to new markets.

By 1913, the impact of corporations on American life was so pronounced that Woodrow Wilson was moved to write, "We are in the presence of a new organization of society. Our life has broken away from the past."[6]

Wilson could not have imagined the size of the break. By the year 2000, of the 100 largest economies in the world, fifty-one were global corporations, forty-nine were countries. Mitsubishi's revenue was greater than the gross domestic product (GDP) of the fourth most populous nation on earth: Indonesia. On that same scale, General Motors was bigger than Denmark; Ford, bigger than South Africa; Toyota, bigger than Norway; Philip Morris, bigger than New Zealand. And Wal-Mart, number twelve on the list, was bigger than 161 countries, including Israel, Poland, and Greece. In fact, if Wal-Mart were a country, in 2000, it would have been China's sixth-largest export market (after Germany) and its eighth-largest trading partner. Just 200 corporations controlled well over a quarter of the world's economic activity.

By 2006, American companies dominated any list of the world's top 200 firms. Six of the top ten companies were American, and U.S. firms accounted for 39 percent of the top 200's sales. But this rise to dominance can't completely account for anti-American feelings. In the 1980s and 1990s, Japanese firms were in a similar position. In 1995, for example, they accounted for 39 percent of the top 200 firms' sales compared to U.S. companies' 28 percent. But no one marched on the local Toyota dealership or Sony office to protest globalization.

VARIETIES OF CAPITALISM

The reason may lie in the divergent paths corporate forms took in the United States as compared to the rest of the world. From the beginning, U.S. companies naturally chose to incorporate in states that placed the fewest restrictions on their activities. This set off a race to the bottom, as states vied with each other to capture lucrative franchise fees by attracting companies to incorporate within their borders. Some observers believe the U.S. courts found that bottom in a 1919 decision that a "business corporation is organized and carried on primarily for the profit of stockholders."[7]

While lawyers, ethicists, and business people have argued the merits of this singularly narrow view of a corporation's purpose, the precedent stands with only minor tinkering nearly ninety years since it was rendered.

This turn of events was perfectly natural, since the corporate form was much faster off the starting blocks in the United States than in Europe. The widely dispersed ownership of American corporations made ensuring that a company's managers were not ripping off its owners the biggest legal and ethical challenge. In Europe, by contrast, the corporate form was slower to be adopted, ownership was more concentrated, and institutions with large stakes in a company usually had a seat on its board. As a result, the central controversy was not the rights of shareholders in relation to managers, but the rights of the community in relation to the corporation itself.

That difference shows up in Europe not only in higher taxes and a thicker safety net of social services, but in greater regulation. The European Union, for example, regulates everything from the size of condoms to the curvature of bananas and cucumbers. EU privacy regulations as of mid-2006 prevented airlines from including passenger meal preferences in preflight reports filed with the U.S. Department of Homeland Security because it might reveal their religious preferences. While many of these regulations are necessary to rationalize standards across countries, they also reflect the social welfare model of the EU's founding members.

In recent years, European economies appeared to be moving closer to the Anglo-Saxon model, though at different speeds. In the 1990s, European governments privatized and deregulated industries ranging from telecommunications to natural gas. Corporate restructurings, factory closings, and massive layoffs have become more common as European companies face greater global competition—and as U.S. investors increase their holdings in them. But there has also been a strong backlash.

Some observers interpreted the 2005 failure to pass a new EU constitution as the public's attempt to correct the European economy's course. What most Europeans voted on was "not the EU constitution but the future of capitalism itself," wrote Jeremy Rifkin. "An increasing number of Europeans are asking themselves whether the liberal market model or the social market model is the best approach to charting the economic future."[8] And in early 2006, when the French government tried to stimulate employment by taking relatively timid steps to make it easier for employers to fire newly hired workers, riots broke out in the streets of Paris and the country's president ultimately had to back down.

The Centre for European Reform summarized the situation well: "When Brits think about 'social Europe,' they are haunted by pre-Thatcher memories of high taxes, state industries, and social unrest. When the French or Germans talk about 'Anglo-Saxon liberalism' they envisage a future of cutthroat capitalism where social safety nets have dissolved and all workers earn Chinese wages."[9] What characterizes the state of capitalism in Europe today is the struggle to preserve a decent level of social welfare and public services in the face of growing global competition and aging populations.

THE PURPOSE OF CORPORATIONS

Organizational specialists Charles Hampden-Turner and Alfons Trompenaars surveyed 15,000 managers from around the world, asking them to choose from the following two statements the one that accurately expressed the proper goal of a corporation:

1. The only real goal of a corporation is making profit.

2. A company, besides making profit, has the goal of attaining the well-being of various stakeholders, such as employees, customers, etc.

Out of the twelve nationalities surveyed, 40 percent of American managers claimed that the sole goal of the corporation was to make a profit, compared to only 33 percent of their counterparts in the United Kingdom, 28 percent in Italy, 27 percent in Sweden, 26 percent in the

Netherlands, 25 percent in Belgium, 24 percent in Germany, and just 16 percent in France.

This difference is also reflected in attitudes toward competition. For example, Trompenaars and Hampden-Turner found that while nearly 70 percent of American managers believed increased competition, rather than cooperation between firms, would benefit society most, only 41 percent of German and 45 percent of French managers had the same view.[10]

To paraphrase Robert Kagan's now classic observation, it seems that American business people are from Mars, Europeans from Venus.[11] The American legal concept of "employment at will," for example, stands in sharp contrast with the German notions of "labor rights" and union participation on corporate supervisory boards. In fact, while only 18 percent of American workers carry union cards, more than half of European workers are unionized—90 percent in Germany.

These facts should not suggest that European corporations are universally beloved in their own countries. When Deutsche Bank announced plans to lay off 1,940 German employees in September 2005, on the heels of an 87 percent profit improvement, it was roundly criticized, not incidentally because it seemed to be following the American model of putting shareholders first. Deutsche Bank was in good company: Insurance giant Allianz tripled its profits in 2004, but cut staff by 17 percent. Pharmaceutical company Schering's earnings jumped by 13 percent in 2004, but it cut 2,000 jobs. Engineering firm Siemens announced drastic job cuts despite an improving bottom line. All four companies explained that they needed to ensure their competitiveness in a global economy.

Well, guess what. As *New York Times* columnist Thomas Friedman observed, "Globalization is so much Americanization. It wears Mickey Mouse ears and it drinks Coke, and it eats Big Macs."[12] While six out of ten Europeans are in favor of globalization, three out of four believe the United States "exercises too much influence on the process."[13] To their minds, the "process" is an endless round of cost-cutting, layoffs, and plant closings.

Globalization is not only crowding Hello Kitty and Orangina off the shelves, it's forcing local companies to change their social contract in another race to the bottom, where Deutsche Bank will be no more German than Citigroup.

SHAREHOLDER VS. STAKEHOLDER

The battle between shareholder and stakeholder capitalism may command less television time than the war in Iraq, but it is no less real. Clark Judge, a former speechwriter for President Ronald Reagan, sees the conflict in historic terms. "The great battle of the twentieth century was between freedom and totalitarianism—an entirely political conflict," he writes. "The great battle of the twenty-first century may well be between the forces of creative destruction and those of destructive preservation—much more a social and cultural conflict."[14]

"Creative destruction," of course, is the colorful phrase coined by economist Joseph Schumpeter to describe the Darwinian process of constant competition, innovation, and entrepreneurship that sustains long-term economic growth even as it destroys established firms and puts people with obsolete skills out of work. "Destructive preservation" is Judge's perhaps slanted characterization of efforts in some countries to soften the impact of full-throttle competition on jobs, communities, the environment, and traditional ways of life, even at the cost of economic growth.

When Europeans protest against globalization, many of them are resisting what they perceive as American efforts to change their very concept of the corporation and its place in society. Many worry that American-style capitalism will eventually lead to massive layoffs, shorter vacations for those who survive, and a general "meaning and leaning" of the workplace.

In short, anti-Americanism can't be blamed entirely on Washington, D.C. It is not only the Bush administration that is seen as arrogant, heavy-handed, and self-centered—so is American business. Even the American public feels that way. A *Business Week*/Harris poll conducted in the summer of 2000—*before* the Enron, WorldCom, Adelphia, and other scandals broke into the headlines—showed that two-thirds of Americans believed large profits are more important to big companies than developing safe, reliable, quality products for consumers.[15] Two years after the scandals broke, public opinion polls from Gallup, National Opinion Research Center, and Harris Interactive (see Figure 8-1) all pegged confidence in big business at thirty-year lows.[16]

By the end of 2005, *The New York Times* opined that Americans have never trusted big business, and they like the people who run it even less: "Pollsters, researchers, even many corporate chiefs them-

Percent (%) "Very Trustworthy"	
President Bush	27
Supreme Court	25
Congress	4
The media	4
Fortune 500 CEOs	2

Figure 8-1. Measures of trust.

Source: Harris Interactive telephone survey of 1,001 investors between July 28 and August 10, 2005.

selves say that business is under attack by a majority of the public, which believes that executives are bent on destroying the environment, cooking the books, and lining their own pockets."[17]

In Europe, public opinion polls about U.S. business unearthed some mixed, if not contradictory, feelings. In a 2004 Harris Interactive survey of people in five Western European countries, "the American way of business" was viewed more positively than negatively, but "American multinationals" were viewed more negatively.[18] Even America's staunchest supporter, British Prime Minister Tony Blair, argues there is a "third way" between laissez-faire capitalism and full-throttle socialism—for example, flexible labor markets without American-style hiring and firing. This mixed economy, he argues, is more suitable to the European model's enduring concern with social justice. It recognizes that, just as socialism is inherently inefficient, capitalism without some elements of socialism leads to exploitation.

"My take," explained Keith Reinhard, "is that there is still admiration for the way [Americans] approach business problems—our straightforward strategies with clear, measurable objectives, our 'can-do' spirit, and our insistence on accountability. At the same time, our big companies themselves are negatively perceived."[19]

COWBOY CAPITALISM

Many Europeans consider pious sermons on "shareholder value" a smoke screen for a breed of cutthroat capitalism that takes no prisoners as it advances and leaves only scorched earth behind. When European intellectuals complain about the pervasive influence of American culture, they are not so much bemoaning America's fast-food, gangster rap, and movie violence as its hypercompetitive, share-price-obsessed business culture. Jack Welch scares them much more than Britney Spears. And British novelist Raymond Williams was almost certainly speaking allegorically when he had a character in a novel declare, "All that will ever break capitalism, is capitalists. The faster they run the more strain on their heart."[20]

John Quelch, Harvard Business School dean, has identified "the emergence of a consumer lifestyle with broad international appeal that is grounded in a rejection of American capitalism."[21] The point of salience between Brand America and Corporate America is the brand of capitalism it practices. The Ugly American of the 1950s was loud, boring, and obnoxious. His twenty-first-century descendant is all that, plus a sharp-elbowed, sanctimonious bully who patronizingly assumes that, given the chance, everyone would adopt his way of life in a heartbeat. Meanwhile, he'll force it on them.

According to Thomas Friedman: "The solution is to think about how to democratize globalization . . . how to make people have a sense that they own it, that they're not going to be steamrollered by it."[22] Historically, business corporations have been sources of moral teaching, though few would admit it. After all, what are "corporate codes of conduct," "value statements," "missions," and "visions" but attempts to construct a moral culture? As they globalize, don't corporations become schools in cross-cultural cooperation?

The idea is not as nutty as it may sound. Economist John Stuart Mill considered it one of a corporation's most important roles. He wrote:

> The economical advantages of commerce are surpassed in importance by those of its effects, which are intellectual and moral. It is hardly possible to overstate the value of placing human beings in contact with persons dissimilar to themselves and with modes of thought and action unlike those with which they are familiar.[23]

American businesses can't do much to assuage anger over U.S. foreign policy, but they need to guard against reinforcing an image of "American exceptionalism," the idea that the United States is above the standards of behavior expected in the rest of the world. While U.S.-

style capitalism may have helped win the Cold War, it could lose the peace in many corners of the world unless it wins the public's trust. The solution is not to jettison the economic model that worked so well in the Anglo-Saxon world, but to demonstrate that the system can function in a fair way that takes into account the interests of a broad range of stakeholders rather than a single-minded obsession with stock prices. In a sense, U.S.-based corporations need to reestablish their legitimacy in global markets.

For many citizens of the world, globalization and Americanization are synonyms for the same disease, and U.S.-based corporations are the carrier. The disease may be psychosomatic, but it is no less dangerous. Todd Gitlin, professor of journalism at Columbia University, once put it this way: "Anti-Americanism is an emotion masquerading as an analysis, a morality, an ideal, even an idea about what to do."[24] Gitlin may have provided a good working definition of the power of a brand, this time from the dark side.

CHAPTER 9

THE POWER OF BRANDS

"Products are made in the factory, but brands are created in the mind."[1]

—Walter Landor, founder Landor Associates

"Brand equity is the sum of all the hearts and minds of every single person that comes into contact with your company."[2]

—Christopher Betzter

LARRY SMITH WAS A TWENTY-YEAR VETERAN OF PEPSI-COLA when he was transferred to Texas in 1975 to do something about the soft drink's anemic market share in the Lone Star State. A native of South Carolina, Smith knew firsthand that Coke dominated the South, but Pepsi's 6 percent share of soft drink purchases in Texas, compared to Coke's 35 percent share, was embarrassing, especially since even Dr. Pepper had a 25 percent share.

Smith soon discovered he had his work cut out for him. The first Dallas supermarket chain he called on turned down what would have normally been a no-brainer promotional deal in which Pepsi proposed to pay the chain to stock its soft drinks and to sell it to them at a heavy discount in exchange for some retail advertising and end-of-aisle displays. "They said they didn't need us," Smith recalled later.[3]

When the advertising people back at Pepsi headquarters in Purchase, New York, refused to replace the Pepsi Generation campaign running in Dallas with something more product-specific that would "move the needle," Smith took things into his own hands. He hired the in-house agency of the 7-Eleven chain, which accounted for about half of Pepsi's meager sales in Texas. Charged with coming up with something that would move soda off the shelves, the 7-Eleven folks staged and filmed some taste tests. Avowed Coke drinkers were stopped outside a 7-Eleven store and asked to taste two colas in cups marked M and Q. Asked which they preferred, fifty-two out of a hundred picked M, the cup filled with Pepsi. That gave Smith and the agency the statistical foundation they needed for a claim that "most Coke drinkers prefer Pepsi." They ran some crudely produced commercials based on that claim in May 1975. The double takes of the confirmed Coke drinkers when shown the Pepsi labels were particularly amusing.

But no one at Coke headquarters in Atlanta was laughing. At first, the Coke executives ignored the Pepsi commercials, but when some of their local bottlers started worrying, they issued a news release questioning the validity of the taste tests. They contested everything, from Coke's assignment of the "unpopular" letter Q to the size of the cups used. "One sip is not enough," they sniffed. Then, when Pepsi's market share rose from 6 percent to 14 percent, the Coke people really got nervous, especially since their own taste tests confirmed Pepsi's findings: In blind taste tests, people really do prefer Pepsi by a small but meaningful margin.

THE PEPSI CHALLENGE

By 1983, the Pepsi Challenge, as the taste tests became known, had spread from Texas across the country, and Pepsi's sales volume increased about 5 percent a year.

The taste tests were a supremely sour experience for Coke's top executives. Pepsi's claim of taste superiority hurt their pride, even if the sales impact was minimal, because the overall soft drink market was growing so rapidly. Coke's research people had been working on a new formulation since 1979, and by the fall of 1984 they thought they had a winner. In blind taste tests against Pepsi, the new formula was preferred by a margin of six to eight points, whereas Pepsi had been beating the existing formula by ten to fifteen points. That was as much as a twenty-three point swing. Over the Christmas holidays, following months of testing new formulations, Coke's charismatic chairman, Roberto Goizueta, decided to change the soft drink's formula.

NEW COKE

"New Coke" was introduced to the world on April 23, 1985, in an elaborate coming-out party at the Vivian Beaumont Theater at New York City's Lincoln Center. The immediate reaction from the newspeople in the room was skepticism. After years of saying the Pepsi taste tests weren't meaningful, why was Coke now changing its formula? Of course, newspeople are paid to be skeptical. But the consumer reaction was even more negative than anyone had suspected.

Within a week, the company's 800 number was getting 1,000 calls a day; by the sixth week, it was jammed with 6,000 calls a day and the headquarters mailroom had processed over 40,000 letters. Almost all the callers and letter writers were outraged, and many said they were switching to Pepsi. Local television news programs showed families pouring New Coke down sewers, shoppers hassled Coke's delivery men outside grocery stores, and by June, *Time, Newsweek,* and *Business Week* all carried stories on the growing protests. When Coke's most loyal bottlers started to complain that the negative media was beginning to affect their business, Goizueta caved. "I can put up with flak when sales are up," he said. "But I can't put up with flak when sales are down."[4] Even then, it would take him another month to get his senior executives on board.

On July 10, 1985, Peter Jennings of ABC News interrupted the afternoon soap opera *General Hospital* to report that Coke would return to its old formula. The company hadn't planned to make the announcement until the next day, but like almost everything else about New Coke, nothing went according to plan.

Coke—and the rest of us—learned a new lesson about the power of a brand.

BRANDS

Any cowboy with a hot iron can create a brand. In fact, that's where the term comes from; brands started as a signal of ownership and evolved into a "maker's mark" in the world of artisans and, later, manufactured goods. The red triangle on a bottle of Bass Pale Ale is one of the world's oldest brand marks. It was the very first issued in Britain when the Trademark Registration Law went into effect on January 1, 1875. But it had been in use almost since the Bass & Company Brewery began operations in Burton-on-Trent, England, in the early eighteenth century. Even illiterate non-English-speaking beer drinkers knew to look for the red triangle as a sign that the bottle or barrel held true Bass ale.

In the early nineteenth century, when goods increasingly came out of anonymous distant factories rather than local farms or workshops, marketers began creating personalities and folklore for their products to make them seem familiar or unique, whichever best served their purpose. People started the day with Aunt Jemima's pancake mixes and syrups, ate Uncle Ben's rice for lunch or dinner, and sucked on Smith Brothers cough drops when they had a cold.

Over time, the brand mark came to represent more than an authentic—if fanciful—source. It was also a sign of quality and consistency. When you pass through the Golden Arches of a McDonald's restaurant, you assume that the burgers and fries you scarf down in Budapest will taste just like the ones you had in Boston. You expect the tables, floors, and bathrooms to be clean. And you expect the time between ordering and actually getting your food to be relatively brief. That's your left brain at work. But marketers have also learned to work on the right side of your brain by associating their products with emotional values, such as youthfulness, fun, or luxury.

Brands are most powerful when they ignite those synapses. The power of McDonald's brand, in large part, is not only in its informational content, but in the emotions it evokes. Some of those feelings derive from memories. You remember all the times you ate Big Macs with your dad on Saturday afternoons after a Little League game, or on Friday evenings hanging out in the parking lot with your friends. Brands are not concerned so much with what you think, but with what you *feel*. That distinction can make all the difference. Neurologist Donald Calne argues that the "essential difference between emotion and reason" is that "while reason leads to conclusions, emotion leads to action."[5]

Some of those feelings are based on the company's own efforts to shape the way you think of yourself as a user of its products. For example, the classic McDonald's advertising campaign, "You deserve a break today," set a montage of happy families to a catchy tune and gave moms permission to take the kids to a fast-food restaurant. It not only made them feel good about McDonald's, it made them feel better about themselves. All strong brands have an element of aspiration in them. The Nike Swoosh is a badge that identifies the wearer as someone who's energetic and a bit of the rebel, whether roller-blading or lying in a hammock. An American Express card sends signals of prestige and status. And Whole Foods says you're not just shopping for food, you're taking care of your family while helping to save the planet.

Branding is not the same thing as advertising. For example, the family-owned Chelsea Milling Company hasn't advertised its Jiffy muffin mix in more than fifty years, but it still dominates its category with a 55 percent market share by unit sales. Betty Crocker and Pillsbury have spent decades and untold millions of dollars on advertising trying to catch up. Caterpillar built a strong brand with relatively little advertising by painting all its giant earthmoving machines a bright yellow and marking them with bold black graphics. Caterpillar's core products—many the size of highway billboards—are its most effective branding tool. Over time, the presence of Caterpillar equipment at heavy construction sites created an aura of "toughness," until eventually the company was able to transfer that attitude to a billion-dollar line of footwear and clothing.

Other brands create an entire environment within which they can define themselves. For example, The Body Shop and Starbucks erased the line between product and retail store. The brand isn't sold *in* the shop; the shop *is* the brand.

Finally, brands can also be built through messaging, but rarely through advertising alone. BP transformed itself from just another oil company to a global energy company that cares about the environment by pouring billions of dollars into programs that reinforce the idea, from research and development to philanthropy, not to mention redesigning its gas stations and launching a new corporate logo. The payoff? BP delivered a total shareholder return of 62 percent between 2001 and mid-2006, compared to Exxon Mobil's 49 percent even while Exxon Mobil's profits were far greater. And BP's brand strength helped it emerge with its reputation largely intact after a refinery explosion in Texas that cost fifteen lives and a $21.3 million fine. Many environmentalists were even inclined to give the company the benefit of the doubt when its Alaskan pipeline was discovered to be corroded and leaky. "BP is deserving of censure, but not a vendetta,"[6] wrote one.

The essence of branding is to identify your product or service with a clear, simple idea that sets it apart from competitors and then to deliver it flawlessly. That idea is often built around emotional qualities that can be symbolized verbally and visually, but it has to be relevant to your customers and credible coming from you. It has to be easy to understand and flexible enough to modulate in a wide variety of interactions with a large number of different audiences. Most important, it can't simply be something you stick at the end of an ad or on the side of a building. It has to be the "golden thread" that runs through every internal process and through every interaction with customers. And your promise can't be primarily rational. It has to operate on the deeper level of emotions and feelings.

BRAND COKE

As Coca-Cola learned the hard way with New Coke, brands don't operate on a conscious level; they're *visceral*.

Coke's executives rejiggered the soft drink's famous secret formula because their own blind taste tests showed that people preferred Pepsi to Coke. But they missed the key point of the tests—they were *blind*. When people knew which brown, fizzy liquid was Coke, most said it tasted better. Their taste buds were overwhelmed by the symbology surrounding Coke, the feelings of refreshment it evoked, maybe even the warm memories of small town parades and patriotism.

Researchers at the Baylor School of Medicine have even been able to track the phenomenon on brain scans. Read Montague, the director of the school's Center for Theoretical Neuroscience, dreamed up an experiment that duplicated the Pepsi Challenge to keep his teenage daughter occupied as she helped out in the lab over summer vacation. Montague had volunteers lie supine in a magnetic resonance imaging (MRI) machine that shows blood flow within the brain. Then he had them sip both Coke and Pepsi through a tube while he watched their neural activity. Without knowing what they were drinking, about half of them said they preferred Pepsi. But once Montague told them which samples were Coke, three-fourths said that drink tasted better, and their brain activity changed, too. The brain's dorsolateral prefrontal cortex and hippocampus areas lit up like Christmas trees. Both of these areas are implicated in modifying behavior based on emotion and affect. Montague theorized that the brain was recalling images and ideas associated with Coke, and the brand was overriding the actual quality of the product. Montague said his findings demonstrated how Coke's brand imagery "biases preference judgments."[7] Your taste buds may say you prefer Pepsi, but your hippocampus overrules them.

A brand's power is reinforced by all the symbols surrounding it. In Coke's case, there's the hour-glass contour of its bottle, the American-flag red color of its logo, the white ribbon that sweeps under the Spencerian script of its logo, and years of close identification with Americana. But it's a mistake to think that a brand belongs to the company that created it except in the narrowest legal sense. Brands belong to consumers, and in their most potent forms they exist only in people's heads. A brand sums up the consumer's ideas and feelings about a particular product based on everything she has read, seen, heard, and, most importantly, experienced. Not all such things are under a brand's control.

In fact, brands need not be products at all. The Roman Catholic Church is a brand. So is Tom Cruise, and so are many cities and countries. A brand is not only a familiar name; it is something that elicits a broad range of feelings and associations that give the name meaning, salience, and relevance.

PLACE BRANDS

Some place brands are the result of carefully designed promotions. Commercials for Jamaica, the Bahamas, and the Florida Keys are always beamed at snow-bound New Englanders during winter. But place branding entails unique challenges. While a product can adjust its features in response to consumer feedback, a country can rearrange itself to suit tourist preferences only in limited ways. It can build new roads from the airport to the beach, but it can't move the beach itself and replace it with mountains.

Furthermore, countries are much more complex than products, with many more "brand managers" whose interests may be diametrically opposed. For example, marketing a country as a rustic getaway may work for the minister of tourism, but it may not sit well with the minister in charge of attracting industrial development. Unlike product branding, place branding is seldom under the control of a central authority. And even where it is, controlling all the touch points through which people experience and learn about the country is orders of magnitude more difficult than for a product. As a practical matter, most places acquire brand values through their history and heritage, their exports, their cultural accomplishments, their government policies, and their people, including not only their media and sports stars but the ordinary folk that travelers encounter. But even with deliberate planning, chance occurrences and serendipity have the edge. The slogan "Hong Kong Will Take Your Breath Away" took on an unfortunate meaning when the deadly SARS virus, which causes respiratory distress, struck the city in 2003.

But the stakes are high as countries compete in export markets and for investment dollars and tourists. Tourism alone is the world's fourth largest industry, growing about 9 percent a year. As a result, many countries are are actively trying to manage their brands. The tiny but oil-rich Persian Gulf state of Oman hired Landor Associates in November 2005 to develop a "Brand Oman" campaign. Even Russia has dipped its toe into image management. When polls showed that the brands foreigners most associated with Russia were Kalashnikov rifles and Molotov cocktails, the country's commissars decided that much of the problem stemmed from the stories being filed by Moscow-based foreign correspondents. So they launched an English-language news channel of their own and the Valdai Discussion Club, which holds meet-and-greets with high-level officials, including President Vladimir Putin. Pointedly, only journalists based outside Russia are invited.

Spain turned itself from a lazy backwater of bullfights and siestas into a hip vacation destination in a relatively short time, based on the successful mounting of the 1992 Olympics and the Seville Exposition in the same year, reinforced by an advertising campaign that used Joan Miró's sun symbol to signal modernization and youth. Ireland and Singapore promoted themselves as good places to do business based on low taxes and generous government subsidies. Tourism officials in India credit the "Incredible India" promotion they launched in 2003 with increasing foreign tourist arrivals by 25 percent in one year.

Some countries, such as most of the Eastern European nations, are still struggling to develop meaningful brands. Others, such as France, Germany, and Italy, have long been strong brands, seemingly synonymous with a broad range of positive attributes and effortlessly evoking positive associations in most people's minds. That's not to say they don't also simultaneously evoke negative feelings. The French may be fashionable but they're also snooty; Germans, industrious but humorless; and Italians, creative but excitable. Strong brands, in fact, reconcile these attributes, no matter how contradictory. Creative and excitable becomes passionate. Industrious and humorless becomes exacting. Fashionable and snooty becomes stylish. And India's "Incredible India" promotion would not have worked were it not in sync with people's preconception that the vast country's sharp contrasts make it exotic and mysterious.

NATION BRAND VALUES

Once acquired, brand values move both ways. As Peter van Ham observed in *Foreign Affairs* magazine, "Brands and states often merge in the minds of the global consumer."[8] Thus Mercedes evokes German engineering precision. Hermes brings to mind French élan and style, while Sony epitomizes Japanese ingenuity and Zen-like simplicity and compactness. Häagen-Dazs built its mystique around a Scandinavian-sounding name, even though the company was based in New Jersey. Fcuk, formerly called French Connection, is a dual nationality brand that combines the cheekiness of its British roots with the sexiness of its Frenchness. Since adopting its startling name, Fcuk has increased its revenue and share price dramatically, and the government-sponsored Research On Youth survey found that it is one of the most relevant brands among fifteen- to seventeen-year-olds in Britain.

Such synergy only works when it is accurate and salient. The German people really do have a long history of engineering achievement, and it is obviously relevant to the manufacture of automobiles. Mercedes is smart to link itself to that heritage and to reinforce it in its communications, from the exact machining of its three-pointed star logo to the dominant use of silver in its sales brochures and showrooms. Finally, the car itself delivers on the implicit promise. Audi's efforts to make the same connections were undermined by its refusal to accept responsibility for accelerator problems in the 1980s. On the other hand, an association with German engineering prowess would contribute little to the marketing of silk scarves. The House of Chanel understandably does nothing to play up the German roots of its star designer, Karl Lagerfeld.

The mutual reinforcement of national and corporate brands is not necessarily permanent. Following World War II, "Made in the U.S.A." was a symbol of quality, just as "Made in Japan" connoted shoddiness. In just three decades, the situation was essentially reversed as Japanese manufacturers achieved clear superiority in such markets as automobiles and consumer electronics based on manufacturing quality and designs that connected with consumers. Perrier lost some of its French gourmet cachet in 1990 when an incident of benzene contamination forced it to admit that it was artificially boosting the carbonation of water from its spring. It took years for the brand to recover.

The key to recovery for Perrier, as for Audi and other brands that suffered a devastating reversal, was to focus on the emotional currents into which they had been pulled. It was only when they understood those currents that they could navigate them.

Pollster Frank Lutz has prospected, tapped, and channeled polling data for Republican politicians since the early 1990s. "Eighty percent of our life is emotion, and only 20 percent is intellect," he says. "I can change how you think, but how you feel is something deeper and stronger."[9]

Those who believe America's declining reputation can be restored through a more forceful explanation of its foreign policies are fishing in trees. Doing a better job of explaining itself is certainly part of the answer, but it fails to address the core of the problem. America's declining reputation has less to do with what people think of America than how they feel about it.

CHAPTER 10

BRAND AMERICA

"Americans may have no identity, but they do have wonderful teeth."[1]

—Jean Baudrillard, French cultural theorist

"America's problem is not with its brand—which could scarcely be stronger—but with its product."[2]

—Naomi Klein, author of "Selling Uncle Sam: The Spectacular Failure of Brand USA"

"This is how people see America, the America of fast food, fast computers, MTV, and Hollywood. This crisis has made clear that Americans have no idea how they're perceived around the world."[3]

—Benjamin R. Barber, author of *Jihad vs. McWorld*

JUST BEFORE CHRISTMAS IN 2005, KAREN P. HUGHES, THE NEW undersecretary of state for public diplomacy, gathered her senior team to discuss the results of their efforts to promote the Iraqi elections of the month before. The Bush team considered the elections one of its singular successes in a country still torn by suicide bombings and lacking such niceties as regular electrical service and safe drinking water.

"Would any of you like to guess what was driving the commentary and all the chatter on all the talk shows in Western Europe that weekend?" she asked, with a hint of exasperation. "You know what it was? It was the death penalty case in California!"

Stanley "Tookie" Williams, the Los Angeles gang leader turned peace activist, had been executed on December 13, two days before 11 million Iraqis went to the polls. Instead of celebrating America's success in restoring democracy to Iraq, most Europeans were scratching their heads wondering how a country that seems so advanced can also be so barbaric.

Such is the challenge faced by Brand America abroad.

BRAND AMERICA

For decades, Brand America provided stability and even lift to a wide range of products that were "Made in the U.S.A." Levi's, Coca-Cola, and McDonald's were, respectively, wearable, drinkable, eatable, and affordable bits of the American experience for millions of people around the world. Even foreign companies bought in to the American mystique. Brooklyn chewing gum, made in Milan, has been on Italian candy store shelves since the end of World War II. Not to be outdone, the French launched Hollywood chewing gum at about the same time and currently export it throughout Europe, Africa, and the Far East.

America is, as British consultant Simon Anholt christened it, "the mother of all brands,"[4] by which he meant no other brand is known as broadly or as intimately. "To a villager in Papua New Guinea, a taxi driver in Mumbai, or a hairdresser in Latvia," he writes, "America stands for pretty much the same things: money, freedom, and the pursuit of happiness."[5] On the other hand, another British branding expert, Wally Olins, summarizes the American brand as "opportunity, technology, and junk"—junk food, junk entertainment, junk news, and junk psychology.[6]

Brand America's strength, it seems, is matched only by its ability to polarize. For every person who admires America's accomplishments, there is at least another who decries its arrogance. While some people admire its vitality and creativity, others criticize its self-absorption and ignorance. Those who celebrate its generosity are offset by others who consider it greedy and selfish. And while some expect America to use its power and influence to help the less fortunate, others accuse it of quarrelsome meddling. The cycle from admiration to envy to criticism to antipathy gets ever shorter when you are the biggest kid on the block.

FLUENT LISTENING

That's why rebuilding Brand America needs to start with a clear-eyed, unapologetic assessment of how the rest of the world perceives it.

That's the easy part, and much of it has already been done. You can practically Google the results. The harder part is understanding *why,* without making excuses, discounting uncomfortable or inconvenient facts, or seeking shelter in bromides like "It comes with the territory." Understanding "why" requires a depth of fluent listening that has never come easy to a people who are so practical and so impatient they want to move immediately to solutions. But it is critical to understanding all the forces tugging and pulling at America's brand.

Pete Peterson, a tough-minded businessman, secretary of commerce under President Richard Nixon, and chairman of the Council on Foreign Relations, provided a real-world example of how fluent listening might have informed a decision that remains unpopular in much of the world—the United States' refusal to ratify the Kyoto Protocol on climate control.

"We came out and said we disagree with the Kyoto agreement," he said. "But if we had listened more, we might have at least shown empathy for the problem and then indicated what the flaws might be and then talked about what we thought should be done about global warming."[7]

Peterson's suggested approach stands in sharp contrast to the way America's foreign policy machine normally works. Ironically, fluent listening is more typical of the executive branch's approach to domestic policy, where most administrations do a lot of research and consult a wide range of constituents before launching an initiative. Domestic policy is almost always informed in this way, and occasionally what the administration "hears" may even cause it to amend its plans if that isn't too inconsistent with long-term policy goals.

On the foreign policy side, however, most administrations adopt a take-it-or-leave-it attitude. The American public has traditionally given the president far more leeway on matters of foreign policy than on domestic matters, probably on the assumption that he knows things they don't. Furthermore, in domestic affairs, public officials know they are dealing with voters who can express their displeasure at the ballot box, whereas foreigners don't vote in U.S. elections. Faced with constituents who can vote but don't care and stakeholders who care but can't vote, few politicians would waste much time plumbing the attitudes or soliciting the input of either.

This is short-sighted in several ways. First, American voters have a way of reasserting their voice in foreign policy when they lose confidence in their leaders' ability to manage it effectively. Public attitudes toward the war in Iraq appeared to have reached that point in 2005, and the issues of outsourcing U.S. jobs, illegal immigration, and America's dependence on foreign oil all seemed to be reaching a similar point in mid-2006.[8] Furthermore, while foreigners may not vote in U.S. elections, they have other ways to express their displeasure, and America needs their support in the long run.

KNOWLEDGE DEFICIT

Unfortunately, while every administration comes into office with world-class domestic polling capabilities, the government's research on foreign public opinion couldn't support the global ambitions of a midsize rug merchant. According to a study by the Defense Science Board Task Force on Strategic Communication, the State Department's Bureau of Intelligence and Research has a budget of about $6 million for public opinion research and media analysis.[9] No U.S. political candidate would budget so little for a nationwide campaign, let alone a global one.

While embassies do their own local soundings and other departments and agencies, such as the Broadcasting Board of Governors, the Defense Department, and the Central Intelligence Agency, also hire commercial polling firms to gather proprietary data, most of their research is stovepiped. Some of this information is classified and unavailable to the State Department's public diplomacy officers. Some is quarantined by the Smith-Mundt Act,[10] which prevents the State Department Office of Media and Opinion Research from distributing it to other government agencies. The government often doesn't know what it knows. The people formulating foreign policy seldom ask for data to inform their deliberations. When data does come in, it often goes unanalyzed because trend research has a low priority compared to polling on the issue of the moment. Of course, once you have the data, you need to know what to do with it.

No country should base its foreign policy, or any other issue of importance to the welfare of its people, solely on what it hears from others. Listening does not impart a veto to anyone, but truly understanding why others believe and feel as they do can inform the way a decision is made, announced, or implemented. And it can inform behavior afterward.

Consider the Kyoto Protocol again. When the United Nations Conference on Climate Change reconvened in Montreal at the end of 2005, the Bush administration had a golden opportunity to patch things up with the rest of the world. It didn't have to cave in to demands that it submit the Kyoto Protocol to Congress for ratification. Not even the Clinton administration had been willing to do that, fearing it would lose. All the administration's representatives had to do was show some concern about greenhouse gases, whatever their source. They could even have discussed steps the administration and private industry in the United States were taking to limit greenhouse gases despite not ratifying the treaty. In fact, they had a relatively good story in many areas because the United States appeared to be doing better than many of the countries that were signatories to the protocol.

Instead, the Bush administration had a hissy fit when it heard that former President Clinton was scheduled to address the conference. The White House reportedly threatened to abandon any consideration of participating in Kyoto if Clinton spoke. Hearing about the controversy, the former president withdrew his name from the speakers list, declaring he didn't want to "play petty politics."[11] But the U.N. refused to back down and kept Clinton on the schedule. Still peeved, the administration's top representative reportedly stormed out of one session because he disagreed with the *title* of a draft declaration.

As Joseph Nye has observed, "Politics has become a contest about credibility. Politics in an information age is about whose story wins."[12] That kind of credibility can only be built on a record of fluent listening. An America that truly listens to the rest of the world, that possesses that kind of empathy, will be in a much better position to develop a compelling vision of what it stands for and what it means to its own people and the people of the world.

HOW OTHERS SEE THE UNITED STATES

What's interesting about recent surveys of world opinion about the United States is how out of sync Americans are with what others think of them. For example, whereas large majorities of people in Europe and the Middle East don't think the United States takes their interests into account in making foreign policy decisions, nearly seven out of ten Americans do.

Majorities in France and the Netherlands and pluralities in Great Britain and Germany consider Americans too religious. By contrast, a 58 percent majority of Americans say the United States is not sufficiently religious, strangely enough agreeing with the Muslim populations of Indonesia, Pakistan, Lebanon, and Turkey.

Americans also see U.S. conduct in the world much differently than people in Europe, the Middle East, and Asia. In response to a hypothetical question, more than seven out of ten Americans consider the United States the major power most likely to come to the aid of people threatened by genocide. Only Poles, Canadians, and Germans see the United States this way in any significant numbers. And fewer than one in ten Western Europeans trust the United States to do right by the environment while more than half of Americans do.

Americans aren't completely oblivious to how the world feels about them. Only one out of four Americans thinks the United States is well liked by people around the world, ranking them with the Turks and the Russians on the diffidence scale (only 30 percent and 32 percent consider their countries well liked, respectively). Americans are more likely than people in most other countries to see themselves as greedy and immoral, though not as inclined to see themselves as violent or rude. And while majorities in most of the world are inclined to agree, Americans are far more likely to consider themselves hardworking, inventive, and honest.[13]

DOES THE UNITED STATES CARE?

Many blame President Bush's policies for this turn of events, forgetting that it was President Clinton's secretary of state, Madeleine Albright, who offended foreign sensibilities by calling the United States "the indispensable nation," and it was during the Clinton administration that the French felt the need to invent a new word—*hyperpuissance* ("hyperpower")—to capture the full arrogance of American pretensions. To be fair, even the French might have written off America's posturing as the boastful bad manners of youth were the United States not also, to their tastes, so awfully trigger-happy. Robert Kagan explains the difference between the European and American approaches to resolving intractable problems as the natural consequence of their relative places in history. When a country has power, it is inclined to use it; when a country no longer has power, it is inclined to diplomacy.[14]

Furthermore, America's very geography has given it fewer opportunities to practice the art of diplomacy than European countries. The United States abuts only two other countries, its borders have been essentially settled since 1848, and it has dominated its immediate neighbors for most of its history. European countries, on the other hand, have seen their borders shrink and expand many times over thousands of years of history, often as the result of calamitous wars. They are more accustomed to making painful tradeoffs and adjusting to new situations. Americans, by comparison, are more used to getting their own way. Whatever the case, an America prone to throw its weight around makes the world nervous.

WHAT, ME WORRY?

Some people are also incredulous that, for all the official fuss over America's declining popularity in the world, the average American seems relatively unperturbed. "It would be no exaggeration to say that for the rest of the world, Americans have become like goldfish in a bowl," says Singaporean diplomat Kishore Mahbubani, "absorbed and self-contained in their little universe with, apparently, little or no awareness of the eyes watching them from the outside."[15]

Indeed, while many American business people in recent decades acquired their first passports to travel the world seeking opportunity, most Americans turned inward and lived in a media climate devoid of international news, except for those acts of God or war that involved other Americans or were so devastating they could not be ignored. The term *globalization* didn't even enter the mainstream American media until mass street protests shut down the 1999 World Trade Organization Ministerial Conference in Seattle. According to a 2004 Columbia University survey, the number of foreign news stories in American newspapers has been dropping since the late 1980s. In 1987, overseas news accounted for about 27 percent of front-page stories in American newspapers—about the same as a decade earlier. By 2003, foreign news accounted for just 21 percent of front-page stories, while coverage of domestic affairs more than doubled over the same period.[16] According to a report by the Project for Excellence in Journalism, 20 percent of *Time* magazine covers in the mid-seventies dealt with foreign affairs compared to about 6 percent in the mid-nineties. *Newsweek*'s numbers were similar.[17] As for television, the former chairman of *Agence Presse,* Claude Moisy, reported that international coverage on CBS, NBC, and ABC declined from more than 40 percent of total news time in the 1970s to less than 15 percent by 1995.[18]

According to a survey taken by the Canadian Tourism Commission in 2005, 34 percent of Americans over eighteen years old have a passport, compared to 41 percent of Canadians of the same age.[19] The percentage of American university students studying a foreign language has steadily declined. According to a report funded by the U.S. Department of Education, in 1965 more than 16 percent of all American university students studied a foreign language. Now only 8.6 percent do. And when *National Geographic* fielded a Global Literacy Study of eighteen- to twenty-four-year-old Americans in 2002, the editors were shocked to discover that less than half could find India on a map, one out of five couldn't find Mexico, four out of five couldn't find Israel, and one out of three couldn't point to the Pacific Ocean.[20]

AMERICAN EXCEPTIONALISM

This apparent self-absorption and insularity operates out of a sense of "exceptionalism" that few non-Americans fail to notice. Based on United States decisions to go its own way on matters ranging from international treaties to waging war in Iraq, many non-Americans have developed a sense that "American exceptionalism" means "except America."

However, the term was originally meant to signal differences that lay even deeper than matters of government policy or practice. The expression was actually coined by Alexis de Tocqueville during his visit to America in 1831. He meant it as shorthand for the general observation that, though initially settled by Europeans, America was different from the Old Country in striking and important ways. It was not a value judgment, but an indication of America's uniqueness.

De Tocqueville was a young French aristocrat who parlayed the change of government following the French "July Revolution" of 1830 into an assignment to study America's prisons. What resulted was not a report on penology but a well-received book, *Democracy in America,* that explored the uniquely American interpretations of liberty and equality. Although the original French Revolution of 1789 was launched under the slogan *Liberté, égalité, fraternité, ou la mort!* ("Freedom, equality, fraternity, or death!"), de Tocqueville held that, in America, notions of "liberty" and "equality" produced a rugged individualism that was unknown in Europe.

De Tocqueville was also struck that an American's idea of "nationality" was different, based less on common history or ethnicity than on common beliefs. And those beliefs were fairly unique for the time: relatively distrustful of public authority, self-reliant, inclusive, egalitarian, classless, and democratic. The other belief that Americans of that time shared was the lively expectation that they could somehow make their lives better economically, religiously, or politically if they only worked hard enough.

America's qualitative differences continue to this day. For example, of all the managers surveyed by Trompenaars and Hampden-Turner, Americans were by far the most individualistic. Europeans, on the other hand, appear to place greater value in "community." Furthermore, the University of Michigan's World Values Survey indicates that on values such as patriotism, religion, and family ties, Americans tend to be "traditionalists." A remarkable 80 percent say they hold "old-fashioned values" about family and marriage.

Europeans tend to be "secular-rationalists" who believe religion is a personal, optional matter; patriotism is not a big concern; and children have their own lives to lead. In fact, except for some Eastern European countries such as Poland, and the legions of Muslim immigrants crowding Western European cities, contemporary Europe may be even more godless than the atheistic former Soviet Union.

On this spectrum of values, America is indeed exceptional. And that frankly concerns many Europeans, who find religion the strangest and most disturbing feature of American exceptionalism. Europeans find it extraordinary that three times as many Americans believe in the virgin birth as in evolution, and they worry that religious fundamentalists are hijacking the country.

The idealized country described by de Tocqueville in *Democracy in America* is no longer as attractive to Europeans as it once was and it is far from the global ideal. When respondents to a 2005 Pew Research

Center survey were asked to name one country they would recommend a young person go to for a better life, only the people of India named the United States as their top choice.[21] It seems that, for many others, the American Dream of opportunity and happiness has degenerated into a reality of greed and acquisition.

CHAPTER 11

CEOs IN HANDCUFFS

"Society has come to believe that the term 'crooked CEO' is redundant."[1]

—Robert S. Miller, CEO, Delphi

"Today's companies are run not by entrepreneurs, but by traders who are increasingly preoccupied with short-term gain and profits."[2]

—Henry B. Schacht, former CEO of both
Cummins Engine and Lucent Technologies

LATE-AFTERNOON COMMUTER TRAFFIC HADN'T STARTED TO build yet, but Postal Inspector Ralph Nardo had no difficulty concealing his nondescript government sedan in the stream of cars crossing the George Washington Bridge. But as they were passing through New Jersey on Route 80, the suspects' car suddenly veered toward an exit. "They made me," Nardo thought. But then instead of trying to lose him, the suspects' car turned left at the bottom of the exit ramp, shot across the bridge over the highway, and turned left again to reenter Route 80 going east. They were heading back to New York.

Meanwhile, Eleanor Berry and Rich Gutierrez, also postal inspectors, tailed a third suspect to Grand Central Terminal in midtown New York and followed him onto a commuter train bound for Greenwich, Connecticut. In Greenwich, they hopped into a waiting, unmarked car like any other suburban couple meeting friends and followed the suspect as he walked to an auto repair shop, where he picked up his car and drove back to New York.

By evening, all three suspects were in their apartment on Manhattan's Upper East Side. Postal inspectors Bill Hessle and Lou LaFleur settled in for a long night of surveillance from across the street. At 6 A.M. the next day, July 24, 2002, a small posse of postal inspectors walked into the apartment building, flashed their badges to the doorman, and told him to ring the suspects' apartment. Taking the receiver from the doorman, the ranking postal inspector identified himself and ordered all three men down to the lobby to be arrested.

Within minutes, John Rigas, the seventy-eight-year-old chairman of Adelphia Communications, and his two adult sons, Timothy and Michael, stepped off the elevator in sports jackets and open-necked shirts, hands out in front, palms up, as instructed. The postal inspectors told them they were under arrest, read them their rights, handcuffed them, and led them out to the street to waiting sedans and news photographers who had been tipped off. John Rigas, a short man, his thick white hair uncombed, looked like someone's grandfather reluctantly allowing himself to be led back to his nursing home.

THE PICTURE OF OUR TIMES

Writing for *The Wall Street Journal*, Peggy Noonan drew just the conclusion that the government was after. "That perp walk, that look," she wrote, "are as much a picture of our times as bankers jumping from windows and Okies selling apples on the street."[3] And, sadly, it was. Just weeks before, at a similarly early hour, federal agents had paraded the CEO of Imclone, Sam Waksal, before photographers in front of his apartment in the fashionable Tribeca section of Lower Manhattan. Waksal was charged with—and ultimately convicted of—insider trading.

John Rigas and his son Timothy, Adelphia's chief financial officer, were eventually convicted of conspiracy, securities fraud, and bank fraud for looting the company and lying about its finances. The elder Rigas was sentenced to fifteen years in jail; Timothy got twenty years. The jury couldn't reach a verdict on the charges against Michael Rigas, but he later pled guilty to a lesser charge in exchange for a sentence of ten months of home confinement.

One week after the Rigases were arrested, WorldCom's chief financial officer and its comptroller would also be arrested and paraded in handcuffs before the waiting news media. The company's chief executive officer, Bernie Ebbers, would soon follow, as would top officers of Tyco, Enron, HealthSouth, Rite Aid, and numerous other companies with lower public profiles. In fact, in the coming months, the U.S. Justice Department would open so many criminal investigations of corporate fraud that its website would list them in alphabetical categories, A through C, D through G, etc. There would be entries under every letter except O, V, and X.[4]

BAD APPLES OR DISEASED ORCHARD?

By the time the last of the high-profile CEOs indicted in those early days of corporate crime-fighting actually went on trial in February 2006, there was a general sense that the tidal wave of corporate scandals was receding. Congress had passed the Sarbanes-Oxley Act, requiring CEOs and CFOs to certify their companies' financial statements and restricting the nonaudit work auditors can take on for their clients. If corporate boards hadn't developed tighter fists in compensating CEOs, they had at least holstered their rubber stamps. Nevertheless, the harm had been done.

"There is a mistrust of big business . . . and I think the degree of mistrust is higher than it has been in the past,"[5] William B. Harrison, Jr., chairman of JPMorgan Chase, told a session of the 2006 World Economic Forum in Davos. The latest corporate scandals not only contributed to an erosion in trust, they have almost certainly exacerbated levels of anti-Americanism around the world. Indeed, the corporate scandals at the end of the twentieth century confirmed what many people outside the United States suspected: American business is run for the benefit of the few who control it. They can understand—if not excuse—multiple cases of corporate felony. But they are dumbfounded by the way American corporations compensate their executives. It all seems to be of a piece.

CORPORATE GREED

Crooks can pop up anywhere, they concede, but personal greed seems to be endemic to the American business system. "I find that executive compensation is a much bigger problem with Europeans and Asians," says Vic Pelson, the former chairman of global operations for AT&T who sits on the boards of three U.S. global companies. "They consider it immoral and indefensible." The Chinese, he says, don't dislike American businesses, "they simply don't respect us, which is a bigger problem."[6]

In the summer of 2002, *Fortune* magazine revealed what it called "the not-so-secret dirty secret" of the 2000–2002 stock market crash. "Even as investors were losing 70 percent, 90 percent, even in some cases all of their holdings," *Fortune* reported, "top officials of many of the companies that have crashed the hardest were getting immensely, extraordinarily, obscenely wealthy." Of the 1,035 corporations the magazine studied, insiders "took out . . . roughly $66 billion. Of that amount, a total haul of $23 billion went to 466 insiders at the twenty-five corporations where the executives cashed out the most."[7]

According to Mercer Human Resources Consulting, which did a study for *The Wall Street Journal* of 350 U.S. corporations with revenue exceeding $1 billion, total compensation for CEOs rose an average of 15.8 percent in 2005.[8] By comparison, white-collar workers' pay increased 3.6 percent in the same period. The average CEO's pay was 262 times the average worker's pay in 2005, contrasted to a 107-to-1 ratio in 1990, which was already up from a 41-to-1 ratio in 1980.[9]

European and Japanese CEOs, who run companies comparable to U.S. enterprises, are paid only a third of what their U.S. counterparts bank.[10] To those who counter that American CEOs are worth more because they create greater wealth for their shareowners, critics point to Britain. According to Hewitt Associates, the median CEO of the top-100 British companies makes 18 percent less than his counterpart on the Standard & Poor's list of the top-500 U.S. companies. And while American CEOs saw their compensation increase by double-digit percentages in 2005, British CEOs tried to get by with raises of only 5 percent.[11] So the gap is widening. But in 2005, those top-100 British companies averaged a total return of 21.2 percent, while the S&P 500 average was just 4.9 percent.[12]

HAPPY LANDINGS

American CEOs apparently don't even expect to back away from the feeding trough when they leave. When General Electric's Jack Welch became involved in a messy divorce, the world discovered that his retirement package entitled him to millions of dollars of lifetime perks, including free use of a midtown Manhattan apartment, free tickets to sporting events, unlimited use of the corporate jets, and even free laundry service. Welch volunteered to give up most of the perks to get out from under the relentless media criticism. In fact, Welch's retirement arrangements were not that uncommon in Corporate America and might have gone unnoticed if his divorce hadn't put them on the public record.

CEOs often benefit from corporate marriages as well, when shareowners are unlikely to pay much attention to matters of compensation, assuming they even bother to read the company filings. When Gillette's shareowners voted for its merger with Procter and Gamble, how many knew that its former CEO, James Kilts, would pocket $188 million from it? The size of his payout even prompted one of Gillette's former vice chairmen, Joseph Mullaney, to exclaim, "It is obscene what he is getting paid."[13]

Kilts could at least point to a successful corporate turnaround and a 50 percent increase in Gillette's stock price. In fact, more than 60 percent of his payout came from the increase in Gillette's share price. David Dorman, on the other hand, had been with AT&T for just a year when he started shopping it around. He finally found a buyer in SBC Communications, which took control in 2005, paying about the same per share that the company was worth when Dorman took over at the end of 2002. Dorman, however, received a personal payout of about $55 million in cash, stock, and other benefits just to go away.[14] He will also draw an annual pension of more than $2 million for the rest of his life.

Corporate largess has also extended to CEOs with even less stellar records. When forty-seven-year-old Joseph Galli, Jr. quit the helm of Newell Rubbermaid after an unsuccessful turnaround effort, the maker of household products didn't owe him a thing. He didn't have an employment contract. Yet the company agreed to give him about $4.6 million in separation pay and other benefits. Few eyebrows were raised in corporate boardrooms. That's simply how such situations are usually handled in Corporate America.

On the other hand, when Deutsche Telekom fired its CEO, Ron Sommer, and gave him a separation payment of 11.6 million euros, eyebrows went up in boardrooms—and living rooms—across Europe.

The contrasts may finally be getting through. When Watson Wyatt surveyed institutional investors at the beginning of 2006, some 90 percent said that corporate executives are overpaid. And almost as many believed that U.S. executive compensation systems have hurt Corporate America's image.[15]

STOCK MARKET CAPITALISM

Ironically, since the 1980s, more than 60 percent of most CEOs' compensation has come in the form of an equity grant in an effort to align the interests of managers and owners—which has been a uniquely American obsession since the nineteenth century. According to compensation consultant Equilar, 99.7 percent of companies listed on the New York Stock Exchange gave some form of equity grant to their five highest-paid executives between 2002 and 2005. Only eight NYSE companies didn't.

Whether stock grants align management and shareholder interests is open to debate, but there is no question that they focus senior executives on the day-to-day movements of their companies' stock prices. Executives across America who never touched a personal computer learned to turn them on just so they could watch the stock ticker on their own screens.

Through the 1990s into the new century, companies that would never dream of fudging their books didn't hesitate to use legitimate accounting methods to manage their earnings to the expectations of investment analysts. In some cases, that degenerated to outright fraud. But even the most honest American business leaders myopically focused on one expression of wealth—an ever-climbing stock price—and on one group of stakeholders—professional money managers, a small subsegment whose fortunes rise and fall with the stock tables. Non-American CEOs, whose compensation is far less dependent on equity grants, seem to pay far less attention to the short-term gyrations of the stock tables.

LAW AND SUNLIGHT

Government believes it has done its part to correct corporate abuses by punishing a few high-profile wrongdoers and passing new laws to close accounting loopholes, toughen the penalties for transgressions, and pull companies' compensation policies into full sunlight. But as always, legislation will not be the decisive factor in determining whether executives rush to embrace honesty, transparency, and good corporate governance. It's the market itself that will decide.

Companies didn't start deemphasizing the use of stock options for compensation when the laws required greater disclosure; they did it when the accounting rules required their value to be factored into a company's financial results. According to Equilar, although nearly twice as many CEOs in S&P 500 companies receive stock options as restricted stock, the average value of their option grants declined by 4.8 percent in 2005, while the value of restricted stock increased by 17.5 percent.[16]

Efforts to improve transparency aren't likely to have much effect, either. A study by three professors at Wharton and Stanford demonstrated that it is very difficult to shame a CEO into taking less compensation. The writers analyzed more than 15,000 articles between 1994 and 2002, categorizing mentions of CEO as positive or negative. Even the most negative articles made barely a dent in the CEOs' fat pay packages. David Larcker, a Stanford University accounting professor, believes such stories have little impact because people consider it little more than "fun reading."[17]

Furthermore, such an astute investor as Warren Buffett worries that more exposure of executive pay practices will become "a shopping list for CEOs." The rise in executive pay does, in fact, coincide with SEC efforts to require greater disclosure. "Of the seven deadly sins," Buffet maintains, "the one that seems to work more than greed is envy."[18]

SYMPTOMS OF BIGGER CONCERNS

From the perspective of Europeans and Asians, however, the compensation excesses of American business are not only distasteful, they are symptoms of the greed that drives the American system. That's a problem, because nothing undermines trust as much as the nagging feeling that one of the parties is greedy and selfish. And trust is the lubricant that keeps any economy or government moving.

Some companies have taken steps to correct the perception that they are driven primarily by a short-term focus on their stock price.

The National Investor Relations Institute published a survey in March 2006 showing that barely half (52 percent) of publicly owned companies were issuing quarterly earnings projections, down from six out of ten (61 percent) the year before.[19] Instead, companies such as McDonald's, Coca-Cola, and Motorola give analysts periodic reports on factors that drive the creation of long-term value. Companies in Europe and Asia have long declined to issue quarterly forecasts, instead focusing on semiannual or annual data.

At a practical level, however, American companies will regain trust only if they get control of executive compensation. While executive pay is generally insignificant in a company's overall finances, it has such symbolic value that little progress is likely on other issues until it is resolved. There is probably no one-size-fits-all solution, but much more can be done to make compensation decisions truly independent of CEO influence.

One step that is gaining in popularity is to separate the roles of CEO and chairman. According to executive recruiters Russell Reynolds Associates, 29 percent of the companies in the Standard & Poor's 500 and 45 percent of companies in the NASDAQ 100 had separated the jobs as of the end of 2005.[20] While having an independent director as chairman doesn't guarantee good governance, supporters of the move—which, according to Russell Reynolds, now includes 59 percent of corporate directors—say it improves board oversight of the CEO. And, according to the search firm Spencer Stuart, 94 percent of S&P 500 companies now have a lead presiding director—up from just 36 percent in 2003. Most importantly, the vast majority of boards now meet regularly in executive session—without the CEO. About one in five independent board members even meets alone with shareholder groups—up from zero five years ago.[21] All these moves can also make compensation discussions more arm's-length. In fact, some boards now insist that compensation specialists report directly to them rather than to company management.

BOARD DISCIPLINE

Some governance experts believe it's corporate boards themselves that require greater oversight. In 2006, shareowners submitted more than 140 proxy resolutions requiring directors to be elected by majority vote, rather than by only a plurality of votes cast. Corporate governance expert Charles Elson thinks board members should have a significant stake in the company. A study he conducted in 1992 showed that companies whose directors owned an average of $100,000 in shares were much less likely to overpay their executives.[22]

Some companies are taking a step in that direction. Coca-Cola, for example, pays its board members entirely in company stock that can only be sold when certain long-term performance goals are met. General Electric, which is often a trendsetter in these practices, has adopted a similar policy for the majority of its board members' compensation. Most companies can do more to tie executive and board compensation to the long-term success of their business rather than to quarterly or annual earnings targets that can be manipulated and are often the result of industrywide factors beyond anyone's control.

Fixing executive compensation is more than a matter of conforming to other countries' notions of propriety, however. Out-of-control CEO compensation is not only a symptom of the excesses of American capitalism, it may be one of the causes. John Bogle, founder of the Vanguard Group of mutual funds, blames it for the stock market bubble of the late 1990s. He said:

> If we had to name a single father of the bubble, we would hardly need a DNA test to do so. That father is executive compensation, made manifest in the fixed-price stock option. When executives are paid for raising their company's stock price, rather than for increasing their company's value, that is exactly what they will do.[23]

The result is stock-ticker capitalism.

CREATING WEALTH

American corporations have a bad image in many global markets not because they are too focused on creating wealth, but because they have defined the beneficiaries of that wealth creation too narrowly. The prevailing view outside the Anglo-Saxon world is that corporations exist to create wealth for *all* who provide their resources and bear the risks of their failure. Such wealth comes in the form of dividends, rising stock prices, jobs, careers, healthier communities, and valuable products and services. As British business philosopher Charles Handy explained it, corporations have a moral obligation to serve their customers honestly, to give their employees an opportunity to develop and grow so they can care for their families, to give their shareowners a fair return on their investment, and to help build a civil society.[24]

Running a business isn't about creating short-term trading value—it's about building a long-lasting institution. Even though only a small minority of American CEOs have done perp walks up the courthouse steps, the rest won't truly earn the world's respect until they can demonstrate that they have a broader sense of purpose than moving their share price. No number of postal inspectors armed with the latest statutes and all the subpoena power in Washington can do that.

CHAPTER 12

PLAGUE OR PARANOIA?

"Brand USA is in trouble . . . it's a problem for business."[1]
—Bono, speaking at the 2005 World Economic Forum

"Wars and boycotts, both fade away."[2]
—Jan Lindemann, Interbrand

KEITH REINHARD WAS FRUSTRATED. AT THE END OF 2004, MORE than three years into his quest to find a cure for anti-Americanism, the file cabinets outside his Madison Avenue office suite bulged with research showing that American brands were in a free fall. Two separate surveys showed that 20 percent to 25 percent of Asians, Europeans, and Canadians were consciously avoiding U.S. brands.[3] His desk was covered with news clips about American brands being summarily "fired" by businesses in Europe. A German bicycle manufacturer canceled all parts orders with six American suppliers; restaurants across Germany and France stopped serving Coke, selling Marlboros, or letting customers pay with American Express cards.[4] The videotape deck in his conference room was piled with tapes of foreign consumers unloading about the arrogance and ignorance of American companies and the American people.

Reinhard felt like a doctor with reams of diagnostic data that indicated his patient should be in a coma, but who was watching him play tennis. And win. He was frustrated because everything he knew about advertising and marketing said American brands should be sucking air overseas, but he had no empirical data to show it was actually happening. In fact, companies that practically shouted "Americanness"—McDonald's, Coca-Cola, and Nike—were reporting strong gains in international sales.

So he sent John Zogby out to personally interview senior executives at iconic American companies. Reinhard could understand why none of them would stand up in public to describe how anti-Americanism was wrecking their franchises overseas. Who would want to lead that parade? It would look disloyal to the Bush administration. It would send a horrible signal to Wall Street. And it would invite a lot of unwanted scrutiny. But certainly in the privacy of their own offices, with a promise of complete confidentiality, interviewed not by a young pollster fresh out of college but by the prince of pollsters himself, the most skittish CEOs would open up.

THE ZOGBY INTERVIEWS

In the end, Zogby secured appointments with thirty-four senior executives, including seven sitting CEOs from companies such as Anheuser-Busch, UPS, and Levi Strauss. He supplemented those interviews with fourteen "thought leaders," ranging from academics to former ambassadors. On a scale of 1 to 5, with the higher numbers indicating greater degrees of "seriousness," the respondents rated anti-Americanism a 3.5, which Zogby characterized as "showing concern." Overall, the thought leaders were much more worked up about the issue than the business leaders. "I am seeing anti-Americanism spreading from dislike of U.S. policies to dislike of Americans," one thought leader said, "and it is now heading toward dislike of doing business with U.S. companies."[5]

A handful of the business leaders said there was nothing new about anti-Americanism and they weren't particularly concerned about it; none were willing to concede that it was a current problem for his company; most said it was a long-term, potential problem for "less established U.S. brands entering foreign markets," but not them.[6] "We see anti-Americanism in some places," FedEx's Bill Margaritis said in the same time frame, "but we don't feel it."[7] And despite news reports about widespread boycotts, none of the business leaders would admit seeing an impact in their own or their competitors' sales. Jack Daly of McDonald's brushed off the problem, saying, "Any U.S. company that does business around the world will have the wind in its face. . . . But it has not hurt our business. Overseas, 2004 was our best year ever and France led the way."[8] Despite the so-called "culture wars," according to *The Economist* magazine, France was gobbling up American entertainment as well:

> French versions of American reality television and confessional talk shows clog up the schedules, spawning the term *la télé poubelle* ("TV garbage can"). French teenagers download American rap to their iPods. In 2004, the person most searched for on Google France was Britney Spears.[9]

WHAT'S GOING ON?

What is going on here? Two political scientists on sabbatical at California's Center for Advanced Study in the Behavioral Sciences think they broke the code.

Peter Katzenstein, a professor of international studies at Cornell University, and Robert Keohane, a professor of political science at Duke University, studied the revenues of three American companies and three of their European competitors between 2000 and 2004. The American firms were Coca-Cola, McDonald's, and Nike, which surveys had identified as vulnerable to consumer boycott. The three European firms they chose—Cadbury Schweppes, Nestlé, and Adidas-Salomon—compete in many of the same markets.

Katzenstein and Keohane hypothesized that European boycotts of American goods following the invasion of Iraq should have been reflected in the firms' financial results, but they could find no evidence of it. "If anti-Americanism had a significant impact on sales," they told *The Economist*, "one should find U.S.-based firms' sales falling in 2003–04, when anti-American views rose sharply in Europe, compared to 2000–01."[10]

In fact, their analysis showed just the opposite. Between 2000–2001 and 2003–2004, all six firms increased their European sales. In fact, the sales of the American companies grew faster than their European rivals. What gives? Are European boycotters that addicted to Big Macs, Cokes, and the Nike Swoosh? Are German bicycle manufacturers and French cafés the only ones who can make a boycott stick?

Europeans also have a long tradition of mixing America-bashing with the consumption of American goods. In his history of postwar Europe, Tony Judt notes that Coca-Cola's rapid expansion in France in the late 1940s "unleashed a public storm." Intellectuals were aghast at rumors that Coke planned to stick a billboard on the Eiffel Tower. *Le Monde* called Coca-Cola "the Danzig of European Culture." But Parisians guzzled it anyway.[11] The CEO of European operations for McDonald's explained the long lines at the fast-food outpost on Les Champs Elysées by observing that the French are "schizophrenic— their head goes one way, and their feet go another."[12]

It is far easier to politicize a brand than consumers' behavior. And a study reported in *Harvard Business Review* found that negative attitudes toward the United States played a negligible role in consumers' purchase decisions for global brands, surprising the authors because their study was conducted at the height of the controversy surrounding the war in Iraq.[13]

TYPES OF ANTI-AMERICANS

Keohane and Katzenstein suggest that trying to measure anti-Americanism through public opinion polls is like trying to sort colored marbles with a steam shovel. It's too crude an instrument. First, few polls are capable of distinguishing between a transient negative opinion and the entrenched bias through which some people view everything American. Most polls capture both ends of the spectrum. Second, many people are simply ambivalent about America, simultaneously attracted and repelled by it. For example, they may love American movies but dislike the violent, materialistic culture portrayed in them. But most significantly, according to Keohane and Katzenstein, anti-Americanism is simply not homogeneous. In fact, they distinguish six different strains:

1. *Liberal Anti-Americans*. People who share America's political and social values, but dislike the United States for not living up to them.

2. *Welfarist Anti-Americans*. People who believe the United States fails to provide a social safety net for its own citizens.

3. *Sovereign-Nationalist Anti-Americans.* People who resent the United States when it acts unilaterally or appears to be taking actions that threaten their country's interests.

4. *Radical Anti-Americans.* People who reject America's dominant role on the world stage and want to weaken U.S. influence.

5. *Cultural Elitist Anti-Americans.* People who reject American culture as commercial and appealing to crude popular taste.

6. *Legacy Anti-Americans.* People who still resent the United States for past wrongs. For example, some Mexicans still resent American seizure of Mexican territory in the nineteenth century.[14]

Each of these strains of anti-Americanism is felt with different levels of intensity and, as described by Keohane and Katzenstein, none are mutually exclusive. For example, Welfarist Anti-Americans may think the United States' broad use of the death penalty is barbaric, but still support its efforts to spread democracy and fight terrorism. Liberal Anti-Americans may tell pollsters that their opinion of the United States has worsened since George W. Bush was reelected, they may even march on the local McDonald's to protest the Iraq War, but when the crowd disperses, they may be just as likely to order a Big Mac with a Coke as any American teenager. They can tell the difference between McDonald's as a political symbol and a hamburger joint. And while Cultural Elitists may refuse to watch *Desperate Housewives,* they aren't about to strap bomb belts to their bodies, though under the right circumstances a Radical Anti-American might.

Broad-based opinion polls sweep all these people into the same net, ask them how much they dislike America, and then ask them what practical steps they intend to take to conform their actions to the opinions they just expressed. To Keohane and Katzenstein, it's no wonder the sales impact of anti-Americanism tends to be highly exaggerated.

BOYCOTT GAP

The Economist suggests the boycott gap results from something as simple as a European's ability to "draw a distinction between President Bush and a Big Mac."[15] Perhaps. But there could also be other reasons anti-Americanism doesn't appear to have affected U.S. international consumer sales.

First, Rob Duboff, the CEO of HawkPartners marketing consultancy, points out that "the addressable market for U.S. goods has greatly expanded since the fall of communism, possibly masking the full effects of anti-Americanism."[16] Furthermore, in the period of Keohane and Katzenstein's study, the U.S. dollar was relatively weak against the euro and other foreign currencies. In the 2000–2001 base period of their study, the U.S. dollar appreciated by 13 percent against the euro. In 2003–2004, it fell by 31 percent.[17] That 44 point swing could account for the apparent strength of the U.S. companies since their sales are calculated in dollars whereas the European companies' are calculated in euros.

But foreign tourist travel to the United States, which would have benefited from the weak dollar, tells a very different story. The number of international travelers visiting the United States in 2005—about 49 million—was about two million fewer than in 2000, and the country's overall share of the international tourism market dwindled from about 17 percent to just 12 percent.[18] As one travel industry expert put it, "While the 'global travel pie' has increased in size, our slice has gotten smaller."[19] According to U.S. Department of Commerce data, between 2000 and 2005, travelers from France declined by 19 percent; from Germany, 24 percent; from Japan, 24 percent; and from Brazil, 34 percent.[20] "It's now 30 percent cheaper to be in the U.S." said Roger Dow, CEO of the Travel Industry Association of America (TIA). "We're on sale, and we're not crowded."

In fact, according to one study, America has fallen from the travel destination people would like to visit most to their sixth destination of choice, behind Australia, Italy, New Zealand, Canada, and Switzerland.[21] In terms of actual visitors, since 2001 the United States has fallen from the second most visited country to the third, behind France and Spain.[22] Even allowing for the extra hassle of getting through stepped-up U.S. security in post-9/11 America, these figures are striking. And discouraging. The Travel Industry Association's research shows that visitors to the United States are significantly more positive about the country than those who have never been here. Overall, 54 percent of people who have visited the United States are positive about it, while just 38 percent of nonvisitors are.[23]

It's also possible that America's very economic dominance insulates some U.S. companies from the full financial impact of boycotts. Until the recent development of open source software, there really hasn't been an appealing alternative to Microsoft's operating system for personal computers. So even though Microsoft is widely viewed as "American" and is even broadly disliked in its own right, its sales don't appear to have suffered. Similarly, although Global Market Insite's poll found that Coca-Cola was widely seen as an American product, few of those who said they planned to boycott U.S. brands singled out Coke. Global consumers seeking alternatives to Microsoft or Coke have few viable choices. For example, a French Muslim lawyer introduced Mecca Cola just a few months before the invasion of Iraq. His timing was impeccable and he garnered reams of news coverage by promising to donate ten cents for every can sold to Muslim causes. But after a strong launch, sales fizzled. In France, the soft drink's biggest market, Mecca Cola's market share is 1 percent or less.

In other cases, American brands have become such a mundane part of people's lives that they fly under the geopolitical radar. Aside from a handful of iconic brands, few consumers can name their favorite brands' country of origin. How many Americans, for example, would say that Alpo dog food, Tender Vittles cat food, and Baby Ruth candy bars are Swiss? Or that Snapple and Dr. Pepper are British? Most consumers are more likely to call a brand "global" than "American," "British," or "Japanese."

Some brands even forge such strong emotional ties with consumers that they become tribal emblems with supranational meaning. The British management consultant Peter York, for example, has argued that Nike's "Swoosh logo means precisely what the crucifix meant to an earlier generation in ghettos—it promises redemption, vindication, and a way out."[24] And like the crucifix during earlier periods of upheaval, Nike's Swoosh appears on T-shirts and caps in street demonstrations from Africa to Asia—ironically, even at anti-American protests.

Finally, there is almost certainly a sector-specific time lag between changes in consumer attitudes and purchasing behavior. John Quelch of the Harvard Business School points out that some of the true sales impact of anti-Americanism may not show up for years as people slowly become less willing to pay a price premium for American products over local goods. "Many consumers were willing to pay this premium to associate themselves with the aspirational American lifestyle," Quelch says. "This price premium will disappear. In fact, because it is no longer cool to be American, the price premium may even turn into a deficit, squeezing Brand America's profit margins." And as American brands lose their appeal and market share, they will find it harder to obtain shelf space.

THE POLITICIZATION OF BRANDS

Even though some American brands may be insulated from the short-term sales impact of anti-Americanism, Quelch points out that none are totally immune. Technological dominance isn't necessarily permanent. And some American cultural icons, such as McDonald's and Starbucks, have already been hit by waves of anti-Americanism simply because they're on every street corner of the world. "The very ubiquity that gives them their power makes them vulnerable," Quelch says. "Some consumers will actively boycott these brands because they are the most available symbols of America."[25] The hard-core activists who refuse to buy global brands are 10 percent to 15 percent of consumers, Quelch estimates, but so far he attributes their behavior to the anti-globalization movement of the late 1990s, not to anti-Americanism.[26] "I'm skeptical the average consumer is going to let their views of American foreign policy affect their brand-choice behavior," he told *Time* magazine.[27]

But "Americanization" and "globalization" have merged into a single boogeyman for many activists. And hard-core anti-American, anti-globalization activists, no matter how small a group, have already demonstrated how they can inflame the emotions of the larger body of consumers when a potential forum (e.g., a meeting of the World Bank) coincides with examples of "bad behavior," either by the American government (e.g., Abu Ghraib prison) or a U.S.-based corporation (e.g., allegations that Coke is stealing water from peasants in India).

In such an environment, iconic American corporations can find themselves the target of attack if only because they have publicity value. Protestors will often march on an American fast-food joint even when the U.S. embassy is more convenient. For example, globalization protestors trashed a McDonald's restaurant in Bern, Switzerland, during the 2001 Davos World Economic Conference, even though it was three hours away by train over the Alps. Protestors in Pakistan burned a KFC restaurant to the ground in Islamabad to protest the U.S. invasion of Afghanistan. Similarly, when the United States invaded Iraq, someone riddled a Ronald McDonald statue in Indonesia with bullets, while someone of like-mind torched another statue in Quito, Ecuador.[28]

Consumer politicization is not always so violent. Indeed, research by the Weber Shandwick public relations firm shows that up to one-third of consumers have boycotted a brand to make a political point. For example, 39 percent of British consumers said they were more likely than five years ago to boycott products in order to make a statement about an issue—whether the war in Iraq, child labor, or an environmental issue.[29] Weber Shandwick's CEO, Jack Leslie, believes the world has entered a permanent era of "constant ebb and flow in which the global acceptance of brands will be tempered by backlashes."[30]

Only the most committed activists persist in such boycotts, but their real danger lies in the atmosphere of political incorrectness they attach to a brand. For example, during the initial phases of the Iraq War, McDonald's counter sales in Egypt declined significantly, but its take-home business in the country grew, suggesting that for a brief period it may have been politically incorrect in Egypt to be seen in a McDonald's restaurant. So consumers simply scarfed their Big Macs in the privacy of their own homes. While McDonald's insists its overall sales in Egypt didn't decline, such incidents surely reinforce attitudes with long-term consequences. We're all wired to keep our thoughts, feelings, and actions in sync one way or another. Anyone who believes action follows feelings knows that the impact of negative attitudes toward America and all things American will one day be felt.

PROBLEMS FROM OUT OF LEFT FIELD

It's not hard to imagine situations in which anti-Americanism would have an even more negative impact than it does today. For example, another Bhopal-style disaster or an Enron-type financial debacle affecting international investors might trigger an outsize consumer response. For example, in late 2005, the Danes learned that something as apparently innocuous as cartoons of the Prophet Muhammad can ignite riots and boycotts.

Left field remains a fertile source of complications for global businesses. "Scandals and environmental mishaps seem as inevitable as the likelihood that these incidents will be subsequently blown out of proportion," according to McKinsey and Company consultants, "thereby fueling resentment and creating a political and regulatory backlash."[31] It's been that way, they note, not for the past five years, but for the past 250.

Furthermore, American companies hold beliefs—for example, the primacy of shareholder value, the benefits of free trade, the sanctity of intellectual property rights, and the solemn right to repatriate profits—that are not well understood, let alone accepted, in many parts of the world. Business people who think everything is just hunky-dory are like the window washer who fell off the scaffolding of a sky-scraper and yelled "So far so good" as he plunged by the thirtieth floor.

OTHER BUSINESS COSTS

Sales may be a lagging indicator of anti-Americanism's true impact. Anti-American feelings already contribute to a hostile business environment, increasing security costs in overseas facilities and making it more difficult to recruit employees outside the United States, as well as to win public approval for mergers or the opening of new facilities. Richard Edelman, CEO of the eponymous public relations firm, says the real impact "will be on the ability of U.S. companies to recruit and retain local talent, engage with regional governments, secure regulatory approval, and establish goodwill that they can draw on in a crisis."[32]

For example, General Electric's merger with Honeywell was supposed to be the crowning achievement of Jack Welch's illustrious career. And it would have been were it not for some European Union bureaucrats in Brussels who blocked it. No one will ever know what role anti-American feelings played in their decision, which was confirmed by EU courts three and a half years later. But there is little question that anti-American feelings erode the social capital that reduces the transaction costs of doing business. That cost is hard to pin down and unlikely to show up on an income statement, but it's no less real, and the potential impact is significant. General Electric, for example, expects 60 percent of its growth to come from developing countries in the next decade versus about 20 percent for the past ten years.[33] Countless American companies share similar ambitions. Standard & Poor's estimates that the companies in the S&P 500 derive about 40 percent of their sales outside their home market and that international sales are growing at a faster rate than domestic.[34]

POLICY IMPACT

Joseph Nye cautions that polls aren't much more than a "good first approximation"[35] of how much attractiveness, or "soft power," a country has and the cost of its unpopularity. While skeptical about the short-term sales impact of anti-Americanism, Keohane and Katzenstein are concerned that it may inhibit U.S. policymaking. It can make it harder for other countries to accede to U.S. requests (or conversely, easier to reject them). And the administration is less likely to ask for cooperation if it thinks its request might be rejected.

Anti-Americanism clearly played a role in Turkey's refusal to allow American troops to invade Iraq from across its border, seriously complicating the war effort. And Keohane and Katzenstein believe the fear of rejection may also have inhibited the Bush administration from requesting more troops from its coalition partners when the scope of the Iraqi insurgency became obvious.

Finally, anti-Americanism is increasingly surfacing as an unexpected factor in local elections around the world. Of course, some European and Latin American politicians have invested entire careers running against Washington in their local elections. But a 2003 report to Congress shows how it is even affecting the local politics of close allies. The report noted that the victor in the previous year's South Korean presidential election won office due in large part "to his criticisms of the United States." He also "benefited from the massive demonstrations in late 2002 protesting the acquittal of two U.S. servicemen who were operating a military vehicle when it killed two Korean schoolgirls."[36] You don't have to have the political instincts of Tip O'Neill to realize that someone who comes to office on those coattails is going to think twice about anything the United States asks him to do.

Richard Haass, the president of the Council on Foreign Relations, warns that "most global issues require global responses."[37] Anti-Americanism can cost the United States the cooperation of other countries (not to mention their willingness to share the burden) in dealing with global climate change, terrorism, HIV/AIDS, avian flu, massive poverty, or the next global security crisis, whether it breaks out in Iran, North Korea, or the Taiwan Strait.

Tamás Dávid-Barrett, who founded Budapest Economics, one of the leading Central European research consultancies, worries that anti-Americanism has caused a backlash against the free-market economic principles with which the United States is so closely identified. For example, he claims that rampant anti-Americanism was encouraging the leaders of some Latin American countries to adopt the socialist policies of Fidel Castro.[38]

GENERATIONAL IMPACT

The cost of anti-Americanism could be felt for generations. As Richard Haass points out, "People who come of age hating the United States will one day come to power mistrustful of the United States, or worse."[39] On the flip side, Joseph Nye worries about how anti-Americanism will impact Americans' behavior. He says:

> As we begin to believe that the rest of the world really does hate us, some Americans begin to hold grudges, to mistrust all Muslims, to re-name French fries, to spread and believe false rumors. Some Americans in turn succumb to residual strands of isolationism, and say that if foreigners are going to be like that, who cares what they think.[40]

To the extent that America tries to build a wall around itself, ignoring the rest of the world on the other side, it reinforces preconceptions of its arrogance. It also emboldens enemies such as Al Qaeda. Isolationism may feel warm and cozy at first, but it leaves America impotent to influence world events until it has no choice but to use military force. And some wars cannot be won with force. Defeating Islamist terrorism depends largely on the strength and determination of moderates within Islamic countries. And their ultimate victory depends on America's attractiveness to them.

That's where Brand America comes in. America's appeal is not based on the number of ships it has at sea or people under arms. It is the product of America's social, economic, and political system as it has evolved over more than 200 years. Not yet perfect, and not easily imitated—much less duplicated—in a single generation, but a model in the breathtaking simplicity of its vision: the freedom to be happy. In small ways and big, that vision comes to life in the products and services of American businesses.

The headline to *Business Week International*'s 2003 special report on U.S. brands—"America has image woes, not its brands"[41]—may have it right, for the moment. But it may also ignore three dangers. First, that U.S.-based companies may jump to the conclusion that negative attitudes toward the United States have no bearing on their commercial success or failure. Second, that the business community considers it a problem to be solved by the professional politicians who caused it. And third, that those politicians will try to solve it the way they solve any "campaign problem"—through better message management and discipline.

But anti-Americanism cannot be spun away. And if American businesses are not the biggest part of the problem, they are a good part of the solution.

PART THREE

CHAPTER 13

IN SEARCH OF
ANTI-ANTI-AMERICANS

"The U.S. can't be sold as a brand, like Cheerios."[1]
—*The Wall Street Journal*, editorial

*"The truly great brands are far more than just labels for products.
They are symbols that encapsulate the desires of consumers . . .
they are standards held aloft under which masses aggregate."*[2]
—Anthony O'Reilly, CEO, H. J. Heinz Company

BERNARD-HENRI LÉVY IS FRENCH. PROTOTYPICALLY FRENCH.
Flamboyantly French. He speaks with such a charming accent you can
practically see the *accent aigu* floating above the "e" in his name.
When he's skeptical about something, which happens several times a
day, his eyebrows rise like two *accents circonflexes* ("ˆ") in his forehead. He kisses ladies' hands and, even in unfamiliar territory, moves
with the easy grace of a maître d' in his own dining room. Well into
his fifties, he still has an unruly mane of dark brown hair and usually
wears crisp black suits with dazzling white shirts open one more but-
ton than would be comfortable on someone with less panache. He's
tall, trim, broad shouldered, and has the aquiline nose of an ancient
Gaul, even though he was born in Algeria to Jewish parents. They
settled in France after the war, where his father founded a lumber company that made him a millionaire and left Bernard-Henri more than
comfortable.

Though educated in France, Lévy's origins may have given him a unique perspective on one of the sources of his countrymen's discomfort with America. "In France, with the nation based on roots, on the idea of soil, on a common memory . . . the very existence of America is a mystery and a scandal," he told *The Wall Street Journal*. America gives the French political right "nightmares," he went on, as the country is based on "a social contract."

"America proves that people can gather at a given moment and decide to form a nation, even if they come from different places," Lévy says. The "ghost that has haunted Europe for two centuries is America's coming together as an act of will, of creed."[3] One can almost hear the café chatter on Les Champs Elysées: America, a country? *Zut!* It's a club!

PUBLIC PHILOSOPHER

People listen—and even take notes—when Lévy expresses such thoughts because he is one of France's most influential and well-known "public philosophers," a profession that currently has no real counterpart in the United States and, were it officially defined anywhere, would include "influence" and "celebrity" among its criteria. A public philosopher plumbs questions so deep they operate at levels far below the flows of political ideology, though they influence them by changing the surrounding currents. Then he surfaces in the public square to apply what he has learned to the issues of the day or to direct people's attention to problems they didn't know they had.[4]

Lévy executed his first deep dive when he was only twenty-eight and wrote *La Barbarie à Visage Humain* ("Barbarism with a Human Face"). The book was a best-seller and made him the most famous member of a group called *les nouveaux philosophes* ("the new philosophers") who had turned against Marxism. Thirty books, numerous magazine articles, and one feature film later, Bernard-Henri Lévy has successfully made so many deep dives he has become a brand in his own right, kind of a Jacques Cousteau of the intellectual world, known throughout France simply as "BHL."

Not unlike the American entertainer Jerry Lewis, Lévy is taken far more seriously outside his native country than within its borders. *Atlantic Monthly* magazine hired BHL to retrace the path taken by Alexis de Tocqueville in the nineteenth century and to report his findings in a three-part series that later became a book, *American Vertigo*. Despite providing BHL (who doesn't drive) with airplane tickets and a young intern to ferry him about, the magazine couldn't get him to follow de Tocqueville's route. But BHL did not disappoint on the two key elements of his profession—publicity and the pose of deep thinking. He was interviewed about the project at virtually every stop on his 15,000-mile trek, and he expressed himself freely on the expected themes—such as America's restlessness, patriotism, and religiosity—offering unique insights into their root causes.

For example, he thought he found the explanation for a peculiarity first noted by de Tocqueville that America is the only nation in the world where freedom and religious faith did not follow separate roads. "In France, liberty has had to be gained over religion," Lévy said. "The less religion we have in France, the more liberty we have."[5] But in America, he noted, liberty was not won from the church, but from another country, and the separation between church and state was established from the beginning, so religion is less threatening to most Americans.

He also found a common thread running through America's restlessness, patriotism, and religiosity that allowed him to tie them together (and inspired the "vertigo" in his book's title). As he told more than one interviewer:

> The faster the pace of change, the more attached Americans become to origins that are mythified, reconstructed, imaginary. This country is in constant motion. "Keep moving"—how many times did I hear that phrase this year? A country whose religion is to keep moving can only avoid neurosis, avoid vertigo, by hanging on to enormous foundation myths. So the two go together.[6]

THE ANTI-ANTI-AMERICAN

BHL did not take the *Atlantic* assignment for the money. He's already rich and has homes in Paris, the south of France, and Marrakech. He doesn't need the added notoriety. He's famous enough to have been hit a record five times by Noël Godin, the infamous anarchist pie-thrower. For Lévy, the assignment constituted binging on empty calories, as intellectual stimulation goes. And it's not because he's blindly in love with America. BHL began a 2003 address at the PEN American Center by declaring:

> I'm not pro-American, because there are a lot of things in the America of today that I dislike and that I'm very strongly against. First of all: the war in Iraq, which I opposed from the first day. The status of the prisoners in Guantánamo, for instance, is a scandal. You cannot be pro-American when America is the country of death penalty—this relic of barbarism does not belong to the culture of America. There are many reasons that I feel offended to be considered pro-American.[7]

But if BHL is not pro-American, he is even more adamantly anti-anti-American. "Anti-Americans don't hate what is worse about America," he said. "They hate what is best in America."[8]

> I traveled a little during these last years in Asia, in Africa, in many parts of the world, and I often saw that this anti-Americanism was a magnet for the worst hatred of democracy, hatred of freedom of spirit, hatred of the bare faces of women, hatred of an idealistic nightmare of America. I am very much anti-anti-American.[9]

In plumbing the depths of the American psyche, Lévy not only helped explain why America is as it is, but why its opponents are as they are. The question remaining, of course, is what to do about it.

The best way to deal with negative attitudes is seldom to challenge them head on, because that often leads to wrestling, bloody noses, and cries of "Fight! Fight!" from fascinated bystanders, just as it does on a schoolyard playground. It is far smarter to acknowledge the other party's feelings, without agreeing to their underlying grudge, find a tiny corner of agreement, and build bridges from there in subsequent encounters. In some ways, this is what the United States has been trying to do, only the common ground it has staked out is not proving very solid.

FINDING COMMON GROUND

The Bush administration's emphasis on "freedom" and "democracy" as its overarching goals is not particularly meaningful or motivating to large swaths of the world's population. That doesn't mean people don't want to be "free" or to live in a democratic society. But as Michael Ignatieff pointed out in *The New York Times*, "Democracy may be a universal value, but democracies differ—mightily—on ultimate questions."[10] Canadians, for example, certainly live in a democracy, but they have very different ideas about exactly what that means in areas ranging from universal health care (they've got it) to gun collecting (they hunt, but don't think people have a "right" to own AK-47s). Unlike many Americans, Canadians interpret democracy to mean the government can't kill people and that gay people can marry.

Anthony Giddens, the dean of the London School of Economics, likes to tell a story to demonstrate that democracy in Britain and the United States isn't understood the same way:

> A British traveler in the U.S. once inquired of an American companion: "How can you bear to be governed by people you wouldn't dream of inviting to dinner?" To which the American replied, "How can you bear to be governed by people who wouldn't dream of inviting you to dinner?"[11]

Many people in the developing world don't give democracy the same weight as Westerners do. When the Dutch, English, French, and Spanish colonial powers set sail to return to Europe in the nineteenth century, they left no democratic models for the indigenous people. Instead, they left them in the hands of ruling elites who invested far more in military and security forces (in order to keep their hold on power) than in democratic institutions. In fact, even people who harbor no reflexive anti-American feelings are not sure what "democracy" really means when the United States seems perfectly comfortable with authoritarian regimes in places such as Egypt and Saudi Arabia. Many Muslims—even many Muslim women—don't feel particularly oppressed or "un-free."[12] And at least one expert believes that many people in the Middle East interpret the United States' calls for greater democracy in the region as "no more than a ploy to perpetuate and consolidate their hegemony over Arab-Muslim lands and resources."[13] Even the United States's most faithful ally, the United Kingdom, has doubts about America's true intentions. In a poll taken in the summer of 2006, 72 percent of Britons said President Bush's claim that he wants to make the world "more democratic" is "merely a cover for pursuing American interests."[14]

ISLAMIC DEMOCRACY?

Some observers suggest that Islamic law—with its restraints on the free exercise of religion, relegation of women to inferior positions, and elevation of clerics to keep secular leaders in line—may be incompatible with modern concepts of democracy. Certainly radical Islamists are violently undemocratic, but even many pacific Muslims adhere to a rigid interpretation of Islam that draws no line between religion and politics.

Their concept of religion is one of total submission to the will of God in every aspect of one's life. The word *Islam* itself is Arabic for "submission (to the will of God)." "It's as if medieval Muslims imagined liberty to be a zero-sum game," wrote Catholic theologian and social thinker Michael Novak in a recent book. "If humans have it, God doesn't. If God has it, humans don't."[15] Obviously, God has it. Ergo, humans don't. That's why "virtue" (i.e., living one's life in accord with the precepts of the Quran) is a more exalted value than "freedom" in the Muslim world.

But Novak points out that many people once believed that being Catholic or Asian was incompatible with democratic values. It's true that the majority Sunni sect follows a school of Muslim theology that is intolerant and determined to impose its interpretation of Islamic law on all of society.[16] But other strains of Islamic thought have been much more accommodating to notions of human liberty. At the beginning of the twentieth century, for example, a Muslim theologian named Muhammad Abduh tried to limit the Islamic code to civil matters, such as family law, leaving matters of governance to political institutions. Unfortunately, his efforts were thwarted by the rise of the Muslim Brotherhood in Egypt and of the Wahhabi sect in Saudi Arabia. Both groups consider such theological and philosophical inquiries the blasphemous work of apostates.

Despite the Saudi government's successful efforts to spread Wahhabism to the far corners of the Islamic World, Novak believes it's worth trying to engage Muslims in a constructive dialogue on Islam and democracy. After all, Indonesia, the world's largest Muslim nation, proves that Islam can be secular, tolerant, and democratic. Indeed, the Islamic scholar Ahmed H. al-Rahim ended his review of Novak's book by summarizing the task facing Muslims and, by implication, the Western world. "The challenge is not merely one of reformulating democratic principles in an Islamic idiom (which has already been done)," he wrote, "but rather of adapting Islam's ethical and legal precepts to the *practice* of democracy."[17]

THE MUSLIM MAJORITY

Novak is encouraged by what he calls "a hopeful majority of Muslims" who want "to live their lives in peace, freedom, and growing prosperity."[18] They cherish their religion as a pure and intense source of transcendence in their lives and abhor the radical Islamists' cynical willingness to suspend traditional values when it serves their political goals. They consider the bombing of mosques and the kidnapping and murder of innocent civilians a subversion of traditional Islamic values.

Indeed, Fareed Zakaria reminds us that "the Quran is a vast, vague book, filled with poetry and contradictions (much like the Bible)."[19] Like many holy books, it speaks through allegory and indirection. Look hard enough and you can find great sweeping exhortations for tolerance and equally fierce condemnations of unbelievers. Similarly, the Quran includes passages that are both congenial and inimical to democracy. "Quotations from it usually tell us more about the person who selected the passages than about Islam,"[20] writes Zakaria.

Recent surveys show widespread support for democracy in Arab societies, even where most citizens have strong Islamic attachments. In the World Values Survey fielded in 2000, the percentage of Arab respondents agreeing that "democracy is a good way to govern countries" ranged from a low of 88 percent in Algeria to a high of 98 percent in Egypt.[21] A 2005 Pew Global Attitudes Project asked people in a number of Muslim countries whether "democracy is a Western way of doing things that would not work here." Large and growing majorities in Morocco (83 percent), Lebanon (83 percent), Jordan (80 percent), and Indonesia (77 percent) said democracy would work where they lived. Pluralities in Turkey (77 percent) and Pakistan (42 percent) also agreed.[22] A 2004 University of Michigan study, done in cooperation with the Baghdad-based Independent Institute for Administration and Civil Society Studies, indicated that more than three-fourths (79 percent) of Iraqis support a democratic political system, though a small majority (51 percent) preferred a strong link between government and religion.[23]

Arab enthusiasm for democracy is borne out by behavior on the ground. When they do have elections, voter turnout in Arab states is usually very high. Some 70 percent of registered Iraqis voted in the December 2005 parliamentary election, despite threats of violence. Nearly 75 percent of Palestinians voted in the January 2006 legislative elections. When political scientist Vali Nasr studied election results in Turkey, Bangladesh, Malaysia, Pakistan, and Indonesia, he was pleasantly surprised to discover that the "vital center" belonged neither to secularist and leftist parties nor to Islamists.

"More likely to rule the strategic middle will be political forces that integrate Muslim values and moderate Islamic politics into broader right-of-center platforms that go beyond exclusively religious concerns,"[24] Nasr wrote. However, the immediate practical results can be mixed. Recent free elections in Afghanistan, Egypt, Lebanon, and the Palestinian territories resulted in gains for warlords, the Muslim Brotherhood, Hezbollah, and Hamas. And the democratic government that the United States installed in Afghanistan considers it a capital offense, punishable by death, for a Muslim to convert to Christianity.

DEMOCRACY AND TERRORISM

If the United States' goal is to "drain the swamp" where terrorism breeds, political scientist Gregory Gause maintains that there's "no solid empirical evidence for a strong link between democracy, or any other regime type, and terrorism."[25] He points out that various terrorist organizations arose in democratic countries during the 1970s and 1980s, including the Red Brigades in Italy, the Provisional Irish Republican Army in Ireland and the United Kingdom, and the Baader-Meinhof Gang in West Germany.

Gause also cites the U.S. State Department's own statistics, which show that around the world, 269 major terrorist incidents occurred between 2000 and 2003 in countries classified as "free" by Freedom House; 119 attacks occurred in "partly free" countries; and 138 incidents happened in "not free" countries. (This count excludes both terrorist attacks by Palestinians on Israel, which would increase the number of attacks in democracies even more, and the September 11, 2001, attacks on the United States, which originated in other countries.) Gause says there's no reason to think that Al Qaeda would be unable to recruit followers under democratic Arab governments. Rather than push for free elections in the Arab world, Gause believes the United States should encourage the growth of "secular, nationalist, and liberal political organizations that could compete on an equal footing with Islamist parties."[26]

For his part, brand consultant Jack Trout has pointed out that "democracy," as nice as it sounds to us, is not what everyone wants. "What people do want are the benefits of a good democracy: security, freedom, and prosperity," he says. "And of the three, my bet is that prosperity would be the most popular."[27] Furthermore, it's wrong to assume that free and democratic societies will, by definition, give their people greater economic opportunities for improving the quality of their lives. Actually, the data suggests just the reverse—democracy and freedom follow economic opportunity, not vice versa.

CHAPTER 14

THE PATH TO HAPPY

"Who has done more good for the planet—Mother Teresa or Bill Gates?"[1]

—John Mackey, CEO, Whole Foods

WITH HIS BALDING HEAD AND CAREFULLY TRIMMED CHIN CUR-
tain, the University of Michigan's Ron Inglehart could easily pass for
an Amish farmer, but what he tends is a massive body of empirical
data from surveys on all six inhabited continents, covering 85 percent
of the world's population. Inglehart directs the World Values Survey,
which has been described as the most comprehensive and wide-ranging
survey of human values ever undertaken. In analyzing the data, Inglehart found an astonishingly strong linkage between the evolution of
industrial society and the rise of democratic political institutions. Hidden in his comparative data across some sixty countries over a number
of years is evidence that, as markets liberalize, people are increasingly
likely to want democratic institutions. And they are increasingly adept
at getting them, despite efforts of entrenched elites to resist giving up
their prerogatives. It seems that economic development increases the
likelihood of greater freedom, gender equality, and democracy.[2]

PERSONAL HAPPINESS

Not surprisingly, Inglehart also found a strong correlation between
economic development and people's sense of personal satisfaction or

happiness. However, the effect appears to level off quickly at a threshold of about $10,000. Beyond that point, there is practically no relationship between income and subjective well-being. For example, according to the World Values Survey data, the Irish are happier than the Germans, although the Germans are twice as wealthy. And the Taiwanese are as happy as the Japanese, even though the Japanese are three times as wealthy.

Once people achieve a reasonably comfortable existence, their happiness depends more on quality-of-life concerns, such as environmental protection, and on lifestyle issues, such as a sense of belonging, opportunities for self-expression, and active participation in society. As Inglehart explains, this condition "has given rise to a wide range of new social movements, from the environmentalist movement to the women's movement, and to new norms concerning cultural diversity."[3] Once people are economically comfortable, they give increasingly higher priority to such values as freedom of speech and political participation. And it is at that point that democracy begins to contribute to human happiness, by creating a social environment within which people are free to express themselves and in which economic development can flourish.

However, Inglehart did *not* find a strong, direct correlation between democracy and human happiness. "Democracy is a good thing, and it probably makes some contribution to human happiness," he wrote, "but it does not seem to have nearly as much impact as other aspects of people's experience."[4] Furthermore, Inglehart cautioned that "democracy is not attained simply by making institutional changes or through elite-level maneuvering. Its survival depends also on the values and beliefs of ordinary citizens."[5] Democracy is not something that can simply be legislated; it must be demanded, nurtured, and supported by society.

Finally, the World Values Survey indicates that there is usually a lag between the attainment of a certain measure of economic security and a shift toward democratic values. It is an intergenerational phenomenon that is decades old in the industrialized world and still under way in developing countries.

MORE TO FREEDOM THAN A BALLOT

In the West, we often conflate the notions of freedom, democracy, and capitalism as if they are all the same thing. What we call "democracy" is a political system for selecting leaders through free and fair elections. In fact, democracy did not become fully developed in the West itself until the twentieth century. Before the First World War, women had the right to vote in only four countries—Finland, Norway, Australia, and New Zealand. In fact, it was 1974 before women could vote in Switzerland. Furthermore, some democratic countries—such as Germany, Italy, Austria, Spain, and Portugal—relapsed into periods of authoritarian rule or military dictatorship during the period from the 1930s to the 1970s.

Even today, "much of the Muslim world remains one of the last outposts of defiantly undemocratic rule—from tyranny to benign authoritarianism,"[6] writes Anthony Shadid. In fact, according to a report by Freedom House, which tracks these things, only one country in the Middle East can be considered "free" (Israel); six Middle East countries and one territory (Palestine) rank as "partly free"; and eleven are "not free."[7] The president of the Palestinian Authority is the only democratically elected leader in the Arab world, proving perhaps that democracy by itself is insufficient.

Even democratically elected leaders can be authoritarian. Adolf Hitler, after all, was democratically elected.[8] And less than fully democratic societies can offer a certain amount of economic freedom. Even under colonial rule, for example, Hong Kong was economically liberal. The key issue is not where a government comes from but where it is going—what its goals are. From its earliest days, America has been characterized as a "liberal democracy"—not in the sense of high-spending, high-taxing, "a chicken in every pot" liberalism, but in the original meaning of the Latin word *libertas,* which means "treated equally under the law," free from coercion by the state, the church, or long custom.

A liberal democracy is a political system in which the individual not only has a say in who governs him, but is also assured that the government's leaders operate under the rule of law, overseen by an independent judiciary. A liberal democracy believes individuals have certain natural rights, including private property rights, the right to worship—or not—as they please, freedom of speech, and a host of other rights developed over the last 200 years.

THE ECONOMIC PATH TO DEMOCRACY

One might wonder, as the German political philosopher Jurgen Hagerman did, how liberal democratic rule could take hold in a closed political system based on the absolute divine right of kings. Were all the monarchs asleep, or were they simply incompetent? Hagerman concluded it was the development of a market economy that made royalty obsolete. Simply put, with the eighteenth-century development of mercantile economies in northern Europe, trade and society grew beyond the ability and authority of kings to govern. As *Newsweek*'s Fareed Zakaria points out, "Nothing has shaped the modern world more powerfully than capitalism."[9] It destroyed monarchism, feudalism, classism, and communism. And it gave society new leaders independent of the state—entrepreneurs and business people.

Non-European countries seem to be following the same path. As Zakaria also points out, those countries that have moved farthest toward the kind of democracy practiced in the West have all followed a familiar pattern: first free enterprise and the rule of law, then democracy. "In much of East Asia—South Korea, Taiwan, Thailand, Malaysia—a dominant ruling elite liberalized the economy and the legal system," he writes.[10]

For example, when the dictator General Augusto Pinochet took over Chile, its economy was in shambles. Inflation was running out of control at a rate of about 1,000 percent a year. Mine workers, truckers, doctors, teachers, students, and small business people had all been on strike at one time or another, sometimes simultaneously. Even housewives had organized marches to protest the lack of food in the groceries. At first, Pinochet tried to run the country as an extension of the army, but when it became clear that that wouldn't work, he brought in a group of Chilean economists trained at the University of Chicago who were disciples of Milton Friedman. Their prescription was a heavy dose of free-market economics, including the privatization of industries taken over by the previous socialist government, slashing tariffs from 94 percent to 10 percent, and lifting nearly all limitations on foreign direct investment.

Economists still argue about whether the "shock treatment" really worked or merely created the illusion of growth. Inflation came down dramatically, but unemployment grew. And there is little question that while the Chicago school economists were fiddling with the economy, Pinochet's henchmen were ruthlessly suppressing political opposition.

But Pinochet's free-market reforms had one more effect. In opening the economy he made a return to democracy inevitable. As Zakaria explains it, "Capitalism created a middle class that then pressured the government to open up the political system. It nurtured an independent civil society that has helped consolidate democracy."[11] And once the door to open markets is ajar, it's difficult to slam shut. The left-leaning governments that followed Pinochet in Chile, for example, have taken a relatively pragmatic approach to the country's economy since they are dependent on outside investment and foreign loans to pay for populist social programs.

DEVIL IN THE DETAILS

Bolivia, which also implemented many of the reforms that appeared to work so well in Chile, stands as an example of the rule that the devil is in the details. Starting in 1985, Bolivia eliminated price controls, slashed government spending, removed barriers to trade, deregulated its banks, and privatized the biggest state-owned companies. The reforms brought hyperinflation under control, but inequality worsened, creating an even bigger chasm between the few rich and the many poor. Friedman's disciples claim the reforms failed because of massive corruption, patronage, and an obstinate government bureaucracy that makes incorporating a business a fifty-nine-day gauntlet that costs twice the average Bolivian's annual income. In any case, the poor reacted in 2005 by electing an avowed socialist as their first indigenous president. And populist leaders were gaining political footholds in other Latin American countries through 2006.

Even the most ardent free marketers have been chastened. They approach the lowering of import barriers and the privatization of industry less precipitously and in less of a cookie-cutter fashion. They acknowledge that multinationals—which provide most of the cross-border investments and account for about one-third of trade—need to take their social responsibilities more seriously in nations where the rule of law is weak. And they put more emphasis on the need for preconditions, such as political stability, sound economic management, and a vibrant civil society that includes professional associations, religious groups, labor unions, and advocacy organizations. Economic development has been a major driver of democratization because it is usually accompanied by rising levels of education and the rise of a middle class that's unbeholden to the state. South Korea and Taiwan stand as the classic examples, but the same pattern can be seen in Thailand, Brazil, Mexico, and South Africa.

And something very similar may be happening in China, which accounts for more than half of the 2.3 billion people Freedom House considers "not free."[12] In some parts of the country, 80 percent of elected village leaders are local businesspeople. And in a 2005 poll, 74 percent of Chinese citizens agreed that "the free enterprise system and free-market economy is the best system on which to base the future of the world."[13] That was an even higher level of agreement than in the United States and twice the level in France. Social scientist Seymour Martin Lipset maintains that "the more well-to-do a nation, the greater its chances to sustain democracy."[14]

Surveys show that there is also a growing appetite in the Middle East and in the developing world to participate in the proverbial middle class. Zogby International surveyed people in five Middle East countries in late 2005, when the Iraq War was still the lead story on most evening broadcasts. They found that the Arab in the street was most concerned with issues such as "expanding employment," followed by "improving health care," "ending nepotism and corruption," and "improving education." "Advancing democracy" was in eighth place, just ahead of "increasing rights for women."[15]

THE MIDDLE CLASS EFFECT

The rise of a new middle class around the world may be the best news ever for Brand America.

Two researchers at the University of North Texas—Audhesh K. Paswan and Dheeraj Sharma—investigated the famous "country-of-origin effect" in 2004. Their study was not exactly unique. There have been more than 766 "major publications" on country-of-origin effects since the 1950s.[16] But their study was noteworthy because Paswan and Sharma were studying brands that most people would consider the exemplars of American "cultural imperialism"—Coke, Pepsi, McDonald's, and KFC. They did their fieldwork at a time when esteem for the United States was at a low ebb and in a country—India—that was still smarting from its own experience as the subservient colony of the British Empire. In fact, while the young researchers were conducting their study, India was having an election in which one party was promising to ban imports of luxury goods and fashions, restrict the use of the English language, and return to the country's precolonial Hindi name.[17] So, what they found was all the more interesting.

It seems that better educated, upwardly mobile consumers were more likely to know where Pepsi, Coke, McDonald's, and KFC come from. And that knowledge *helped* the brands, rather than hurt them. What's more, the good feelings flowed both ways—knowing that Pepsi, Coke, McDonald's, and KFC came from the USA made them feel better about America.

"As people become better off and their position more stable," Paswan and Sharma wrote, "foreign cultures no longer threaten [them] in the way that they often do for the poorer elements in society." And it's true around the world, they theorized—that is, "the successful middle class is not threatened by immigration, does not feel shaped by branded goods and services, and can separate the good and bad in a culture, without branding that culture as innately good or bad." In fact, Paswan and Sharma suggested that America's goods and services are the USA's best ambassadors. "Consistent in quality, respected and enjoyed, these brands portray much of the good about the USA—one of the reasons why they are so successful worldwide."[18]

Brand America may have found its worldwide constituency.

AMERICA'S CONSTITUENCY

A BBC poll of twenty-three nations conducted at the end of 2004 showed the now depressingly familiar pattern of antipathy toward the United States. America edged out Russia for the dubious distinction of having the largest number of countries (sixteen) rate its influence in the world as predominantly negative. But even in the countries that were most negative toward the United States, large numbers of people were pro-American. The BBC's poll showed that some 38 percent of the French, 27 percent of Germans, 42 percent of Brazilians, and 40 percent of Chinese said they like the United States.[19] Who are these people?

In some cases, these are people who experienced America's support firsthand. For example, Europeans of a certain age remain grateful for America's help during the world wars. Closer to our time, many Britons associate America with the economic changes that Margaret Thatcher, and later Tony Blair, ushered in. And many Poles remember Ronald Reagan's support for the Solidarity movement during the 1980s. Of course, nostalgia is at best a wasting asset. But there may be another, separate vein of potential pro-Americanism hidden in this blizzard of statistics. It turns out that patterns emerge when pro- and anti-American sentiments are broken down by age, income, and education.

The Washington Post's Anne Applebaum did precisely that with the BBC's polling data on file at the University of Maryland's Program on International Policy Attitudes. She found that in Britain, for example, 57.6 percent of people with low incomes believe the United States has a positive influence in the world, while only 37.1 percent of those with high incomes feel that way. In South Korea, 69.2 percent of those with low education think the United States is a positive influence, while only 45.8 percent of those with a high degree of education agree. "That trend repeats itself not only across Europe but in many other developed countries," she writes. "Those on their way up are pro-American. Those who have arrived, and perhaps feel threatened by those eager to do the same, are much less so."[20]

In developing countries, such as India, Vietnam, Brazil, Indonesia, and the Philippines, the trend is reversed. According to the Applebaum's analysis, 69 percent of high-income Indians, for example, think the United States is a positive influence in the world, while only 29 percent of those with low incomes agree. The poor and less educated in those countries remain untouched by the effects of globalization, but their younger, wealthier, better educated countrymen have had a taste of economic opportunity and crave more.

And an expectation of personal economic progress, that one's lot in life is improving, seems to correlate with positive feelings about America. People who are upwardly mobile—or would like to be—tend to be pro-American. They are aspirational, and what America symbolizes for them is that dreams *do* come true.

MIDDLE CLASS EXPLOSION

If current trends continue, the upwardly mobile segment of the world's population is about to explode. According to McKinsey and Company, "almost a billion new consumers will enter the global marketplace in the next decade as economic growth in emerging markets pushes them beyond the threshold level of $5,000 in annual household income—a point when people generally begin to spend on discretionary goods."[21] And it's a point when their dreams of a better life seem finally within their grasp.

According to McKinsey, China's rising economy will lift hundreds of millions of households out of poverty. "Today, 77 percent of urban Chinese households live on less than 25,000 renminbi a year (about $3,100)," McKinsey notes. "We estimate that by 2025 that figure will drop to 10 percent." At that point, Chinese urban households will constitute one of the largest consumer markets in the world, spending about 20 trillion renminbi ($2.5 trillion) annually.[22] Based on a ten-year survey it conducted within the country, The Gallup Organization says that the newly prosperous Chinese are ready to spend on improving their lifestyles. Whereas in 1994, the average Chinese household looked forward to buying labor-saving products such as vacuum cleaners and refrigerators, nowadays their consumption leans more toward "products that enhance enjoyment and entertainment that satisfies individual tastes."[23] The percentage of Chinese households with DVD players increased from 7 percent in 1997 to 52 percent in 2004. The proportion with computers grew from 2 percent in 1994 to 13 percent in 2004, and the number with mobile phones jumped from 10 percent in 1999 to 48 percent in 2004.

Interestingly, the World Bank estimates that about the same proportion of the world's population (i.e., 11 percent) is "middle class," which it defines as an equivalent annual income between the poverty line in Western countries and the mean income in Italy, the poorest of the seven largest industrialized nations. The developing world may be reaching a tipping point similar to America's in the eighteenth century, when consumer demand dominated the economy and ignited an explosion of entrepreneurial energy. But the World Bank cautions that "there is no agency whose mandate is to care about it."[24] As a result, middle-class growth is inhibited by natural forces within many countries. Richer Indians, for example, may achieve annual incomes on a par with the worldwide middle class, but further growth is difficult because of high national taxes and potential political instability as people of lower income complain about a growing income gap.

REBUILDING BRAND AMERICA

Just as rebuilding Brand America cannot be accomplished with one ad campaign, people's respect and affection cannot be bought with bags of rice, free concerts, or subsidized trips to Disney World. Worldwide acclaim won't even come from a change in the U.S. administrations, as much as some people would like to believe that's all it will take. Animosity toward America has been building for decades, is rooted in ancient grudges both perceived and real, and is not easily unpacked. It also won't go away by itself.

As in any successful branding effort, America must clearly define itself in terms of what it means to others in highly practical personal terms. America's appeal must be emotional and not simply rational. America needs to sell its benefits, not just its features. And, as in the most effective branding campaigns, America's initiatives must target those constituents who can be moved and are the likeliest to move others—specifically, the upwardly mobile people to whom America represents proof that one can improve one's life. Every other American ideal—equality, liberty, tolerance, individualism, risk taking, and so on—should be positioned within that intellectual and emotional frame.

Millions of people around the world associate America with generalized notions of upward mobility, economic progress, a better quality of life—in other words, "opportunity." For many, it is still aspirational, but aspiration is the essence of the American Dream. It is the essence of branding. And it may even be the key to rebuilding Brand America in the Middle East.

As Fareed Zakaria prophetically warned in 2003, "At the start, the West must recognize that it does not seek democracy in the Middle East—at least not yet. We seek first constitutional liberalism, which is very different."[25] Clarifying one's goals has the distinct advantage of making them that much easier to attain. With a clear goal of economic reform, the U.S. government can marshal its influence to push the autocracies of the Middle East to liberalize their markets, creating a vibrant new business class and reclaiming their historical place as the inventors of the world's greatest bazaars and the center of international trade. Nothing would frustrate the recruitment of terrorists more. And, as it happens, in this case, American companies have a major role to play since they are, almost by definition, vehicles of liberalization.

A MATTER OF TRUST

Ironically, the free flow of information and the increased business contact between people, both of which are characteristic of liberalized markets, tend to increase conflict in the short term as people become more aware of their differences. And, in one of the major contradictions of our time, as the world grows smaller, people are less likely to trust each other. Ron Inglehart's World Values Survey shows that levels of trust have declined in nearly every nation that has liberalized its markets and expanded its global trade (see Figure 14-1).

The average percentage of people who answered "Yes, people can be trusted" as opposed to "You can never be too careful" declined from 38 percent in 1981 to 35 percent in 1990, and 24 percent in the years from 1995 to 1997. Results for individual nations mostly followed this general trend, although with some variation. For instance, according to the World Values Survey data, more than half (52.3 percent) of the Chinese are trusting, while practically no one in Brazil is (2.8 percent).

A global public opinion survey commissioned by the World Economic Forum in 2005 painted the same alarming picture. Trust in national governments, the United Nations, and global companies are all at historic lows.

The first challenge in rebuilding Brand America is to rebuild its credibility. At this point, there has been so much focus on U.S. foreign policy—particularly its relations with the Arab world—that America can't change the subject of the conversation. The U.S. government's ability to influence public opinion in foreign lands is very limited. For Brand America to move forward, the U.S. private sector needs to shift the focus from foreign policy to local society, from what's in the inter-

Percent (%) Agreeing with Statement: "You can trust most people"									
	World Average	U.K.	USA	Australia	Argentina	Brazil	China	Russia	Poland
1981	38.4	43.3	40.5	48.2	26.1	N.A.	N.A.	N.A.	N.A.
1990	34.6	43.7	51.1	N.A.	23.3	6.5	60.3	37.5	34.5
1995–1997	24.3	29.1	35.9	40.0	17.6	2.8	52.3	23.2	16.9

Figure 14-1. Levels of trust.

Source: World Values Survey.

ests of the American people to what matters to people outside the United States, who happen to be their customers. A world shaken by conflict makes for lousy markets. At minimum, American companies should be committed to stable, healthy markets around the world. Alleviating anti-Americanism is not only a matter of patriotism—it is good business.

U.S.-based companies can undercut the legitimacy of terrorists, who spread hatred of America, by spreading opportunity—hiring local people, doing business with local suppliers, and selling products and services that raise local living standards.

By becoming part of the local culture, sharing their customers' cares, and identifying with their dreams, they will build bridges of trust between America and the rest of the world.

CHAPTER 15

SINK ROOTS, DON'T JUST SPREAD BRANCHES

"What people see in America these days is Imperial Rome again."[1]
—Philip Kotler, Northwestern University

"If you can look at the world through the eyes of your customers, you can offer effective products and services. But if you believe other nationalities have to accept your company on your conditions, you're destined for failure."[2]
—Ronald M. DeFeo, CEO, Terex Corporation

EVEN AT THE END OF HIS LIFE, WELL INTO HIS EIGHTIES AND frail, Ted Levitt looked like he might once have been the demanding overseer of a busy loading dock. But for more than forty years, this prematurely balding man with a thick brush mustache, bushy eyebrows, and piercing eyes trafficked not in goods but in ideas, great pallets of ideas that are still taught at business schools around the world. Officially, he taught at the Harvard Business School, where he chaired the marketing area and was listed as "professor emeritus" until his death in mid-2006. But through a prodigious output of books and articles, including a four-year stint as editor of *Harvard Business Review,* Levitt influenced generations of the world's business leaders.

As a lecturer, Levitt prowled the classroom, occasionally tossing chalk to emphasize a point. He was provocative and had a knack for memorable aphorisms packed with meaning. In the first piece he ever wrote for HBR, he asked the now-famous question, "What business are you in?" and scolded railroad executives for failing to see that they were in transportation rather than the railroad business. Lecturing his marketing students, he famously thundered, "People don't want to buy a quarter-inch drill. They want a quarter-inch hole!"

Levitt's remarkable writing career was bookended by a dry-as-dust doctoral thesis titled "World War II Manpower Mobilization and Utilization in a Local Labor Market" and, three decades later, an outrageous opinion piece for *The New York Times* that claimed, "Every sustained wave of technological progress and economic development everywhere has been fueled by greed, profiteering, special privileges, and megalomania."[3] The two pieces neatly demonstrated his evolution from a scholar of economics to an agent provocateur. One former student likened Levitt's genius to grabbing business people by the lapels and shouting "Wake up!"

GLOBAL WAKE-UP

Levitt's most famous wake-up call appeared in the *Harvard Business Review* in 1983. Thanks to "The Globalization of Markets,"[4] a generation of M.B.A.s was brought up thinking that the world was morphing into one global market for standardized products. "The world's needs and desires have been irrevocably homogenized," he pronounced. "This makes the multinational corporation obsolete and the global corporation absolute."[5] Freed from having to worry about local differences, global corporations could concentrate on lowering their costs through economies of scale in production, distribution, marketing, and management.

Levitt may have been ahead of his time by a century or two. The homogenized global market he envisioned has yet to materialize. Most companies that attempted to offer standardized products around the world have been consistently outflanked by local competitors. And companies that acquired local brands as a shortcut into global markets lost touch with their customers if their primary focus was on back-office economies of scale.

Sara Lee Corporation, for example, bought a number of lingerie brands in the United Kingdom, France, and Spain that it thought would complement its Playtex and Hanes lines in the United States. It studiously kept existing local brands, such as Dim in France, and concentrated on centralizing back-office functions such as sourcing and distribution. It focused so much on building economies of scale in the logistical systems supporting its brands that it completely missed changes in the marketplace. Hosiery sales went south as European women began wearing pants suits more often, and department store sales of lingerie declined as specialty retailers such as Victoria's Secret wove a fantasy that made shopping for bras and nightgowns more fun. Eventually, Sara Lee announced a major retrenchment from Europe and put its local brands up for sale. The lesson: Efficiencies in supply chain management only provide competitive advantage if what you're supplying has meaning to consumers. As management consultant Bernard Demeure said, "If all you do is play a good game, you can still wind up playing the wrong game."[6]

On the other hand, one might expect MTV to be the kind of standardized global brand that Levitt envisioned. After all, it is the exemplar of the very technological and social phenomena that inspired his globalization insight. And indeed, MTV entered Europe in 1987 with pan-regional, advertiser-supported English programming. Within a few years, however, MTV discovered that the sum was smaller than its parts, because local ad buys tallied to a much larger figure than ads sold on a pan-European basis. There simply weren't many advertisers who offered the same product across Europe.

For example, when Kellogg's renamed its Coco Pops cereal Cocoa Krispies in 1998 to standardize the name across Europe, many children protested so loudly the company decided to put the matter to a vote. The old name won by a margin of 85 percent and the company decided to forgo the economies of scale in packaging. And Kellogg's found it nearly impossible to produce television commercials that could be run across Europe for those few products that it offered in multiple countries. In a cornflakes commercial, for example, references to iron and vitamins would have to be deleted in the Netherlands, where health claims are strictly regulated; children wearing Kellogg's T-shirts would be edited out in France, where they are banned from endorsing products on TV; and in Germany, rules against making competitive claims would prohibit the use of the advertising line that "Kellogg's makes their cornflakes the best they have ever been."

MTV also discovered that its audience wasn't the universal tribe it had imagined. While young people shared many common attitudes and musical tastes, they were also sharply different from country to country. When local competitors, such as VIVA in Germany and

MCM in France, began to exploit these differences, MTV quickly changed business models. Today, MTV Europe is in 164 countries in multiple languages and formats with nearly 50 percent local programming. In all, MTV runs eighty distinct music programming services in Canada, Asia, Europe, Australia, Latin America, the Caribbean, and Africa.

MTV tailors its channels to local cultural tastes with a mixture of national, regional, and international artists, along with locally produced and globally shared programming. For example, local language and music account for 80 percent of the programming on MTV India. Not surprisingly, Indian young people love it. "When we started MTV Asia in 1992, only one Asian video had been made. So we played that, and everything else was basically American," said former Viacom CEO Tom Freston. "Today, we have MTV China, and 80 percent to 90 percent of the videos we run there are made in China and sung in Chinese."[7]

TRANSFORMATIVE INTERACTION

Levitt's acolytes may have been deflated now that his globalization pronouncement seems at best premature, but they are stolidly unbowed. Richard Tedlow, a business historian at Harvard, takes the long view. "Sometimes, even if they are wrong, ideas can set off a chain of debate that results in greater knowledge," he said at a seminar to celebrate the article's twentieth anniversary. "So a brilliant idea that may not be right but that gets people thinking can be of greater value than a standard idea that doesn't stimulate thought at all."

Revisionist history or not, Tedlow and his copresenter, Rawi Abdelal, claimed that Levitt's deepest insight—that "consumer preferences are constantly shaped and reshaped"—sailed right past most readers, along with its implications. "What constitutes globalization, in Levitt's (and our) way of thinking, is interaction that changes things, rather than leaving them the same," they wrote. "The global market is not solely what firms find. The market is, to some important extent, what firms make of it."[8]

In other words, *globalization* describes more than just shipping products across borders; it describes how the interaction between companies and societies can create something new for both of them. MTV is neither a "multinational" company offering local products in multiple nations, nor an "international" company shipping a standardized product across borders. It is a "global" company intimately engaged with local societies to satisfy universal needs that Levitt described as "the alleviation of life's burdens and the expansion of discretionary time and spending power."[9] In MTV's case, the alleviation of life's burdens may come in the form of something you can dance to, but it is no less real and the culture it represents is as meaningful as any nation's.

LOCALIZING A BRAND

Somewhat paradoxically, the globalization process assumes an intimate understanding of local customers' needs, expectations, and values. Though the world may be getting smaller and flatter, local tastes, customs, and habits still predominate.

"The most important thing that we've done as a group of channels in all of our brands is that we care very much about the point of view of the young person on the street," says Brett Hansen, the president of MTV Europe. MTV works a street that runs from London through Paris and Berlin, Caracas, and Guangdong. MTV's genius lies in developing a feel for what is happening on different stretches of that street and translating it into phone text, websites, television programming, and gaming.

Procter and Gamble learned the importance of localizing brands when it tried to sell toothpaste with a wintergreen flavor in England after the Second World War, not realizing that the Brits associated wintergreen with liniment and weren't about to put it in their mouth. Then the company had to cope with complaints that its Drene shampoo crystallized because bathrooms were a lot colder in England than in the States. After similar experiences in postwar Japan, the company abandoned the idea that it could ship U.S. products to foreign markets with little more change than to translate the copy on the packaging. P&G started paying much closer attention to local habits, tastes, and idiosyncrasies.

For example, in countries such as Japan, where space is at a premium, P&G developed much more highly concentrated formulations of its leading brands, such as Joy dishwashing liquid and Cheer laundry detergent. Some P&G brands—such as Pampers, Pantene, Pringles, and Oil of Olay—have more similarities from country to country than differences, but the variations can be significant. Herbal Essence shampoo smells the same worldwide, but the fragrance is modulated according to country preferences—more subtle in Japan, stronger in Europe.

Sometimes the differences can be more significant. P&G's researchers discovered that in many developing countries, where clothes are often washed by hand, it took too much water to get the suds out. So the company developed a low suds detergent. Tide 1-Rinse cuts in half the amount of water needed to rinse clothes after hand-washing.

Even McDonald's, which built its reputation on consistency, adapts its menu to a country's religious laws, customs, and tastes. For example, in Israel, Big Macs are served without cheese to conform to kosher dietary requirements. In India, where Hindus do not eat beef, Muslims do not eat pork, and many others don't eat meat of any type, McDonald's serves Vegetable McNuggets and a mutton-based Maharaja Mac. In Malaysia and Singapore, McDonald's restaurants undergo rigorous inspections by Muslim clerics to ensure ritual cleanliness. In Indonesia, some McDonald's have a raised area with low tables for diners who want to take off their shoes and sprawl on mats, in the traditional style of central Java. And in Japan, where the "r" sound is rarely pronounced, Ronald McDonald is known as Donald McDonald.[10]

The most successful global companies understand local consumers' latent needs, as well as the ones they can express. For example, Samsung built memory backup into the washing machines it sells in India to compensate for the country's frequent power outages, and it designed a special rinse cycle for saris to prevent them from becoming twisted and knotted. Nokia introduced a mobile phone with a dust-resistant keypad, antislip grip, and a built-in flashlight to appeal to the hundreds of thousands of truck drivers who travel India's poorly lit highways.

On the other hand, when Vodafone retreated from the Japanese market by selling its local mobile service operator, *The Wall Street Journal* headlines said the company was "tripped up by local quirks."[11] Vodafone apparently never quite figured out what kinds of phones and service the gadget-happy but tech-fussy Japanese wanted.

A LOCAL FACE

One of the highest priorities for most successful global companies is to adopt a local face. In 2000, to better penetrate the European market, Boeing stopped flying salespeople in from Seattle and appointed a group of powerful country presidents with political ties to local governments. Two years later, it had taken the same steps in countries such as Japan and China. It appears to have worked because in 2005, although Airbus claimed a larger number of orders, Boeing had the larger share of worldwide revenue for the first time since 2000. And its biggest customer in Europe is Air France, which is introducing the latest Boeing 777 model.

Virtually all of McDonald's top management in Europe worked at one time behind the counters of its restaurants. The manager of the company's first outlet in Moscow is now the president of the entire Russian operation. In fact, every senior executive who reports to him started on the crew in the company's very first Russian restaurant, in Pushkin Square.

Of more than 60,000 people working for UPS outside the United States, fewer than sixty are American. But it isn't simply a numbers game. Hiring local managers also sends a signal that a company has come to stay. "We learned very early in our international development," said UPS CEO Mike Eskew, "that our business ran best when we empowered local people and made long-term commitments."[12] That means identifying with the local culture—not merely fitting in. UPS has learned to marry the local way of doing things with the UPS way. For example, many UPS offices in Thailand have Buddhist shrines, and Latin American facilities might have pictures of the Madonna. But UPS also knows where to draw the line—even though many Germans enjoy a beer with lunch, UPS Deutschland is dry.

Hiring local managers also helps ensure the company understands and respects local culture, and the nuances of language. The hoary story that General Motors tried to use the "Nova" nameplate in Mexico only to discover that it means "Won't Go" is probably apocryphal, as is the fable that Coca-Cola translated its name into Chinese characters as "Bite the wax tadpole" or that the Coors beer slogan "Turn it loose" became "Suffer from diarrhea" in Spanish markets. But sometimes the subtleties of language can trip you up in less obvious ways. For example, pricing goods at 250 renminbi in northern China could be embarrassing, since the Chinese pronunciation of the number 250 (*er-bai-wu*) is very close to a local expression for calling someone "an idiot."

Language can also give marketers real insight into the national culture. The Thai, for example, have no single word for "no." The closest they come is the equivalent of "not yes," signaling a society that is remarkably polite and friendly.[13] The Koreans, on the other hand, have eight different words to express their relationship with the United States, from *chinmi* ("worship America") to *hyommi* ("loathe America"), capturing perhaps both the ambivalence and complexity of their feelings toward the country, as well as its centrality in their national consciousness.[14]

China is a good example of how "local" local can be. The ruling communist party claims that China is basically homogenous, with 95 percent of its people belonging to the Han ethnic group and everyone united by a single written language and a common culture. But demographers, anthropologists, and many Chinese themselves maintain there are many Chinas, perhaps as many as there are countries in Europe. To start, the Chinese speak eight languages that are so different from one another they are mutually unintelligible. To succeed in China, marketers need to take into account wide variations in language, temperament, income, culture, climate, diet, demographics, and history.[15]

P&G

According to *BusinessWeek,* "few companies pay better attention to all these details than P&G."[16] Charles Decker, a management consultant who began his career as a P&G brand manager, explains that P&G's success in global markets is the result of learning from past mistakes when the company treated foreign markets as "opportunistic add-ons to the U.S. business."[17] Now, instead of shipping pallets of packaged goods to foreign markets from Cincinnati, the company treats each new market as a greenfield to be planted and cultivated by a corps of local managers sensitive to the prevailing climate and the country's ways.

A cadre of about a thousand "internationalists"—executives who are steeped in the company's culture and move from country to country—recruits the top people from local universities who seem to have an affinity for the P&G culture. "The cultures of many societies around the world are incompatible with the 'Procter Way' of conducting its business,"[18] Decker writes. For example, in some cultures it's perfectly acceptable—even expected—to start meetings late or to eat up time talking around an issue without reaching a firm conclusion. Some cultures value consensus over decisiveness. Others are hierarchical and don't expect lower-level managers to take initiative. P&G's recruiters spend a lot of time talking about the "Procter Way" and pass over candidates who don't seem comfortable with it. Those they hire are given extensive training. Meanwhile, the P&G people brought into the country to start up operations get their own training on the local culture, history, and language. In this way, P&G is building a unique hybrid of its own culture and its host country's.

When P&G entered the Chinese market in the late 1980s, one of its first steps was to recruit the top students at the twenty-five leading Chinese universities. It hired about 200 students a year in the early years, and today the company is a net exporter of talent from China to other countries, meaning that there are more Chinese P&G people abroad than P&G people from other countries in China.

In addition to hiring and developing local managers, P&G dispatches hundreds of researchers to live with Chinese families and observe how they approach everyday tasks, from changing the baby to brushing their teeth. The resulting knowledge plays in everything from the names of products to their formulas to their advertising. For example, P&G's brands in China have distinctly Chinese names. "Pampers" is translated into three Chinese characters meaning "help," "baby's," and "comfort." And wherever possible, P&G formulates products using local flavors, colors, and textures. Jasmine-flavored Crest toothpaste, for example, capitalizes on the Chinese belief that tea is good for controlling bad breath.

P&G is the most successful foreign marketer in China as measured by market share. It holds the number-one position in four of the seven product categories in which it competes, including laundry, hair care, baby care, feminine care, personal-cleansing products (such as body washes and soap bars), skin care, and dentifrice. But the company does not consider any of the brands it offers in China as "global." It considers them "Chinese." Laurent Philippe, former head of P&G's Greater China Region, made the distinction clear in terms Professor Levitt prematurely claimed were obsolete more than two decades ago:

These brands happen to benefit from the breadth of our company expertise and know-how in the areas of branding and technology. But we are trying to build Chinese brands for the Chinese consumer. I think Chinese consumers see our brands as Chinese brands from a global company with a great reputation.[19]

P&G doesn't leave the discovery of that corporate reputation to chance, either. Unlike in the United States, where the P&G name is relegated to small type on the packaging of its products, the company works at reinforcing its corporate commitment to its host countries. It cultivates constructive relationships with the local media, meets with opinion leaders at universities and in the community, and even conducts extensive corporate advertising in some markets. In Japan, for example, consumers pay close attention to the reputation of the companies they buy products from. That put P&G at a disadvantage compared to Kao Corporation, the mammoth Japanese packaged-goods company and its principal local competitor. So P&G runs corporate advertising in Japan and even devotes a few seconds at the end of product-specific TV commercials to associate the brand being advertised with the company. It's all part of being perceived as a local company.

CORE BRAND VALUES

Localization is not abdication. In fact, doing business globally probably requires an even deeper understanding of a company's core values and business processes than operating in its home territory. Training and performance reviews are essential to ensure that a company's standards don't slowly erode when it ventures into global markets. For example, local managers for Starbucks get thirteen weeks of training at company headquarters in Seattle. They not only learn how to brew coffee, they absorb the company's values and worldview. They are taught that as long as the core product stays true to its quality and principles, other elements of the offer can adapt to local market needs. For example, in the Middle East, Starbucks has separate areas for men and families; in China, it offers special snacks for local celebrations, like the annual mid-Autumn Moon Festival. But some things are sacrosanct—no smoking, even in smoking cultures such as Russia, and comfortable couches, even where space is at a premium as in Japan.

When MTV sets up a local network, it always gives the local production team a specific set of standards within which they have to work. Says MTV Europe president, Brett Hansen:

> At every network group around the world, we have creative heads whose job it is to bring people up to speed, to help coach people, to help hire people locally, and if necessary, to make sure that if there is a weakness in an area, we can help cover that. Because obviously an MTV channel that doesn't look good enough is not going to do the business for us, let alone for the audience. There's a higher expectation.[20]

Effective brand management means ensuring that a customer's experience is consistent with a company's brand values, even if the way those values are expressed varies from market to market. McDonald's core values of food, family, and fun are broad enough to include beer and wine, where that is an expected—not just accepted—menu item. But they are incompatible with gambling, even if plenty of other Las Vegas fast-food restaurants have slot machines near the indoor playground. In an organization as large as McDonald's restaurant network, every decision can't be made at headquarters. Local restaurant operators are given a great deal of leeway to operate within the McDonald's "brand envelope." But instilling those brand values is not left to chance. A worldwide Brand Values Committee shares best practices and sets broad policy. More important, every restaurant owner and operator is drilled on McDonald's values.

Courses at McDonald's famous Hamburger University outside Chicago, Illinois, are taught in twenty-eight languages because restaurant managers from around the world are expected to cycle through. There are additional training centers in Munich, Tokyo, Sydney, London, and mainland China. The training centers teach managers the temperature at which hamburgers should be cooked, how to conduct performance reviews of restaurant staff, and how to inspect facilities, from kitchen to parking lot, to ensure that quality standards are met.

Managers leave Hamburger University with an operating manual that is six inches thick. McDonald's standards have to be met the world over. For example, one out of two fries must measure 75 millimeters in length. Meat for a Big Mac must weigh 45 grams and have 20 percent fat. Buns must be 9.5 to 9.8 centimeters in diameter and 6 centimeters high. If suppliers can't meet McDonald's specifications, the company does it itself or finds other sources. For example, when the beef available in Russia didn't meet McDonald's standards, the company set up its own source of supply for its restaurant.

McDonald's menu recipes are identical everywhere and every restaurant has the same kitchen layout. Employees worldwide ring up sales on machines that display symbols of Big Macs, French fries, or colas instead of words or numerals. Walk-in orders have to be filled within ninety seconds and drive-through orders in less than three-and-a-half minutes. Company representatives monitor performance by making surprise visits to McDonald's outlets every quarter.

McDonald's is so ubiquitous around the world, so local yet still basically the same everywhere, that *The Economist* magazine uses the price of a Big Mac as a predictor of changes in currency exchange rates. The magazine reports its Big Mac Index twice a year. No countries have moved to the "hamburger standard" yet, however.

"GLOCALIZATION"

At about the same time Ted Levitt was writing "The Globalization of Markets" in the 1980s, the Japanese coined a term for a phenomenon they considered a more meaningful and accurate description of what was happening—simultaneous globalization and localization. They called it *dochakuka,* which consists of three ideograms: *do, chaku,* and *ka,* meaning "land," "arrive at," and "process of." A literal translation of *dochakuka* conceptualizes not *where* a company does business—globally or locally—but *how* it does business. It means to be assimilated or "nativized."

To the Japanese, a people very aware of their status as an island nation separated from the world by vast oceans, a company arriving in a new country must not only show respect for local customs but adapt to them, just as a farmer would adapt his agricultural techniques to the land he is cultivating. As marketing professor Johny K. Johansson puts it, "The Japanese do not approach foreign markets with the assumption that their values are universal and with the confidence in their own system that Americans possess."[21] That attitude makes local adaptation as natural for the Japanese as it is foreign for Americans.

In the 1990s, sociologist Roland Robertson translated the term as "glocalization," a neologism of "global" and "local" that captured the paradoxical nature of globalization: that it could be, "in and of itself, simultaneously homogenizing—making things the same—and, at the same time, making things different."[22] Robertson believes that the defining characteristic of contemporary society is the "interpenetration" of the global and the local. In marketing terms, it means that global companies have to deal not only with worldwide considerations but with the particular conditions of every country in which they do business. Courtesy is such a precious value in Asia, for example, that McDonald's restaurants in Beijing assign five to ten female receptionists to take care of children and talk with parents. Not only is that unnecessary—and unaffordable—in Western countries, it would probably be looked on suspiciously in some quarters.

American brands have to avoid collisions with other cultures. Coca-Cola cannot allow itself to be perceived as rolling over the tea culture of India, and McDonald's can't be seen to be undermining the sacred, leisurely meal of the French. That doesn't mean American companies have to leave their values at home. It means they have to be careful how they express them. Being global doesn't mean being supernational or nomadic. It means being multinational and multilocal. It means being global and local at the same time.

CHAPTER 16

GO GLOCAL

"Think global, act local."[1]
—Rene Dubos, biologist and environmentalist in 1972

"Think local, act global."[2]
—Izumi Aizu, Japanese Internet pioneer in 1985

WILLIAM THOMAS STEAD WAS ONE OF THE MOST PROMINENT newspaper editors of Victorian England, a muckraking journalist who was once jailed for buying a young girl in London's slums and reselling her to a brothel to prove that the city was infested with child prostitution. Always controversial, he was a teetotaling puritan, a pacifist, and a spiritualist with a snow-white beard and striking blue eyes.

In 1893, Stead decided to visit the Centennial Exposition in Chicago, but because he arrived from New York the evening it closed, he didn't see it until the next day. The contrast between the pristine, practically empty fairgrounds and the crowded tenements of the city impressed him sufficiently to provide the fodder for two books. *If Christ Came to Chicago* contrasted the "Ivory City" of the World's Fair to the darkness of the city's crowded slums. That book is credited with launching the City Beautiful movement that tried to bring American cities up the standards of those in Europe. But it was the second book that had the greater impact on his European readers.

The Americanization of the World saw an ominous future laid out in the gleaming white pavilions of the Chicago World's Fair. It was a future of Ferris wheels, electric light displays, and food novelties such as Cracker Jacks, Juicy Fruit gum, Shredded Wheat cereal, and Aunt Jemima's pancake mix. It was all-electric kitchens, belly dancers, kinetoscopes, and Buffalo Bill's Wild West Show. It was raw, exciting, and beguiling. And Stead could see it swamping both the homey traditions and the refined culture of Europe. What would happen to French crêpes and Dutch pancakes when anyone could achieve the same result with a little water and Aunt Jemima's magic powder? Stead could see national languages, cultures, and identities caving under the weight of this American "progress."

AMERICANIZATION

Such fears are not limited to effete Europeans. In fact, Stead would have felt right at home on the modern-day Upper West Side of Manhattan, where neighborhood activists protested the opening of a Barnes & Noble megastore that put corner bookshops out of business just as they predicted. Or in Hercules, California, where Wal-Mart withdrew its application to open a store because of community concerns that it would change the character of the town. There's an element of elitism in such protests, but they are also grounded in a genuine desire to preserve the ineffable qualities that distinguish one small town from another. America's "modernity" and eagerness to try new things troubles people who cherish their heritage.

Stead went down with the *Titanic* a decade after committing his fears to paper. But his apprehensions live on. Academics, journalists, politicians, and social pundits of all stripes on both sides of the world decry the "homogenization" of local cultures, by which they invariably mean its Americanization. They fear that Hollywood, McDonald's, and Mickey Mouse will drown out, or at minimum water down, local cultures and traditions. But many sociologists point out that America has imported as much culture as it has exported—if not more.

As a nation of immigrants that gave refuge to scores of scholars and artists during the 1930s and 1940s, America couldn't do otherwise. And if American culture has also found a receptive home in other countries, it may be because it incorporated those influences into its own style and ideas. For example, Starbucks' founder, Howard Schultz, frankly admits that he was deeply influenced by the European coffeehouse tradition in designing his shops. Eric Almquist, of Mercer

Management, points out that coffee consumption in the United States had been in decline since its peak in 1962 until the European-inspired gourmet coffees were introduced in the early 1990s. "In fact, America has really Europeanized over the last twenty or thirty years," he says. "It's reflected more and more in the clothes we wear, the foods we eat."[3] And the youth of the United States and Asia are similarly oriented to each other's cultures to a greater extent than ever before.

"What Americans have done more brilliantly than their competitors overseas is repackage the cultural products we receive from abroad and then retransmit them to the rest of the planet," writes Richard Pells of the University of Texas. "In effect, Americans have specialized in selling the dreams, fears, and folklore of other people back to them. That is why a global mass culture has come to be identified, however simplistically, with the United States."[4] Disneyland, after all, was based on Tivoli Gardens in Copenhagen, and many of its most famous characters, including Snow White, Cinderella, and Pinocchio, are drawn from European fairy tales.

Besides, cultures are not static. They are constantly changing, even in land-locked areas that have little contact with the outside world. By definition, cultures are the living DNA of a community, and every generation leaves its mark. Just as a culture is affected by outside influences, it also affects the outside influences. You'll find a busy McDonald's on Les Champs Elysées in Paris, but you'll also find Chinese and Italian restaurants there, just as you'll find French restaurants and clothing shops on Madison Avenue in Manhattan. French writer and economist Philippe Legrain points out that the cross-fertilization of cultures is a force for good:

> If critics of globalization were less obsessed with "Coca-colonization," they might notice a rich feast of cultural mixing that belies fears about Americanized uniformity. Algerians in Paris practice Thai boxing; Asian rappers in London snack on Turkish pizza; Salman Rushdie delights readers everywhere with his Anglo-Indian tales. Globalization not only increases individual freedom, but also revitalizes cultures through foreign influences.[5]

Indeed, the book you are holding is the result of innovations from China (the paper), Phoenicia (the Western alphabet), Arabia and India (numbers), Germany, China, and Korea (the printing press), and France (the author's ancestors, by way of Canada).

CROSS-FERTILIZATION

Many of Europe's commercial innovations resulted from careful study of American models. The French hypermarkets came about after Carrefour studied the operations of Jewel supermarkets in the United States and then opened even bigger stores in their own country. Carrefour now has more than 900 hypermarkets worldwide. The French lodging company Accor based its Novotel motel chain on the U.S. model. Now it operates the Motel 6 chain in the United States, a brand that is as American as big fins on cars.

The arts, in particular, benefit from cross-pollination, from the steel bands of Trinidad that turned cast-off, fifty-gallon oil drums into joyous musical instruments to the ancient Celtic fiddle traditions still alive in Appalachia. Even with the easy availability of recorded music practically anywhere in the world, people in developing countries still hunger most for music made at home. In India, domestically produced music makes up 96 percent of the market; in Egypt, 81 percent; and in Brazil, 73 percent.

Metal knives didn't make the people of Papua New Guinea lazy, but made it easier for them to carve their distinctive totem poles. When they first came into regular contact with people from the south, the Inuit weren't inhibited from producing their soapstone carvings; they were encouraged to make more carvings, because they now had an appreciative market for their craft. The beads used in South African Ndebele art aren't indigenous to Africa, but were imported from Czechoslovakia in the early-nineteenth century, just as the mirrors, coral, cotton cloth, and bits of paper incorporated in "traditional" African art came from contacts with Europeans.[6]

Reflecting on all these influences, famed French anthropologist Claude Lévi-Strauss noted that "diversity is less a function of the isolation of groups than of the relationships which unite them."[7] The fear that all the world's cultures will be forced through a stars-and-stripes blender has no basis in history, nor in contemporary observation.

McWORLD

Nevertheless, more than a century after William Stead's cautionary tome first appeared, fears of an American cultural hegemony persist.

Among contemporary culture police, Stead's intellectual descendant might be Benjamin Barber, who brought a new twist to fears of cultural imperialism in his book *Jihad vs. McWorld*. The world, he held, was being attacked on two sides—from America by encroaching and smothering commercialization, typified by McDonald's, and from the East by a radical Islamic theocracy that would put all women in burqas and force all men to stop shaving.

Others aren't so sure it's a two-front battle. Dr. James L. Watson looked at how McDonald's franchises have affected communities in Asia in a book entitled *Golden Arches East*. He found that in most communities, McDonald's has conformed to local culture, not the other way around. In fact, he cites the experience of one Hong Kong entrepreneur who studied McDonald's local operations so closely he was inspired to open a chain of Chinese restaurants in the United States. Watson maintains that in most of the countries he studied, McDonald's has been "Asianized" far more than its host countries have been "supersized." In fact, seven of the ten busiest McDonald's in the world are in Hong Kong.[8] Jack Daly, a McDonald's executive, says the key is to "inculcate the local culture" into everything you do. "We have over 4,000 restaurants in Japan," he says. "When Japanese families travel to the United States, their kids say 'Oh look, they have McDonald's here, too.'"[9]

And when McDonald's French restaurants came under attack as a symbol of American culinary and cultural imperialism, the local managers ran ads in French newspapers making fun of Americans and their food choices. One depicted a beefy American cowboy and said that, although McDonald's was born in the United States, its food was made in France, by French suppliers using French products. Since the president of McDonald's in Europe is a Frenchman who started behind the counter in a store on the outskirts of Paris, he not only understood the issue the ads were designed to address, he had no qualms about approving them.

"We don't *act* local; we *are* local," said Walt Riker, a spokesman at McDonald's.[10] Indeed, McDonald's has been so successful in this regard that when the Bern demonstrators returned on the second day of the World Economic Forum to take another run at the local McDonald's, they found not only the staff guarding the store but neighboring shopkeepers and even customers who considered the restaurant "theirs." "It's localization, not globalization," says McDonald's Riker. "We're exporting the business dynamics."

But the assimilation of McDonald's was not left to chance like so many oil drums cast over the sides of freighters and turned into steel drums by musically gifted beachcombers. It is a conscious and highly structured process that has at its core the development and empowerment of local management attuned to the culture of the host country. Other companies have learned that lesson the hard way.

DISNEY

When Disney opened its first park outside the United States in Paris, it was determined to recreate the American experience as religiously as possible. "Cast members" who took tickets and operated the rides were instructed to shave off any facial hair, to use lots of deodorant, and to smile more. None of the park restaurants served wine or beer. Everything was done "the American Disney Way."

Labor costs were twice as high as projected because of high turnover among the young staff who resented being told what to wear and how to act. The French called the park "a cultural Chernobyl." The weather was colder and wetter than back home in California and Florida, resulting in empty parking lots and hotels. The park hemorrhaged cash. A nasty recession accounted for many of the park's initial problems, but even its biggest boosters had to admit that Disney had seriously misread its local market.

By the time the company opened its overseas park in Hong Kong, it was hiring *feng shui* experts to help lay out the rides and was so intent on satisfying local tastes that it got into a minor controversy with environmentalists over plans to serve shark fin soup in its banquet halls. The Hong Kong park has done much better, although Disney is still learning that visitors from mainland China have very different expectations. For example, most visitors from the mainland travel on package tours that normally include group dinners. Initially, the Hong Kong park couldn't accommodate such large groups and, even if it had, the ticket prices didn't include adequate commissions for the tour operators, so few of them put Disney on their itineraries. As a result, a Hong Kong transvestite bar was actually pulling in more visitors from the mainland.

Furthermore, once in the park, many Chinese visitors considered it little more than a backdrop for family snapshots, so the company began distributing brochures explaining how to enjoy the rides. Disney even hired "guestologists" to follow park visitors around with a stopwatch. When they discovered that Chinese guests took ten minutes longer to eat than Americans, Disney added 700 seats to park dining areas. The park's managing director, Bill Ernest, conceded that Disney is "still learning" about Chinese culture. "We are probably as critical on ourselves as anybody is with us,"[11] he said. That humility will go a long way in helping Disney assimilate into Chinese life. It was only after the company stopped trying to turn its European staff into Californian clones and started making accommodations to local preferences, such as serving beer and wine, that Disneyland Paris became the number-one paid attraction in Europe.

WAL-MART

After a false start in several European countries, Wal-Mart may be matching its U.S. success story in China by applying these lessons. Since entering the country in 1996, the company has opened forty-three stores and trained 25,000 local employees. There is only a small group of expatriates in Wal-Mart China, 99.9 percent of staff are local people, and every store is run by a local manager.

"The culture of Wal-Mart is stronger in China than anywhere else in the world," says Joe Hatfield, the company veteran who heads up its operations in China. It's more than a matter of translating "Sam's Sayings" into Chinese characters, clothing store employees in red vests, or stationing greeters at the front door (though Wal-Mart has done all three).

Wal-Mart has identified the business processes (e.g., efficient sourcing and real-time logistics) and core values (e.g., everyday low pricing and deep inventories) that differentiate it. Then it "localized" them sensitively. For example, meat is sold unwrapped, not because it saves money on packaging, but because the Chinese consider it fresher that way. Individual employees are not singled out for praise because it would embarrass them; instead, the performance of their whole department is celebrated. The stores even smell different—a blend of live poultry, earthy mushrooms, and fragrant spices, not unlike the markets of Chinatown.

Many of the company's young Chinese employees find Wal-Mart's management style energizing. Most Chinese managers are typically tight-lipped, sharing little information with employees, and advancement usually depends on knowing somebody higher in the hierarchy. Wal-Mart is different. Store managers gather employees in daily morning sessions, complete with the Wal-Mart cheer in Mandarin, Wu, or Cantonese. They encourage workers to contribute ideas and to tell them what's going on.

SESAME STREET

Sesame Workshop, producer of *Sesame Street,* even left Bert, Ernie, and Big Bird at home when it branched out overseas. Gary Knell, chief executive in New York, explained how his team established 120 locally produced and staffed productions of the *Sesame Street* television program around the world. "Our model," he said, "is to build a local research facility, usually with a university in that country, train the production team locally, and hire local actors. Our goal is to empower our local partners wherever we have taken the program."[12] That way, the program deals with local problems, such as the stigma of AIDS in South Africa, female illiteracy in Egypt, and intercommunal conflict in Israel, Palestine, and Jordan. But it also means that iconic *Sesame Street* characters sometimes get bumped aside, as in France, where Big Bird was replaced by an enormous yellow character, Nac, whose trumpet nose and whimsical nature were tested with children and vetted by French psychologists. In India, Big Bird had to make room for a seven-foot-tall lion named Boombah, who will eventually speak all sixteen languages spoken in his native country. Knell said that Sesame Workshop is providing alternatives to local broadcasting that tends to be anti-American. But he and his producers never lose sight of the fact that they must mirror the values of the country they are in.

CULTIVATING THE LOCAL LANDSCAPE

Many other U.S. brands have made themselves part of the local landscape wherever they do business. Heinz, Ford, General Motors, Kellogg's, McDonald's, Starbucks, KFC, Coca-Cola, Frito-Lay, and many others never underestimate the importance of local knowledge. Instead of promoting an American lifestyle to which most international consumers no longer aspire, they became part of the local community.

For example, Starbucks has gone out of its way to position its stores in China as staples of the local neighborhood, supporting school sports teams and participating in local festivals. In 1999, when U.S. bombers mistakenly hit the Chinese embassy in Belgrade during air strikes on Yugoslavia, protesters in Beijing took a shortcut through a Starbucks to the United States embassy, buying coffee en route. David Sun, then chairman of Starbucks' twenty-nine-store Beijing franchise, said sales actually rose that day.[13]

Interestingly, according to the Edelman Trust Barometer, some of the companies that have seen the biggest turnaround in reputation in Europe are those that have faced the most hostile public scrutiny. For example, although Monsanto was caught in the controversy surrounding genetically engineered food, its credibility level rose from 12 percent to 28 percent in recent years. And though Nike was targeted because it allegedly used sweatshop labor in developing countries, its level of trust improved from 6 percent four years ago to 43 percent in 2005. According to Richard Edelman:

> While each turnaround is distinct, there are some common traits. Not only have these companies taken concrete business action to rectify their shortcomings, they've also been conscientious about informing local markets of the upgrades, so the communities where customers and employees live and work are aware of the progress. They've demonstrated through action their commitment to these communities.[14]

From small things—like using the Queen's English and A4-size paper in the United Kingdom—to big things—like sourcing their raw materials and management talent locally—all these companies have demonstrated a commitment to their local communities.

ETHICAL DILEMMAS

While adopting local standards can be relatively straightforward when it comes to buying paper or remembering to use the plural form in referring to companies, it can also result in ethical dilemmas. Yahoo!

for example, was widely criticized for giving Chinese authorities the Internet address of a journalist who had been exchanging e-mail with a democracy group in New York. The information led to the journalist's arrest in 2003 and he was subsequently sentenced to eight years in prison. In September of the same year, Yahoo! responded to a similar government request that led to the arrest of another journalist who was given a ten-year prison sentence.

Microsoft's MSN Spaces came under fire when it shut down the blog of a popular Chinese writer who rubbed government censors the wrong way. Cisco Systems was roundly criticized for selling the Chinese government equipment it could use to block websites and images it considers subversive, such as photos of the Dalai Lama of Tibet. And when Google agreed to censor the results of its search engines based in China to omit subjects deemed "offensive" or "subversive" by the Chinese authorities, a Republican congressman from New Jersey accused the company of "collaborating . . . with persecutors" who imprison and torture Chinese citizens "in the service of truth."[15]

Despite all the rhetoric flying around over these incidents, there is little question that American companies have to obey the laws of their host countries if they want to operate within their borders. The real question American global companies need to address is whether or not to operate within certain countries. Consider the dilemma Yahoo! Microsoft, and Google face. China has the world's second largest online population with about 103 million users. Since that's only 8 percent of the country's population of 1.3 billion, China will soon surpass the United States in Internet use. It's too big a market to ignore.

As in many ethical questions, it all comes down to finding the right balance between benefits and costs. But, in these cases, the relevant costs/benefits are not those the company will endure or enjoy—lost market opportunity if it stays out, revenue and criticism if it stays in— but the effect *on the people of China*. The ethical question is whether the benefits to the Chinese people of continuing to operate in China, even under less than ideal conditions, outweigh the costs.

"DO NO EVIL"

Google, which says it makes business decisions under the motto "Do No Evil," had to ask itself whether doing business in China under these conditions is "evil." The answer, for now, is that providing some, albeit censored, search capabilities is better than nothing, which was the only other choice for the company (Google, after all, needed Chinese government approval to locate its computers in the country). Google cofounder Sergey Brin explained his reasoning to *Fortune* magazine:

> We felt that by participating there, and making our services more available, even if not to the 100 percent that we ideally would like, that it will be better for Chinese Web users, because ultimately they would get more information, though not quite all of it.[16]

In fact, because of bandwidth constraints on the country's international communications links, access to Google was unreliable and very expensive before the company reached agreement with the government to put its search engines on Chinese soil. Google has done nothing to censor the results of its search engines located outside China. So Brin's contention that the local search engines are a net benefit to the Chinese people rings true.

But Google neither started nor stopped there. Before making its decision, the company consulted with human rights groups and nongovernmental organizations; Brin personally talked to Internet experts in China several times; and finally, when the company made its decision to operate within the Chinese government's constraints, it made all the limitations of its China service known. If a computer user types "Tiananmen Square" into the Google China search engine, for instance, the results pages won't show the protestors and government tanks that come up on the same search from any other country, but it will show a small disclaimer at the bottom of the page that reads, "Local regulations prevent us from showing all the results." Meanwhile, Google is not shutting down the existing, uncensored search engines located outside China that take longer to access, but it is staying away from Chinese e-mail or blogging services for now to avoid future government demands to cough up user identities.

Ironically, in about the same period, Google challenged the legality of a U.S. government request that it turn over a sample of one million search requests for the declared purpose of uncovering trends in pedophilia. Google got little credit for its principled stand in its home country (which cost it 9 percent of its market value), but it was widely criticized for its "surrender" to the Chinese. No one should approach these ethical questions looking for win-win answers. Doing the right thing is its own reward.

Sometimes—as in South Africa during apartheid—the answer to these ethical questions will be, "No, doing business here will cost the local people more than it will benefit them." There are no general rules of thumb to make these decisions easier. Different companies, operating under different conditions, may even come to different conclusions. But a global company needs to know how to make those decisions, drawing on the best available advice, if possible from the people most directly affected, and with clear transparency. Part of the secret to global success is knowing how to be local. And that involves a lot more than knowing what side of the road to drive on.

CHAPTER 17

SHARE YOUR
CUSTOMERS' CARES

"Globalization can be a strong force in the fight against poverty. But globalization must mean more than creating bigger markets, and experience confirms that growth alone cannot reduce poverty and income inequality."[1]

—Kofi Annan, U.N. Secretary-General

"Few trends would so thoroughly undermine the very foundations of our free society as the acceptance by corporate officials of a social responsibility other than to make as much money for their shareholders as they possibly can."[2]

—Milton Friedman, 1976 Nobel Prize Winner in Economics

POSED IN FRONT OF A MUD HUT IN WESTERN KENYA, WITH HIS arm around the shoulder of a local sheep herder, Greg Allgood looks like he just stepped out of the air-conditioned Land Rover of a high-end safari excursion company. He's dressed in spotless white sneakers, neatly pressed khaki shorts, and a light blue polo shirt. No cap or sunglasses, despite the potentially dangerous combination of equatorial sun, a fair complexion, and a forehead that ends in the middle of his skull. But Allgood is not on vacation. He's checking in on a product trial his employer, Procter and Gamble, is conducting in the bush country.

As products go, this one is not in the league of Allgood's last two projects—the fat substitute, Olestra, and over-the-counter heartburn medication, Prilosec. It will never generate that much revenue, and the working assumption at P&G is that it will never account for a penny of profit.

CLEAN WATER

Allgood has a Ph.D. in toxicology, and the product he is testing is a specially formulated powder that can clear and disinfect water. Branded and packaged in "the P&G Way," the PUR household water treatment comes in a small foil packet that can purify ten liters, or two and a half U.S. gallons, of the dirtiest water after a few minutes of vigorous stirring. PUR powder is a virtual "dirt magnet" that causes sediment to clump together and sink to the bottom. More significantly, it kills bacterial diseases such as typhoid and cholera and even eliminates toxic compounds such as arsenic. After filtering the water through a clean cloth to separate any debris, it is clean enough to drink. A packet of the powder costs about the same as a single egg in many poor countries and has been shown to reduce diarrheal illness by 50 percent.

That's a big deal in most of the developing world, where about 5,000 children a day die from diarrheal illnesses, most under two years old. In fact, P&G scientists, working with researchers from the U.S. Centers for Disease Control and Prevention, invested four years and $10 million developing the powder. Initially, when the company introduced PUR in 2002, it thought it could commercialize the product, but market tests in Pakistan showed that it would be very difficult to get enough sustained use to cover its manufacturing, marketing, and distribution costs. On the other hand, there was a clear need for PUR, and the technology was cheaper, easier to use, and more palatable than the alternatives of boiling water or adding chlorine bleach. Bleach has an unpleasant taste and odor. Firewood is precious in much of the developing world, and boiling water over a fire is time-consuming.

P&G continued to experiment with different distribution approaches in Africa, Asia, and Latin America. It tried selling the packets to consumers in places like Guatemala and the Philippines for nine to ten cents each. It sold the packets to nonprofits for eight or nine cents. And it sold them to emergency relief agencies such as the International Rescue Committee for use in refugee camps, at its cost of about three and a half cents. By November 2004, P&G decided that PUR would never turn a profit and shut down production. Allgood wondered how he was going to get rid of the PUR packets sitting on the shelves of a P&G warehouse in Manila.

TSUNAMI

Then a tsunami hit East Asia the day after Christmas in 2004, killing 283,100 people and leaving millions more homeless in a ring of destruction that stretched from the east coast of Africa to the shores of Indonesia, Sri Lanka, South India, and Thailand. Allgood was vacationing in New York City when relief agencies such as the Red Cross and UNICEF started calling his cell phone. They all knew that one of the things the tsunami victims would need almost immediately is pure water. Their normal water sources would likely be contaminated by ocean salt and decomposing bodies.

Allgood committed to contribute all the packets of PUR on hand and to ship more as fast as it could be manufactured at a P&G factory in Pakistan. At first, P&G offered to sell the packets at cost, but when the scale of the disaster became obvious, it decided to simply donate them. In the end, P&G donated 28 million packets of PUR powder to the tsunami relief effort, enough to purify 280 million liters of water or nearly 74 million U.S. gallons. That was nearly six times more than P&G had shipped to victims of every other disaster in 2004. According to Allgood, "After the product failed commercially, PUR had a lot of baggage. The tsunami not only revived the product, it established it within P&G."[3]

In fact, P&G decided to make the world's clean water crisis its primary philanthropic mission. The company now sells PUR packets to nongovernmental organizations in more than a dozen developing countries at less than its costs. But the nongovernmental organizations still require donor support to come up with even that bargain-basement price, so Allgood has been working with Population Services International (PSI) in Haiti and Uganda to devise a distribution system that could make the product self-sustaining by generating enough long-term usage to cover P&G and PSI's costs. Meanwhile, a group of retired P&G senior executives has contributed $700,000 to underwrite the product's distribution in two additional African countries.

Despite his last name, Allgood doesn't consider P&G's involvement in PUR as only charity. "It's a cause-related issue," he says, "but we'll also learn things about low-income consumers that are going to help P&G overall."[4] For example, Allgood points out that the commercial potential of many developing countries is limited, because they don't have the basic infrastructure. "To be successful here would be outside our capability," he says, "because we would not have the necessary distribution channels."[5] Nongovernmental organizations are among the only multinational groups with feet on the ground in many of the world's poorest countries. Organizations such as the Red Cross and Catholic Relief Services were the first international groups to put people into the areas devastated by the East Asian tsunami, and for weeks they had the only reliable distribution networks.

While P&G won't make any money from PUR directly, it's a good long-term investment. Allgood is frank about the eventual commercial value: "We will learn about consumers in countries that we are not in now and that will translate into top-line growth over time," he says. "In Haiti and so on, we are opening up the way for a whole portfolio of P&G products."[6]

CORPORATE RESPONSIBILITY

Economists might argue whether P&G, on this issue at least, has thrown its lot in with Kofi Annan or Milton Friedman, who may represent the opposite ends of the spectrum on the issue of a corporation's responsibilities to society.

In 1970, Friedman wrote that "there is one and only one social responsibility of business—to use its resources and engage in activities designed to increase its profits so long as it stays within the rules of the game, which is to say, engages in open and free competition without deception or fraud."[7] That's the orthodox view among free-market economists: that the only social responsibility a law-abiding business has is to maximize profits for its shareholders. All within the rules of the game. Well, in global markets, the rules of the game appear to be different.

According to research in forty-one countries, about eight out of ten consumers outside the United States prefer a global brand over the local one—all else being equal.[8] Global brands seem to have an aura of higher quality in much of the world. But being global comes at a price. Most of those consumers hold global brands to even higher standards of social responsibility than local companies. "They expect (global) firms to address social problems linked to what they sell and how they do business."[9] They don't demand that the corner gas station try to solve the global warming problem, but they expect the giant oil companies to.

This seems to confirm a poll taken at the turn of the century among 25,000 people in twenty-three countries. Some 60 percent of the respondents said they judged a company on its social record, 40 percent took a negative view of companies they felt were not socially responsible, and 90 percent wanted companies to focus on more than just their profitability.[10]

TRANSMITTING VALUES

Global consumers consider multinational companies as the most powerful institutions on the planet. As Thomas Friedman (no relation to Milton) observed, they believe those companies command the power, "not only to create value but also to transmit values."[11] Many American business leaders say they get it. For example, the President's Export Council, the principal national advisory committee on international trade, issued a special report on "U.S. Corporate Stewardship Around the World" in 2005. The council's message was that good international corporate citizenship is also good business.

Consumers outside the United States assume that global companies will "do no harm." But they expect more than that, and they don't define it as "philanthropy" or "charity." John D. Rockefeller may have softened his image by dispensing shiny new dimes to street urchins, but benevolent paternalism isn't enough today. And image-polishing mega-grants, especially if they are designed to distract attention from substantive problems, also fall short. The pool of goodwill bought that way will evaporate when exposed to the least heat.

Chuck Prince, Citigroup's CEO, believes that aligning public and private interests will require companies like his to assume a more prominent public role. The example he discussed at the 2006 World Economic Forum was his company's "Equator Principles," a set of guidelines developed to ensure that the development projects Citigroup finances meet certain environmental standards. "We stepped out ahead of others in the banking industry," he said. "Now many other banks have followed. Private institutions have the power to play a vital role in leading the way for positive change."[12]

GLOBAL COMPACT

For its part, in 2000 the United Nations published the Global Compact, ten principles relating to human rights, labor, the environment, and honest business conduct. The principles are less a legal contract than a statement of how companies in a civilized society should behave. (See the box on the facing page.)

Global companies were invited to sign on and to share best practices with each other. But American companies hesitated to join for fear that signing the compact would expose them to litigation if someone believed they weren't living up to the standards. That was not an entirely unrealistic fear in a country where people have successfully sued someone else for spilling hot coffee on themselves. In May 2004, the American Bar Association helped draft a boilerplate-laden letter intended to limit the liability of signatory companies; subsequently, more U.S. companies signed on. At the end of 2005, 2,400 companies in fifty countries had agreed to participate, including about 100 American companies.

That low level of U.S. participation may be a mistake. McKinsey and Company points out that a reputation for socially responsible behavior is the price of entry into some of the world's most lucrative markets. It reports:

Many of today's most exciting opportunities lie in . . . products and services targeted at low-income consumers in poor countries. These opportunities are large, and . . . [c]orporations have to be recognized as socially responsible simply to gain access to these debates. To influence the outcome, however, it will be necessary to do more than just check boxes on a corporate-responsibility scorecard; unless companies can understand, engage with, and respond to the interests of all parties that have an interest in a contentious business opportunity, they are unlikely to win a society's permission to explore it."[13]

U.N. Global Compact

Human Rights

Principle 1: Business should support and respect the protection of internationally proclaimed human rights; and

Principle 2: Make sure that they are not complicit in human rights abuses.

Labor

Principle 3: Businesses should uphold the freedom of association and the effective recognition of the right to collective bargaining;

Principle 4: The elimination of all forms of forced and compulsory labor;

Principle 5: The effective abolition of child labor; and

Principle 6: The elimination of discrimination in respect of employment and occupation.

Environment

Principle 7: Businesses should support a precautionary approach to environmental challenges;

Principle 8: Undertake initiatives to promote greater environmental responsibility; and

Principle 9: Encourage the development and diffusion of environmentally friendly technologies.

Honest Business Conduct

Principle 10: Business should work against all forms of corruption, including extortion and bribery.

Without that permission, McKinsey notes, companies will never be able to convert these opportunities into sustainable and profitable markets.

PUBLIC PERMISSION, PUBLIC APPROVAL

The basic concept is not exactly new. Back in 1926, Walter Gifford, the chairman of AT&T, asked Arthur W. Page to take over the company's public relations department. Page had been the editor of *The World's Work* (that era's version of *Business Week*) and he told Gifford if he was looking for a press agent, he could keep looking. Somehow, Gifford convinced Page that he needed someone who could help the company navigate the cross-currents of public opinion in an era of doubt and skepticism toward big business. He not only hired Page and made him an officer of the company, he put him on its board of directors. Page's basic advice at the time rings just as true today: "All business lives by public approval and, roughly speaking, the more approval you have, the better you live." Of course, he also pointed out that "the fundamental way to get approval is to deserve it."[14]

But Page would have agreed with Milton Friedman on at least one point—no number of good works can compensate for a corporation that fails in its most basic obligation of staying in business so it can serve all the stakeholders who depend on it. In Page's day, the saying at the AT&T monopoly was "we earn to serve," which seems to have means and ends in the right order. Friedman himself conceded as much in a widely discussed debate in the pages of *Reason* magazine. "Maximizing profits is an end from the private point of view," he wrote, "it is a means from the social point of view."[15]

In other words, the profit motive of the free-market system has proven to be the most efficient means to encourage people to cooperate in their economic activities and to ensure that resources are put to their most productive use. The end purpose of a business is to create wealth for all who contribute resources to it and accept the risks of its failure—a group which includes its employees, its customers, and the communities in which it operates, in addition to its investors. Management's job is to balance these groups' sometimes competing interests.

Page was no starry-eyed ideologue. His stance was also coldly pragmatic. He knew that if businesses fail to balance those interests fairly, government intervention is inevitable. The accounting scandals that ushered in the twenty-first century eroded public trust and the Sarbanes-Oxley Act of 2002 was the result. If Milton Friedman's goal is a free market, corporate social responsibility is the way to get it.

SOCIAL RESPONSIBILITY IS NOT "PR"

To be sustainable, and to truly warrant lessened regulation, social responsibility must be integrated into a company's operations at every level, not simply into the glad-handing and do-gooding of its public relations department. It should flow from the corporation's business strategy, not its CEO's social ambitions.

The European Commission defines corporate social responsibility as "a concept whereby companies integrate social and environmental concerns in their business operations."[16] And that is precisely what global consumers expect of global companies. Socially responsible behavior is not something ancillary to a business; it is the way you do business.

Heightened expectations of social responsibility don't stop at the company gate. Prominent brands are now held accountable for links in their value chain that they don't even control. Thus, apparel companies are held responsible for the labor practices of their subcontractors; food processors and fast-food restaurants, for the environmental practices of their suppliers. Bain and Company calls the added costs of monitoring suppliers a "Brand Tax."[17] Nike, Gap, and other clothing and footwear manufacturers have taken steps to improve labor standards in the contract factories that manufacture their products. HP, Dell, and IBM forged an alliance in 2004 to establish socially responsible manufacturing standards not only for their own far-flung factories, but for all their suppliers.

FOCUS, CONSISTENCY, RELEVANCE

My good friend and former boss, Marilyn Laurie, sat at Arthur Page's desk for nearly two decades as the head of AT&T public relations. She used to say that effective social responsibility had three components: focus, consistency, and relevance. She said:

> True caring is not something that comes and goes with the popularity of a particular issue. Plus, if your programs are diffused, they can't be linked with your product—or your company—in the customer's mind. Finally, if they're not relevant, they won't touch your customers' emotions. And, make no mistake, trust is more an emotional response than a rational one.[18]

Relevance flows both ways, she would always add. If the program isn't relevant to your company, it won't have meaning and any association your customers make will be happenstance.

The key is to give back to the community in a way that becomes identified with your company, meets real community needs, and reflects your company's competencies and brand values. McDonald's core customer, for example, is a family with children. Ken Barun, the president and CEO of Ronald McDonald House Charities, says the company concentrates its charitable work on helping "seek solutions for the problems facing children and families today."[19] But it isn't all dictated from the company's Chicago headquarters. There are 160 local Ronald McDonald House Charities in twenty-seven countries, all aimed at the specific needs of improving the lives of underprivileged children in their communities. McDonald's attacks this global problem by addressing the problems locally.

Avon's decade-long breast cancer crusade, IBM's education initiatives, Johnson & Johnson's support of nurses, American Express's campaigns to feed the hungry, and General Mills's youth fitness programs are other examples that show how focus, consistency, and relevance can build highly credible reputations for social responsibility.

Local giving may seem like the most obvious—and painless—form of social responsibility. But when sociologist Doug Guthrie studied the charitable gifts of 2,776 companies in fifty U.S. cities, he discovered that 77 percent of their giving stayed within their headquarters' communities.[20] Companies may be globalizing their sales, but their social spending is still mainly a local production.

LEVERAGING OPERATIONS

While charitable contributions are always welcome, social responsibility is even more meaningful when it flows from a company's actual operations. Some companies are leveraging their procurement dollars to achieve social goals.

"At McDonald's, we don't grow, raise, or produce food, crops, or animals. We're simply a food retail company," says the company's director of corporate social responsibility, Bob Langert. "But we do purchase a lot and so have influence on our suppliers. We try to use this influence responsibly."[21] McDonald's struck an agreement with Conservation International in 2002 to set environmental standards for a global supply chain that draws beef, fish, chicken, pork, bread, lettuce, pickles, tomatoes, and potatoes from larders in all four corners of the world. Since the program began, the company's suppliers have reduced waste in all categories tracked. For example, suppliers' water savings ranged from 12 percent to 42 percent.

Starbucks also worked with Conservation International to source coffee directly from farmers in the Chiapas region of Mexico who take pains to grow coffee beans in shade rather than full sun to preserve the habitat of migratory songbirds. Starbucks markets the product to U.S. consumers as a high-quality, premium coffee; the Mexican farmers make more money because the sourcing arrangement eliminates middlemen.

Unilever, the largest buyer of fish in the world for its Birds Eye and Gorton's brands,[22] partnered with the World Wildlife Fund to form the Marine Stewardship Council (MSC), which promotes responsible fishing practices worldwide. MSC was established in 1997, when the United Nations estimated that nine of the world's seventeen largest fishing grounds were being overharvested and Greenpeace was on Unilever's back for allegedly depleting whitefish stocks in the North Sea. Now an independent organization with offices in London, Seattle, and Miranda, Australia, the MSC certifies fishing fleets that follow sustainable practices that avoid depleting fish stocks and preserve the fishing grounds' ecosystems.

At the end of 2005, the Marine Stewardship Council had certified twelve fishing areas, including the largest grounds for whitefish, Australian rock lobster, Bering Sea pollock, and Alaskan wild salmon. An additional seventeen fishing grounds were in the process of being assessed, including the American Albacore Fishing Association, which accounts for more than 20 percent of the canned tuna caught in the Pacific. In all, more than 223 seafood products sold in twenty-four countries bear the council's eco-label. More than 250 retailers, ranging from Tesco and Sainsbury's in the United Kingdom to Wal-Mart and

Whole Foods in the United States have pledged support for the program, as have major processors such as Unilever itself.

ENLIGHTENED SELF-INTEREST

Other companies leverage their distinctive capabilities to further social causes related to their primary business interests. For example, Nike worked with the United Nations to help design a *hajib* for young Muslim girls who play volleyball in refugee camps. Nike sent four of its designers to a camp in Kenya, where they worked with young Somali girls on a design that would allow freer movement while still covering most of their bodies. After teaching the girls how to sew the uniforms, the company donated enough material for several hundred outfits.

Pfizer's Global Health Fellows program matches employees with nongovernmental organizations in developing countries to help fight HIV/AIDS, tuberculosis, and malaria. More than thirty Fellows, including doctors, epidemiologists, and lab technicians, spend up to six months in one of fourteen countries. The NGOs receive skills in analysis, planning, and training; and Pfizer gains a better on-the-ground understanding of the needs in treating infectious diseases.

While these initiatives might qualify as "good works," they are unapologetically rooted in the companies' self-interest because they help develop new markets. After P&G's Crest toothpaste started a national dental-health program for underserved kids in 2000, it gained 15 percent more of the Hispanic market.[23] Similarly, capital equipment companies have discovered that it is in their long-term interests to nurture the development of the markets they sell into. Cisco Systems, for example, has established network training academies in technical schools, colleges, and community-based organizations across more than 150 countries. To date, the Cisco networking academies have prepared more than 1.5 million students for careers in the information technology industries, including several thousand women in Middle Eastern countries such as Saudi Arabia and the United Arab Emirates.

EMPLOYEE VOLUNTEERISM

Corporate social responsibility is most credible when it taps the greatest resource a company has—its own people. With more than eight million employees overseas, American businesses have more natural ambassadors than the U.S. government itself. Through their memberships in local religious and civic groups, they know more about the local country than any embassy does. Though some employees are expat Americans, most are locals and, because they are exposed to American business values every day, they are—for good or ill—a company's most credible spokespeople. In fact, one of the major findings of the 2006 Edelman Trust Barometer was a significant shift in where people place their trust, away from institutions and figures of authority to "colleagues," "friends and family," and "a person like yourself."[24]

That's one reason many leading global companies engage their people in their social responsibility efforts through employee volunteer programs. Marilyn Laurie used to paraphrase Humphrey Bogart in *Casablanca*: "Cash is appreciated. But cash plus expertise . . . cash plus more hands to do the work . . . cash plus a sharing of the recipient's goals and values . . . that's the beginning of a beautiful friendship!"[25]

General Electric is making friends through more than 4,000 employee projects around the world, all designed to communicate the same message—"We are part of your community." Some companies give their employees paid time away from the job to participate in community service projects. Timberland, for example, gives every full-time employee up to forty hours of paid leave to help meet local community needs in more than twenty-seven countries. The Body Shop requires employees to do a certain amount of community service on company time. Other companies provide less paid time for volunteer work but use community projects for on-the-job team building. More than 20,000 UPS employees in forty-five countries, for example, donated about 100,000 hours of service to their local communities during the company's 2005 "Global Volunteer Week."

Global accounting giant PricewaterhouseCoopers uses an employee volunteer program to groom high-performing young partners the firm considers potential leaders. After an intensive one-week orientation program, the firm deploys them on eight-week assignments helping NGOs with their work in developing countries. From 2001 through 2006, more than fifty-eight partners from twenty-nine different countries have participated in eighteen development initiatives around the world. The teams' projects have ranged from helping an NGO in Belize develop an ecotourism plan to helping a United Nations agency in Tajikistan create a model for microfinanced enterprises. The program has not only helped PWC retain talented managers, it has helped them develop as responsible leaders attuned to cultural differences.

Other companies encourage employee volunteerism through flexible work schedules and special grants to community projects with significant employee support. Cisco Systems matches the time its employees spend volunteering by making an equivalent cash contribution to the organization of up to $1,000 per year, per employee. Hewlett-Packard created a mentoring program that matches employees with elementary and secondary school students in the United States, Canada, Australia, and France. All communication between students and volunteers is conducted via e-mail.

When asked what they think of American business, politics, society, and popular entertainment, many global consumers give a thumbs-up only to American popular culture. Why? Bruce Bawer suggests it's "because they've experienced American movies and music firsthand and can judge for themselves, whereas their social and political views are based on what they've been taught in school and told by their media."[26] Employee volunteerism can fill this gap by giving global consumers a new firsthand experience.

CHAPTER 18

STIFF-NECKED,
TREE-HUGGING CRITICS

"International nongovernmental organizations are pressure groups, whose resonance comes from some form of moral claim and whose influence derives from their colonization of the U.N. and its specialized agencies."[1]

—Deepak Lal, professor of International Development, University of California

"For all their strengths, nongovernmental organizations are special interests. A society in which the piling up of special interests replaces a single strong voice for the common good is unlikely to fare well."[2]

—Jessica Mathews in *Foreign Affairs*

WHEN EXXONMOBIL BEGAN PLANNING A NEW OIL PIPELINE IN Chad and Cameroon, it turned to the World Bank to help the two countries fund their portion of the cost. Even though the project promised to create 5,000 construction jobs and to pay billions of dollars in royalties and taxes to two of the poorest nations on earth, it took five years to win World Bank support.

The reason? The World Bank now invites nongovernmental organizations (NGOs) to review major projects. According to ExxonMobil's vice president of public affairs at the time, the NGOs "helped improve the project in several ways, but they also almost killed it."[3]

Some of the NGOs were opposed to development of any kind.

Some of them didn't think the countries should get loans until they fixed their governance and human rights problems. But others believed the economic benefits that would flow from the pipeline project were worth the risk that project money would go astray. They not only advised ExxonMobil on pipeline routes and labor practices, they helped devise a payment system that would ensure that pipeline taxes and royalties would benefit the country's people and not line the pockets of local politicians. Sadly, once the oil revenue started flowing, Chad started spending some of it on the military as well as schools, hospitals, and roads, forcing the World Bank to suspend its loans in January 2006. ExxonMobil found itself caught between the World Bank and NGOs on one side and, on the other, the government that controlled access to the oil fields it had spent more than $4 billion developing.

THE EVOLUTION OF NGOs

ExxonMobil's experience was a microcosm of the evolution many nongovernmental organizations have undergone, as well as the inherent risks of doing business in the developing world. In the beginning, many NGOs were moral absolutists incapable of compromise. Obsessed with a single issue, their driving purpose was to block an action. Their default setting was a high-profile media campaign, designed to embarrass their opponents into submission. They used companies or brands as springboards to publicize their cause. In fact, one NGO leader has been widely quoted as saying that "targeting brands for us was like discovering gunpowder."[4]

Nothing generates ink like a good fight, especially with a well-known brand. It became such a staple in the NGO kit bag that even the threat of bad publicity could move big companies. For example, in 2003, Nestlé promptly forgave a six million pound debt that Ethiopia owed it when Oxfam criticized the company for trying to collect.

But over the years, many NGOs have realized that even the most successful media campaign can only accomplish so much. It's an inherently negative strategy, and most NGOs want to stand *for* something, not just against seemingly every aspect of modern life. Randall Hayes, founder of the Rainforest Action Network, explained it well in a talk he gave to other activists: "If you [as an NGO] are not talking to business, you are just preaching to the choir. Real change . . . is going to come from the business sector; we can't depend on government regulation to solve our problems."[5]

Peter Drucker called NGOs "human change institutions."[6] Lester Salamon, founding director of John Hopkins Institute for Policy Studies, claims that the role of NGOs in the twenty-first century will be as significant as the role of the nation state in the twentieth. He estimates more than 60,000 international NGOs are active on the world stage. They range from Oxfam and Save the Children to Shack Dwellers International, which claims membership on three continents. They include many religious organizations, such as the World Council of Churches and Catholic Relief Services, which enjoy broad public support. Their causes range from Aarskog syndrome[7] to zoonotic bacterial diseases,[8] but are generally grouped into three main areas: human rights, development, and the environment, all of which impinge on a company's global expansion. Some NGOs specialize in the distribution of aid and providing services; others, in campaigning and propaganda. More than 2,000 NGOs have consultative status with the United Nations.

Just adding up the fast-growing budgets of the biggest NGOs suggests these increasingly visible players on the global political scene have become a multibillion-dollar industry in their own right. Plus, NGOs have accumulated even more precious capital—trust. The public's confidence in NGOs has consistently outpaced trust in governments, businesses, and the media. In fact, the 2006 Edelman Trust Barometer shows that, for the first time, more than half of Americans consider NGOs the "most trusted institutions," a status they have held in Europe for all six years the survey has been conducted. Tellingly, even though the survey asked respondents to name trusted global *companies,* many volunteered NGOs such as the Red Cross in France and the U.K. and Greenpeace in Germany. According to Edelman, NGOs are now the most-trusted institution in every market except Japan and Brazil, where they are catching up. The widespread rise in trust of NGOs has now extended to Asia, especially in China, where NGO trust ratings went from 36 percent to 60 percent in 2005.[9]

While headline-grabbing stunts by some groups attract less than flattering attention, the vast majority of NGOs are highly professional organizations, dedicated to worthy causes and commanding impressive resources in some of the world's most hostile environments. Indeed, in January 2005, in the aftermath of the Asian tsunami, many corporations turned to NGOs to distribute the products that they were donating to the relief effort. In fact, about 10 percent of all development aid is now channeled through NGOs.[10] In the developing world, NGOs are the point of entry to what is known as "civil society"—the thought leaders, opinion makers, and voluntary associations that constitute a country's nonelected leaders.

NGO CRITICS

That's not to say NGOs don't have their share of critics. Some people charge that NGOs are hijacking other elements of "civil society" to support their cause or risk being labeled collaborators with the enemy of the moment. Others accuse them of covertly sowing the seeds of anarchy through their myopic, noncompromising, and confrontational tactics. Sebastian Mallaby's book about former World Bank president James Wolfensohn argues that NGOs are often ill-informed and incoherent, unaccountable and uncompromising, and even damaging to the development causes they proclaim to champion.[11] "For all their strengths, NGOs are special interests," wrote Jessica Mathews in an influential article in *Foreign Affairs* magazine. "The best of them often suffer from tunnel vision, judging every public act by how it affects their particular interest."[12] Unlike corporations or governments, NGOs do not have to consider trade-offs or the overall impact and unintended consequences of their policies. They have the luxury of obstinate single-mindedness.

As a consequence, the world of NGOs is hardly monolithic. They sometimes disagree among themselves, not only on tactics, but on goals. The World Wildlife Fund, for example, does not oppose the "sustainable use" of wildlife—such as through recreational hunting—as long as it doesn't endanger a species. Other groups, such as the equally moderate International Fund for Animal Welfare, oppose hunting on the grounds of cruelty. They even oppose the culling of African elephants, which many wildlife officials say is needed in places such as South Africa to alleviate hunger among the swelling herds of the world's largest land mammal.

And though the general public is inclined to give NGOs a lot of slack, there is something of an anti-NGO bandwagon rolling through some quarters. Critics question everything from their legitimacy (whom do they speak for?) to their accountability (whom do they answer to?).

As a result, some major donors are setting tighter standards on how their contributions can be used. National governments, as well as the United Nations, are discussing ways to tighten NGO accreditation without cramping their flexibility. Some countries, such as Russia, and most autocratic regimes, such as Iran, restrict NGOs' activities or ban them completely.

Many NGOs are beginning to follow the advice they have long been giving global companies in terms of openness, transparency, and ethical standards of behavior. The top leadership of such NGOs as Oxfam and Amnesty International have even attended workshops at the Harvard Business School to sharpen their management and strategic planning skills.

THE NGO PUSH

But as businesslike as NGOs become, business people will not always see eye-to-eye with them. Like a good exercise coach, the NGO's function in life is to push companies and governments to go further than they would if left at their own comfort levels.

NGOs also make no excuses for their rationale in picking targets. When the Campaign for Food Safety launched a drive to force Starbucks to buy more fair-trade coffee and eliminate milk taken from cows fed bovine growth hormone, some reporters asked why the group wasn't targeting the company's much larger competitors. The national director of the Campaign admitted his group considered targeting conglomerates such as Kraft, Nestlé, or Procter and Gamble, which account for the majority of U.S. coffee sales. But the group ultimately decided on Starbucks because the company "is highly visible—they're everywhere," the group's leader said. "Everywhere there are socially conscious consumers, there are also Starbucks outlets. It's hard to get at Kraft because they're just one of thousands of products in grocery stores."[13] After vandals glued the locks of fourteen Starbucks stores and customers had to navigate picket lines to buy their morning coffee, the company agreed to step up its purchases of fair-trade coffee and to offer organic milk for an extra forty cents a cup.

Perversely, Starbucks has long been generally regarded as a socially conscious firm. Its "guiding principles," include such values as "providing a great work environment" and "contributing positively to our communities." Nancy Koehn, a business historian at Harvard Business School, says that "[Starbucks' founder] recognized ahead of most executives that customers today vote with their dollars and will spend more money at companies with values they admire."[14] Even back in 2001, when the Campaign for Food Safety painted a bull's eye on the Starbucks mermaid logo, the company had already contributed millions of dollars to literacy programs, Conservation International, and CARE. It was one of very few companies to offer health insurance and stock options to any employee working twenty hours a week. Considering that record, Starbucks' president could be forgiven for saying, "It's a pretty unfair and short-sighted point of view for those organizations to go after the ones that are trying, versus the ones that say, 'I don't give a damn.' "[15]

HOW TO DEAL WITH NGOs

If that doesn't seem fair, it's only because it isn't.

The public will almost always give NGOs the benefit of the doubt and even forgive their excesses. One way to deal with NGOs is to stonewall them; another is to embrace them, using their feedback as a catalyst for growth and innovation.

Nike, for example, endured more than a decade of high-profile attacks for failing to police its suppliers. A series of media exposés described how Nike workers were earning below-subsistence wages and forced to work overtime, how some Nike plants used toxic chemicals, and how some factories even used child labor. At first, the company tried to ignore the attacks. Then it argued that it wasn't responsible for what its suppliers did and, anyway, the wages they paid were better than average for the area. Then it tried to outadvertise its critics. Then it hired a former U.S. ambassador to the United Nations to conduct a speedy (and, some say, superficial) audit of labor practices in the plants where its sneakers were manufactured. (Interestingly, in early 2006, Wal-Mart hired the same official—Andrew Young—to lead a pro-company group challenging WakeUpWalMart.com. He had to resign less than a year later because of racist remarks he made about Arabs, Koreans, and Jews in a newspaper interview.)

Finally, Nike got serious. It created a labor practices division, appointed a vice president of corporate and social responsibility, and created a board committee on corporate responsibility. But it really made progress when it engaged selected NGOs in a dialogue on the issues. Ultimately, the discussion led to new labor and environmental standards for all its contract manufacturing plants, including programs for monitoring performance across its supply chain. Nike even submits its "corporate responsibility report" to a third party of NGOs and academics for review and publishes their comments along with the report on its website. And in 2005, in the ultimate sign of its seriousness, Nike became the first footwear and apparel manufacturer to release the complete list of all the factories producing Nike-branded products.

THE 800-POUND GORILLA

On the other hand, working with NGOs is like dancing with an 800-pound gorilla. You don't get to quit—without suffering a few bruises—until she's ready. John Elkington, chairman of the consultancy SustainAbility in the United Kingdom, told the World Economic Forum of his group's efforts to facilitate a dialogue between Ford Motor Company and some of its NGO critics. According to Elkington, although the effort included sixteen different groups, participants were able to agree on a three-point agenda: combating global climate change, promoting human rights, and persuading Wall Street analysts to include social criteria in their company evaluations. "We showed you can get a diverse group of stakeholders together and boil their demands down to a manageable set of strategic priorities," Elkington said. But the project also taught a less positive lesson when Ford joined a coalition of automakers seeking to ease federal gasoline mileage standards. "Many NGOs saw it as an absolute betrayal," Elkington said. "It showed how important it is not to make commitments you can't keep."[16]

Companies have long entered new markets with partners who know the lay of the land. Today, when the landscape includes social and political issues as foreign to corporate managers as indigenous languages, those partners are likely to include nongovernmental organizations. Sir Douglas Hurd remembers that when he was the U.K.'s foreign minister, one of his deputies seemed to surround herself with NGOs, and not just for defensive reasons. "If you want to know about the Sudan, you don't go to the foreign office anymore," Hurd explained. "You go to the Church of England or to Oxfam. They actually do have a much wider experience of information than the representatives of government in dealing with that country."[17] In addition to providing intelligence on the new market, they also bring perspectives that can help avoid missteps.

You don't find potential NGO partners in the yellow pages. First, NGOs are very jealous of the independence that is the wellspring of their credibility. There can be nothing about your relationship that would even create the appearance of compromising the NGO's accountability to its stakeholders or its independence. Second, NGOs have no real interest in helping corporations; they are totally dedicated to furthering their cause. They will not even consider working with you unless you can demonstrate that you are not only serious about change, but well positioned to influence activity across your industry. But as Richard Edelman once counseled, "No NGO will roll over. But you can do better than have the stuffing kicked out of you."[18] So choose to partner with an organization that has a track record of constructive relationships. And that includes an understanding that any restraints or conditions you agree to will also apply to your competitors.

As in any other partnership, both partners need to understand how the other benefits. For their part, NGOs are more inclined to trust companies that point to the profit motive, as opposed to vague notions of "corporate citizenship," as the key driver in their decision making. Peter Melchett, the former executive director of Greenpeace in the United Kingdom, says:

> I think the key thing in relationships with NGOs is to look at the core business of what you actually do, what the products are, what the processes are. [An NGO relationship] is not something about media spin [and] press coverage in the long run. There may be some short-term gains. But they're going to be very short-term.[19]

With that in mind, at the very beginning of the partnership, the roles, rules, and even the risks of a partnership need to be crystal clear to all parties. Both partners need to agree to the scope of their work together, their mutual expectations, how they will make decisions, how they will evaluate progress, and how they will resolve conflicts.

It can work. DuPont and the Alliance for Environmental Innovation have agreed to collaborate on a framework for the responsible development, production, use, and disposal of nanoscale materials.

FedEx partnered with the same group to reduce the environmental impact of its vehicle fleet. And McDonald's worked with the group to curb the use of antibiotics in its suppliers' poultry farms.

HIDDEN OPPORTUNITIES

Constructive relationships with NGOs can even be the source of competitive advantage by keeping companies in touch with emerging social trends. As Ian Davis of McKinsey and Company writes, "Large companies must build social issues into strategy in a way that reflects their actual business importance."[20] Putting things in terms of sheer shareholder value, Davis points out that 80 percent of the market value of U.S. and Western European companies is based on projected cash flows more than three years out. And the long-term financial impact of social issues has already been demonstrated in industries ranging from tobacco, oil, and mining to pharmaceuticals, financial services, and food processing. Far from being tangential to the creation of shareowner value, social issues are at their core, both from defensive and value-creation points of view.

Furthermore, emerging social and political issues are often wrapped around unexpected areas of opportunity, ripe for new product or marketing strategies. Toyota, for example, anticipated growing interest in environmentally friendly products when it introduced the Prius. At the beginning of 2006, there was a six-month wait to buy the car in California. The Prius became a cultural icon featured on television shows from *Gilmore Girls* to *South Park* and attracting high-profile drivers from Larry David to Cameron Diaz.

But that doesn't mean companies should try to take on all the world's problems. Even religious orders bring some focus to their work. Peter Drucker, for one, thought it was a mistake for companies to allow themselves to be sucked in to social causes far removed from their area of expertise. But he didn't think corporations could hide from the world's problems, either. Corporations are in the community. "They cannot retreat into isolation," he argued, "when the world around them goes to pieces."[21] The trick is to find the intersection of a company's specific competence and society's needs.

For example, at the beginning of the twentieth century, Sears Roebuck realized that its mail-order business depended more on what farmers could afford to buy than on what it was trying to sell. But farmers of the time were dirt-poor, isolated, and ignorant of modern agricultural techniques. So Sears invented the Farm Agent and financed the program for ten years until it was so successful in introducing new methods that the government took it over. By then, farm families had sufficient purchasing power to buy from the Sears Roebuck catalog. And Sears became the world's largest, most profitable retailer for several decades.

More recently, food giant Cargill faced bitter opposition to its entry into the market for sunflower seeds in India where local farmers accounted for as much as 70 percent of seed production. Its local offices were set on fire twice. Instead of hopping on the next plane back to Minneapolis, the company's executives set up a program to teach Indian farmers how to improve their crop yields. As a result, the local farmers' productivity increased more than 50 percent. Once Cargill had provided them with a palpable economic benefit, they understood that the company aspired to be their partner rather than their exploiter.[22]

STRATEGIC SOCIAL ACTIVISM

Socially responsible behavior shouldn't be an add-on to a company's "real" business. It shouldn't be a response to the first good cause to make it past the receptionist. And it certainly shouldn't be a response to looming or erupting crises. Global companies need to develop specific processes to ensure that social issues are explicitly considered as part of overall strategic planning, both as risks and as opportunities. Constructive NGO relationships should be part of that process.

Emerging social trends can change an industry's landscape as well as threaten the reputations of individual companies within it. Claude Smadja, a business strategist who directed the World Economic Forum's annual meetings for five years, believes businesses today are undergoing structural and environmental stresses akin to those of the Great Depression. "Nonbusiness factors now loom as large as the business or financial ones," he says.[23]

Because it was slow to respond to an oil spill by one of its tankers, ExxonMobil spent $2 billion on the cleanup and another $5 billion in lawsuits. If the company had taken a different tack, it arguably might have limited its financial exposure, not to mention the damage to its reputation.

Global companies need to develop broad metrics to track relevant social issues, just as they have long analyzed customer trends. The issues that consumer groups and the media will mobilize arund can be roughly estimated. For example, the growing interest in fuel-efficient cars could not have been clearer in the last years of the twentieth century, and few food companies would have been surprised by the obesity debate if they had tracked growing government expenditures on obesity-related health problems. The movie *Super Size Me* was the natural result of that movement, not its instigation. Combined with the obvious interest of both the media and lawyers looking for litigation targets, the issue was obviously huge. But by the time most food companies took the issue seriously, they were in a defensive posture, struggling to catch up with the public debate.

This is a familiar syndrome to some executives who spent their careers calling their colleagues in the executive suite to arms, like modern-day Paul Reveres, but with less satisfactory results. "All large bureaucracies are defensive, self-absorbed, constantly in denial, and don't care about the outside world," Marilyn Laurie wryly observes.[24] Ironically, nongovernmental organizations can be a corporation's best friend in understanding, and staying rooted in, the real world.

WHAT GETS MEASURED GETS DONE

Finally, while no corporate social responsibility program should be designed with the goal of generating publicity, if it is central to a company's competency and competitiveness, it deserves to be reported, if only because what gets measured gets done. The global accounting firm KPMG reports that in 2005, 80 percent of the largest Japanese companies and 71 percent of the largest British companies issued separate social responsibility reports, while only about a third of U.S. companies did.[25] While the quality of the reports is gradually improving, they seldom reflect the same rigor and transparency as financial results—warts and all.

After a bumpy record in this area, Gap, Inc. issued a model social responsibility report in 2003 that one newsletter applauded as a "no-holds-barred report on its labor practices throughout the world."[26]

Gap even had its report reviewed by a group of NGOs and social investment groups and gave them a page in the report to express their own opinions. The report, which included the news that the company had terminated contracts with factories that violated its code of vendor conduct, positioned Gap as an ethical company exerting moral leadership.

Unilever monitors its social responsibility goals and publishes yearly progress reports, showing hard metrics—for example, how the wages it pays around the world compare to local standards—and displaying the company's on-the-job accident record over a five-year period.[27]

The era of instant communication and one-to-many publishing represents great challenges for businesses of all size. What Howard Rheingold has termed "smart mobs"[28] can be organized and deployed against a company in a matter of hours using e-mail, websites, and mobile telephones. Anyone with a computer hooked to the Internet can launch a website, podcast, or a blog attacking the biggest company. Within minutes, it will be linked to thousands, maybe millions, of other like-minded sites. At times, it seems that David has been armed with weapons of mass destruction.

If anything, the playing field has been leveled, after years of tilting in the direction of Big Business and Big Media. That's not all bad. For example, whereas business people could do little more than complain when they were quoted out of context by the mainstream media, now they can post the entire interview to their company's website—even before the story appears—to give the public the full story. Businesses can use e-mail to share timely information with allies, many of whom may have their own blogs. Most important, they can use the Internet to engage their stakeholders in a meaningful dialogue. For example, when P&G put toll-free numbers on the packaging of products sold in Japan, it was an innovative signal that it was open to questions. Now, with 44 local language websites from Albania to Yugoslavia, the company has broadened and deepened the conversation. And in addition to putting its social responsibility report online, in 2006 McDonald's linked it to a blog where readers can contribute comments or ask questions.[29]

American companies need to adopt higher standards of social responsibility, not only because it's expected in other countries, but because it's the new standard of liberal democracies.

CHAPTER 19

SHARE YOUR
CUSTOMERS' DREAMS

*"We share common values—the common values of freedom, human
rights and democracy."*[1]
—George W. Bush, forty-third president of the United States

*"It is time to stop pretending that Europeans and Americans share
a common view of the world. . . . Americans are from Mars and
Europeans are from Venus: They agree on little and understand one
another less and less."*[2]
—Robert Kagan, The Carnegie Endowment for International Peace

SUPER BOWL XVIII DIDN'T WARRANT THE GRANDIOSE USE OF
Roman numerals that has characterized the game since its earliest
days. It was a rout. The Los Angeles Raiders dominated the Washington Redskins from the first kickoff and achieved one of the most lop-
sided victories in Super Bowl history, winning 38–9.[3]

Viewers had to find their entertainment in the commercials, as is
often the case, since marketers pull out all the stops for what is usually
one of the most viewed programs of the year. In 1984, they were
treated to a number of commercials for a new product called a personal computer. Bill Bixby, TV's *Incredible Hulk,* pitched RadioShack's
model. Alan Alda, fresh from his eleven-year tour on *M*A*S*H,*
hawked Atari's computers. And an actor dressed like Charlie Chaplin
toddled around for IBM. But decades later most people remember only

one TV spot from that Super Bowl—the Apple Computer commercial in which a young blonde woman in red running shorts dashes into an auditorium filled with row after row of slack-jawed, zoned-out spectators and throws a sledgehammer through a giant TV screen on which a Big Brother–type figure is droning on about "information" something or other. Except for another play on local television in Boca Raton, Florida, where IBM's personal computer division was headquartered, the commercial ran only that one time. But it struck such a chord that it was replayed for free on local and national news broadcasts.

It was a great commercial, although it reportedly made the Apple executives who approved it, despite the reservations of their own board, more than a little nervous. What made it memorable were not the production values, though the director, Ridley Scott, spared no expense in giving it the polish of a feature-length movie. It didn't have much plot—girl runs in, throw sledgehammer, TV screen explodes, cue announcer and Apple logo. It was darkly wry rather than slap-your-knee funny.

No, what made it truly great—and memorable—was that it tapped into a set of feelings and ideas that everyone watching shared. It tapped into the fear of Big Brother, first articulated in exactly those words by George Orwell in a novel entitled, not coincidentally, *1984*.

Orwell didn't invent the idea of Big Brother; he gave it expression. The notion of an all-seeing, all-knowing force that could manipulate people's lives without their knowledge had probably been around since the dawn of the Industrial Age, if not earlier. It's one of those myths entwined in the underlying fabric of modern society. By exploiting that myth, Apple created a television commercial—and a brand—that endures to this day. It attached moral values to its brand, essentially saying that "their computers enslave you, ours set you free." Quite a feat, considering that Apple's products—from the Mac computer to the iPod music player—all run on closed, proprietary technology while its competitors use relatively standard, open software. Nevertheless, the Apple brand remains in equal measure virtuous and hip.

BIG BROTHER USA

Less than a week before the September 11, 2001, terrorist attacks, the man who created the 1984 Apple commercial, Steve Hayden, spoke to hundreds of State Department diplomats on how the United States could shed its reputation as the foreign policy equivalent of a hegemonic Big Brother. Hayden urged his audience to take a page from the corporate handbook in presenting America to the world. "People like leadership, not dominance," Hayden said. "If you had to deal with the world's only superpower, what would you want it to be like? Fair? Reasonable? Participatory?"[4]

In a post-9/11 interview with *Foreign Policy* magazine, Hayden conceded that corporate analogies are "lightweight" compared to the problems the United States faced. But he still believed that public diplomacy would be more effective if it followed the example of successful advertising and took more of an "emotional rather than rational approach." For example, if U.S. officials had paid more attention to negative attitudes, he said, "we wouldn't have used words like *crusade* or *infinite justice.*' "

Although Hayden made his career in advertising, and although he had been invited to speak by his former boss, Charlotte Beers, he was not arguing for TV commercials or print ads to "sell" America to the world. On the contrary, he was encouraging the U.S. State Department to connect with people around the world on the most elemental level of their dreams and hopes. In hindsight, that was a point of view shared by Beers, though it got lost in the furor surrounding her Shared Values campaign.

Several years later, in assessing the shambles of America's public diplomacy, a small group of former diplomats, well-schooled in the ways of Washington, echoed Hayden's warning. They issued a stinging dissent to those who would simply pour more money into the dissemination of information and the countering of propaganda. They wrote:

> Americans, who control a disproportionate share of global wealth, who contribute 42 percent of all carbon emissions to global warming, who have the largest nuclear arsenal on the planet are not necessarily loved more by being seen more clearly. We become credible in this world to the extent that we are seen to be working to solve global problems that affect their lives. We become credible to the extent that we recognize their hopes, aspirations, and fears.[5]

America would only gain people's trust, they said, if it identified with their hopes, aspirations, and fears. The story America should tell is not its own, but "the human story and how America relates to those outside our borders."

THE POWER OF STORIES

Ever since the first man (or woman) drew on a cave wall, one of the ways we've made sense of the world is by telling stories. Brands serve the same function. They are the stories that run through people's minds and hearts as they wheel their cart up and down the supermarket aisles or examine a business card. Those stories drive awareness, consideration, trial, and purchase. Marketers recognized this tendency from the earliest days of branding. Aunt Jemima's and Uncle Ben's became the symbols for a new pancake mix and a particular brand of white rice not only because they gave the products personality, but because they subtly told a back story of "happy slaves" who were dedicated to their "family's" well-being. St. Joseph's aspirin and Father John's cough syrup created the impression they came from the selfless staffs of Catholic hospitals.

The clarity, consistency, and credibility of a company's brand story is what sets it apart from its competitors. The most successful global brands tell stories that are so responsive to their customers' values, hopes, and aspirations that they rise to the level of myths.

The popular definition of myth today is a "tall tale" or a "lie." But it actually has a deeper psychological meaning. King Arthur, the Knights of the Round Table, and Camelot may not have existed, but the Arthurian legend tells us a lot about the worldview of the people who embraced the story and kept it alive through retelling. At its core, it is a story of chivalry, a value lost in our modern age.

Similarly, a simple pair of denim blue jeans—Levi's—took on mythic quality, first, in America as a retelling of Gold Rush stories, then in postwar Europe as a symbol of the youthful, fun-loving country of its liberators. By the 1980s, a pair of used Levi's were so packed with meaning that they were a form of currency in parts of Eastern Europe for traveling Americans.

Marketers create brands to give their products a heritage grounded in consumers' aspirations. Saab's advertising, for example, stresses that the company's founders started out designing airplanes. In addition to the obvious associations with engineering prowess and high-performance, the ads lay the foundation for a story of speed, freedom, and exhilaration.

People use global brands to create an imagined identity that they share with like-minded people. One of the purposes of myth is to express the values that bind people together in society. Myths have held tribes together for millennia. Today, the myths underlying the world's great brands have created cohorts of new "consumer tribes."

Global consumers identify with like-minded people without regard to their national affiliations. In some ways, the nation-state is actually taking a back seat to affiliations that many people find more meaningful because they are based on deeply felt common values and concerns. Ethnic and religious conflicts characterize one end of the spectrum; brand loyalty, the other, thankfully more peaceful, end. The Nike Swoosh, a Porsche key fob, and an Apple iPod are tribal badges in their own right. The Internet, global entertainment media, and a celebrity culture keep members of these new "tribes" plugged in to each other. In such a tribal society, the products that companies make are less important than the relationships they forge with those who share an affinity for their brands. Product features come and go, innovations are copied, but brand values endure.

Starbucks, for example, is more than a cup of coffee. It's a total experience. Customers order in an idiosyncratic language where "tall" means "small," "grande" means "medium," and "venti" means "large." A "barista" makes the coffee fresh, customer by customer, right across the counter. Patrons can take their cup to a comfortable chair or a sofa, and if they pass someone on the street carrying the familiar cup in a safety liner they know they're members of the same club, what many brand experts call a "coffeehouse community."

Brand myths also help people reconcile ideas that are apparently contradictory. For example, AT&T became the mythic Ma Bell on the strength of its ability to nurture its customers by collapsing the contradiction between "distance" and "closeness." When AT&T invited families to "reach out and touch someone," it resolved the logical contradiction between "being there" and "being somewhere else."

Brand America once had such mythic quality. In fact, many American products rode on its coattails in overseas markets. People around the world could relate to the American Dream. Mothers and fathers everywhere want their children to be better off than they were. The story of Horatio Alger is alive and well in the farthest corners of the world. And although "the pursuit of happiness" may not appear in the foundation documents of other governments, it's spirit is universal. But the story many people today connect with Brand America has a very different plot line. Horatio Alger seems to have pulled the ladder up after himself, downsizing and outsourcing all the good jobs. The U.S. government seems less interested in honoring Emma Lazarus's injunction to "give me your tired, your poor, your huddled masses yearning to breathe free,"[6] than in securing its borders.

BRAND MYTHS

If U.S.-based companies can no longer count on a free ride courtesy of Brand America, they can create their own myths by identifying with their customers' deepest concerns and aspirations.

The way Anglo-Dutch company Unilever markets Dove soap, for example, has tapped into women's deepest feelings about the notions of feminine beauty in the Western media. When Dove surveyed women in ten countries about their attitudes toward beauty, it found a global insecurity complex, especially among young women. Only 2 percent of the women surveyed considered themselves beautiful, and only 9 percent feel comfortable describing themselves as attractive. In response, Dove designed a Campaign for Real Beauty that challenged stereotypes of waif-like, leggy supermodels as the standard of beauty. Dove's ads in the United States, Canada, Brazil, Argentina, the United Kingdom, and Germany featured real women of various body types confidently posing in their underwear. But the campaign is not about self-acceptance or lowering the bar for self-esteem. "We wanted to debunk the . . . beauty stereotype that exists," says Philippe Harousseau, Dove's marketing director. "We are recognizing that beauty comes in different sizes, shapes, and ages."[7] Dove aims to change the status quo and to replace it with a broader, healthier, more democratic view of beauty. As its website says, it's "a view of beauty that all women can own and enjoy every day."[8] Along with Dove soap, of course.

VALUES

Just as beauty is in the eye of the beholder, it's a mistake to assume that values have the same weight—or even the same meaning—in every culture. On issues such as gender equality, divorce, abortion, and gay rights, for example, the Western and Islamic worlds are in different solar systems. When President Bush triumphantly declares "Freedom is on the march!" he may mean democracy is coming to countries previously ruled by dictators and absolute monarchs. He'll face no argument there, as proved by thousands of Iraqis and Afghans who braved roadside bombs and snipers to vote. But freedom can also mean the expression of personal values that clash head-on with entrenched religious beliefs and patterns of personal behavior.

And it would be a mistake to assume that the tenets of traditional Islamic society are embraced only by men. Karen Hughes began her term as undersecretary of state for public diplomacy with a listening tour of the Middle East at the end of 2005. On a mission to explore attitudes toward America, Hughes was challenged by American stereotyping of Arabs. According to *The New York Times*, an audience of about 500 well-educated Saudi women burst into applause when one of their members told Hughes, "The general image of the Arab woman is that she isn't happy. Well, we're all pretty happy."[9] And when Hughes said she hoped Saudi women would one day be able to drive a car and vote, a female obstetrician and gynecologist who runs her own hospital told her, "I don't want to drive a car. I worked hard for my medical degree. Why do I need a driver's license?"

Even Europe, with which so many Americans share a cultural and genetic heritage, has sharply different values. By and large, Americans value individual autonomy; Europeans consider themselves interdependent. Americans seek personal wealth; Europeans tend to emphasize the quality of their lives. Americans focus on economic growth as a measure of progress; Europeans are more concerned with sustainable development. Americans brag about how hard they work; Europeans covet their leisure. Americans are mostly religious; Europeans are ostentatiously secular.

COMMON DREAMS

The homogenized global market that Ted Levitt predicted has yet to jell. What we have instead is more of a stew, with the people of every nation contributing their own ingredients and mixing them with others'. But there's a common broth in that stew. A factory worker in

Taiwan dreams of improving her family's life. A farmer in Peru dreams that his children will receive an education and enjoy a better life than he did. A waitress in Germany dreams of owning her own restaurant. These are dreams of opportunity. They may be expressed in the accent of a particular corner of the world, but they reflect the American experience.

In addition to sharing their customers' cares, global companies must share their customers' dreams by rooting their brands in the myths that nourish those dreams. In the developed world, most people's basic needs are already being met. Successful brands are those that meet people's aspirations.

That doesn't mean global brands should be anything but what they are. Based on surveys of 3,300 consumers in forty-one countries, Research International/USA concluded that "consumers expect global brands to tell their myths from the particular places that are associated with the brand."[10] Nike, for example, has not tried to hide its American roots. Indeed, the values it celebrates—"fun," "competitiveness," "achievement," "spontaneity"—are all ideals closely identified with America, even if they are expressed in French, Spanish, or Swahili. At the same time, Nike has taken pains not to be identified too closely with the sports or hobbies of any particular country. In fact, it celebrates "street games" and has constructed an image of having fun outside of the normal rules. According to marketing consultant Bernard Demeure, "Nike caught the mood of the time perfectly, a feeling that one should simply express himself, that it's okay to have fun without rules."[11] At a time when snowboarding is in and skiing is out, Nike is telling the French kids who *glissent* (i.e., slide on a wet floor) that they're playing a sport as legitimate as soccer. Local adaptations are important, but not sufficient in building a global brand. The trick is to adapt around universal values. Nike's real strength was in understanding young people's willingness to participate in a new trend, to join a new "tribe." "Just do it" and the Nike Swoosh became the tribe's insignia and represent values that cross borders and owe allegiance to no particular country.

Although Coke sells bottled water under the Turkqaz brand in Turkey, it also sticks its name on every blue-tinted bottle, just above the dolphins that symbolize friendship. Even though America's image in Turkey is at an all-time low, the president of Coca-Cola's Eurasia/Middle East division, Ahmet Bozer, says it's a conscious decision. "Our sales force says that is essential, because it tells people it's something they can trust," he told *Fortune* magazine. "People are more skeptical about local products."[12] (Turkqaz, by the way, is the best-selling bottled water in Turkey.)

The Starbucks myth is one of sophistication and community. According to Starbucks' founder Howard Schultz:

> I wanted to blend coffee with romance. One thing I've noticed about romantics, they try to build a new and better world far from the drabness of everyday life. That is Starbucks' aim, too. We try to create in our stores an oasis, a little neighborhood spot where you can take a break, listen to some jazz, and ponder universal or even whimsical questions over a cup of coffee. We see ourselves as the respectful inheritors of the European coffeehouse tradition with all its connotations of art, literature, and progressive ideals.[13]

But reflecting its American roots, Starbucks also offers breathtaking choice. Whereas the finest European coffeehouses might offer espresso, café au lait, and café américain, every Starbucks brews a bewildering range of coffees. In fact, Starbucks has published a twenty-four-page booklet describing all the ways you can order its brew.

Employees in the fast-growing knowledge industries are their company's single biggest asset. The consulting team that calls on clients represents the store, the inventory, and the staff of a company like Accenture. Being perceived as a U.S. company "is a net good because of America's perceived business acumen and technology skills," says Chief Marketing Officer Jim Murphy. Yet Accenture makes sure to have multiple nationalities represented on the project team that's in daily contact with an overseas client. The implicit message: We are part of the global village, just like you. "That piece of brand-building is as important as the advertising," says Murphy.[14]

THE STORYTELLING POWER OF BRANDS

As the Disney executive responsible for negotiating marketing alliances, Larry Vincent acquired a keen understanding of the storytelling power of brands. In his book, *Legendary Brands,* he explains how a shoe stripe came to stand for heroic victory and an apple came to represent individuality and innovation. The secret to Nike's and Apple's success, according to Vincent, lies in the stories that communicate their underlying brand philosophy.[15]

Apple Computer famously started in a garage, but its story is not about nerds in skunk works. Apple's story is that it's different—it's not about the stuff inside a computer, it's all about what you *do* with the thing. Its products are more like kitchen appliances than electronic business equipment. They promise to be just as easy to use and just as versatile. Apple is as homey as, well, an apple.

Nike started when two "running geeks" decided to import Japanese sneakers as an alternative to the expensive German-made athletic shoes they had been buying. But its story isn't about sneaker treads. It's about celebrating the athlete inside you, whether you're shuffling off on a morning jog or competing in a triathlon. Similarly, Harley-Davidson tells a story of grit and the open road. Ralph Lauren is all about Gatsby-era elegance and sophistication. L.L. Bean is Yankee ingenuity, thrift, and honesty, 24/7.

The Brooklyn founders of Snapple stumbled onto their brand's myth because they couldn't get grocery chains and fast-food franchises to stock the drink, so they distributed it in restaurants, delis, street carts, and mom-and-pop groceries. They were so desperate for sales that they rolled out unusual blends like cantaloupe and kiwi strawberry if customers asked for them. And when they had enough money to start advertising, they put offbeat characters like Wendy their receptionist in their commercials. Even though it's now owned by the U.K. confectionary giant Cadbury Schweppes, the Snapple brand still nurtures the "little guy" myth and has taken it to eighty countries. Similarly, even after its acquisition by Unilever and its expansion to twenty countries, to most of its customers, Ben & Jerry's is still a quirky ice cream produced by two aging hippies in Vermont.

Whatever its source, a successful brand myth tells customers a story that they not only find relevant and credible, but compelling. That story may unreel in a specific place at a specific time, but it speaks to values and aspirations that are universal and timeless.

CHAPTER 20

MYTH AMERICA

"It's a complex fate, being an American."[1]

—Henry James

"There is nothing the matter with Americans except their ideals. The real American is all right; it is the ideal American who is all wrong."[2]

—G. K. Chesterton

THURSDAY, NOVEMBER 9, 1989, DAWNED AS GRAY AND COLD IN East Berlin as the concrete wall that separated it from the West. No one suspected that by late afternoon a minor government official would gather reporters together to read from a small piece of paper that East Germans would no longer need special documents to travel west. At first, the reporters didn't understand the significance of what they had just been told. Then it dawned on them—the Berlin Wall, a twenty-eight-mile-long barrier that had divided the city for twenty-eight years, was officially open and would soon come down.

By the time the reporters got to the wall from the government ministry, the guard towers on both sides were empty and the barbed wire had been shoved aside in spiky piles. German kids were dancing on the wall, while others hammered away at it with sledge hammers. And every last one of them seemed to be wearing Levi's jeans.

Those jeans, which were far from cheap (if you could even find them) on the eastern side of the Berlin Wall, were part of the American myth, the stories that remind people they are part of something bigger than themselves and that carry their values from one generation to the next.

Levi's jeans, the quintessential American clothing, were invented by a German immigrant who copied the trousers worn by sailors in the Northern Italian port of Genoa and cut them from a denim cloth traditionally woven in the French town of Nîmes. Like the country they came to represent, Levi's are a hybrid—something completely new created from things that are warmly familiar somewhere else.

Nothing is more American than Levi's jeans, even though the company has operations in seventy countries and sells its products in 110 nations. But wherever Levi's jeans are sold, the company emphasizes its core brand values. "In Europe, the ads talk about the cool fit. In Asia, they talk about the rebirth of an original. In the U.S., ads show real people who are, themselves, originals—ranchers, surfers, great musicians," says spokesman Jeff Beckman. "There's a connected set of values and brand attributes, communicated in a locally relevant way."[3] A common story.

So what is the story they tell? For one thing, Levi's stand for democracy, but not in the narrow political sense of campaigns and ballot boxes. "Levi's blue jeans are worn by the affluent and working people; men, women and children alike," says spokesman Beckman. "They are the quintessential symbol of freedom, rebelliousness, and democracy—ideas that are universally appealing from Maine to the Middle East."[4] Indeed, blue jeans must be the most universally worn apparel in the world. The "democracy" of blue jeans is that of the great leveler, the idea that accidents of birth or other circumstances don't define an individual. That anyone can go as far as his talent and hard work will take him.

Levi Strauss & Company CEO Philip Marineau believes that his company's jeans are a wearable emblem of American values. "I think the core values of Levi's—democracy, freedom, independence—certainly are viewed as the best of America,"[5] he says. And in truth McDonald's, Boeing, Coca-Cola, Nike, and hundreds of other American brands all communicate something about the values of their country of origin.

MYTH AMERICA

The American myth is of men and women who make their own way in the world, free from the shackles of the particular circumstances of their birth. "America's founding ideal was the principle of individual rights. Nothing more—and nothing less," wrote Ayn Rand. "The rest—everything that America achieved, everything she became, everything 'noble and just,' and heroic, and great, and unprecedented in human history—was the logical consequence of fidelity to that one principle."[6]

What an appealing principle that must have been to people locked into a "classless" society where everyone had to settle for the lowest common denominator. Two years after the fall of the Berlin Wall, 30,000 Muscovites lined up on a cold winter day for the opening of the first McDonald's in Russia. As it happens, the restaurant was a joint venture of the Russian government and McDonald's Canadian subsidiary. But to the Muscovites enjoying their first Big Mac and fries, it was a delicious serving of America.

The American myth is of people who are always on the move, restless, hardworking, and optimistic. In little more than 200 years—a blink of the eye on Asian and European calendars—America went from primal wilderness, to colonial backwater, to open frontier, to bustling cities, to a safe refuge for those unwelcome elsewhere. America is a country in a hurry. The Americans in these stories are independent, self-reliant risk takers willing to tackle any challenge. While Europeans were holed up in their walled cities, American settlers were pushing westward in wagon trains. They cleared the forests, plowed the plains, planted corn, chased off coyotes, crossed the Rockies, cut timber, opened shops, raised families, and panned for gold. Americans were certainly not the first people to open frontiers. Europeans and Asians, after all, had led all the great explorations of the world and had conquered countless lands peopled by lesser civilizations. In their earliest days, Canada and Australia were frontiers in their own right, but they belonged to a king who distributed parcels as he saw fit. Following the revolution, America was the first place where lands were not conquered for someone else, but for oneself. What distinguished the American myth was its personal significance—America stood for the pursuit of personal happiness.

Stories of the Wild West shaped America's self-image and arguably its character. The first line of the Mickey Mouse Club pledge, for example, had tykes in the 1950s swearing to be "straight shooters," amiably marrying notions of violence and fairness. But what is most striking about the pervasive influence of these frontier myths is that they were, at best, only partially true.

The American West was settled not by rugged individuals, but by large extended families that moved across the plains together. While homesteaders created more than 372,000 farms, the majority of western land ended up under the control of large cattle, timber, and mining companies. It wasn't so much "free" as stolen from the Native Americans who had lived there for centuries. New York investors financed the laying of the railroads; government troops killed Indians who wouldn't get out of the way and shoved their families onto land no one else wanted. Even the legendary cowboys were unreliable, poorly paid employees of giant cattle corporations. Furthermore, the West was something less than a promised land for many Asians, Mexicans, and blacks who were virtually indentured servants there.

Historians are in general agreement that the opening of the West was hardly the most telling event in American history. It pales in influence compared to slavery and the Civil War, immigration, and the development of industrial capitalism. Nonetheless, the frontier is still the dominant American myth, even if it's less than historically accurate. Stories of exploration and development—and all the images, values, and heroes associated with the American frontier—are not only potent symbols of America's past, but have been attached to products from blue jeans to banks and are reflected in everything from America's popular entertainment to its foreign policy. Its iconic status derives from the most basic value it expressed—the pursuit of personal happiness.

THE PURSUIT OF HAPPINESS

America was founded on a vision of freedom—specifically, the freedom for all its people to "pursue happiness." The words "life, liberty, and the pursuit of happiness" appear in the very document by which Americans declared their independence. Over time, those words have been expanded upon and recast. They have even stimulated heated debate, including a civil war, but they have endured as the essence of the American vision, simple enough to be easily recited by any schoolchild yet grand enough to inspire Nobel laureate V. S. Naipaul:

> It is an elastic idea; it fits all men. It implies a certain kind of society, a certain kind of awakened spirit. So much is contained in it: the idea of

the individual, responsibility, choice, the life of the intellect, the idea of vocation and perfectibility and achievement. It is an immense human idea.[7]

The USA's brand manager in chief, George W. Bush, concurs. The president has been outspoken on the attributes he would associate with Brand America—opportunity, democracy, freedom. But something happens between the president's lips and foreign ears. Americans tend to believe that their ideals are universal," Simon Anholt says, "and are surprised to discover that foreigners either don't understand exactly what they mean, or else they do understand and simply don't invest these ideals with the same importance."[8] Those ideals acquired their meaning for Americans through a combination of history and folklore that is less meaningful to many in the rest of the world.

The world's love affair with America is not over, but it's no longer blind. America has lost its mystery, and increasing familiarity with its ways breeds discernment, if not contempt. Just as a label declaring a product to be "Made in America" is no longer enough to move it off the shelf, America's ideals need to be redefined in terms that are meaningful to the rest of the world.

For example, "freedom" was a powerful brand attribute in the 1940s, 1950s, and 1960s, when so much of the world was enslaved. The imagery of the American cowboy perfectly communicated the essence of freedom: A cowboy was free to come and go as he pleased, ranging far and wide, beholden to no one and making his own future with his own two callused hands. But today, freedom is common across much of the world and suspect in much of the Islamic world, where it is confused with permissiveness. Cowboy imagery tends toward a lone ranger who ignores fences, shoots before asking questions, bathes infrequently, and grabs whatever or whoever he wants. But many non-Americans value "community" more highly than the individual, and that one difference may explain many of the tensions between the United States and the rest of the world.

The World Values Survey discovered that what makes people happy varies from one country to the next. Personal success and self-expression are the most important factor in the United States, while in countries such as Japan and the Philippines, fulfilling the expectations of family and society is valued more highly.[9] "For Filipinos, happiness isn't material—it's social," wrote Philippine journalist Alan Robles in *Time* magazine. "We're happiest in a group: family, friends, immediate community, even strangers. The small group is our bastion against life's unfairness."[10]

Furthermore, in the United States, the ideals of freedom and opportunity have long been more closely intertwined with those of commerce and trade than many Americans realize. Many of the disputes that roiled the colonies in the years leading up to the American Revolution were essentially commercial in nature. The Boston Tea Party of 1773 was the colonists' way of protesting what they saw as an unfair commercial advantage the British Crown had given British merchants by allowing them to sell tea without paying the usual colonial tax. In fact, twenty of the men who signed the Declaration of Independence were businessmen—merchants or farmers—second in profession only to the lawyers and jurists.

Jefferson, Franklin, and Hamilton didn't fight the theory of degeneracy out of pure patriotic pride, but because they feared it would inhibit investment in their young country. Alexis de Tocqueville himself noted that Americans' dominant ethic seemed to be "making money." And for many modern-day Europeans, that remains the prototypical American obsession, feeding their conspicuous consumption of everything from gas-guzzling SUVs to all-you-can-eat buffets. But a later traveler to America's shores, the Dutchman Edward Bok, who immigrated in 1870, saw more in the American spirit than "making a buck." He wrote:

> While between nations as between individuals, comparisons are valueless, it may not be amiss to say, from personal knowledge, that the Dutch worship the guilder infinitely more than do the Americans the dollar. What is not generally understood of the American people is their wonderful idealism. Nothing so completely surprises the foreign-born as the discovery of this trait in the American character.[11]

Bok didn't believe Americans were even conscious of this idealism. In fact, he thought they hid it under a thick veneer of materialism, but "let a great convulsion touching moral questions occur," he promised, "and the result always shows how close to the surface is (their) idealism."[12]

The American ideal was not necessarily to open a shop or own a business, or even to accumulate untold wealth and consumer goods. It was to be free of the European social and economic model that kept everyone firmly in his place. It was a spirit of fair play in which each

man or woman has an equal chance to succeed. "America is another
name for opportunity,"[13] goes Ralph Waldo Emerson's famous epi-
gram. And from the Revolutionary War through the nineteenth century, millions of Europeans and Asians immigrated to America certain
that, with courage and hard work, they could build a better life there,
whether by laying claim to a plot of land in the broad prairies, pros-
pecting for gold in the western mountains, or working on one of the
railroads stretching across the country. The dime-store novelist Horatio Alger kept that dream alive through stories of bootblacks, newspaper boys, and peddlers who went from rags to riches through sheer
pluck and determination.

AN ASPIRATIONAL BRAND

The vast majority of Americans living today are either the descendants
of immigrants or immigrants themselves. Franklin Delano Roosevelt
reportedly once started a speech to the Daughters of the American
Revolution by saying, "My fellow immigrants . . ."[14] In fact, according
to the Census Bureau, nearly 12.4 percent of the U.S. population is
foreign-born.[15] That's higher than any nation but Australia (22 percent) and Canada (19 percent),[16] but greater in absolute terms—some
36 million people—than either country's total population.[17] Until the
Second World War, the foreign-born population of the United States
was seldom less than 13 percent.[18] That long history of immigration
makes America the original aspirational brand. And it also helps explain aspects of the American personality that even its closest allies
sometimes find frustrating. Almost by definition, immigrants are restless. They have a sense that things can be better and they're willing to
accept deep sacrifices to improve their lot.

But it was 1930 before anyone gave the dream a name. Historian
James Truslow Adams coined the expression "the American Dream"
and first used it in his book *The Epic of America*. He wrote:

> The American Dream is of a land in which life should be better and
> richer and fuller for everyone, with opportunity for each according to
> ability or achievement. It is not a dream of motor cars and high wages
> merely, but a dream of social order in which each man and each woman
> shall be able to attain to the fullest stature of which they are innately

capable, and be recognized by others for what they are, regardless of the fortuitous circumstances of birth or position.[19]

At the time Adams wrote those words, America was rapidly industrializing. The railroads had stimulated the development of new markets far from centers of production. A new breed of men personified the American Dream—industrialists like John D. Rockefeller and Andrew Carnegie, who rose from humble circumstances to positions of great wealth and power. During the Great Depression, it seemed to many people that the dream was only an illusion. For some, especially those who were brought to America against their will in the holds of slave ships, the dream was unreachable even when times were good. But it endures as the animating force in American society and its economy, even if for some of its citizens it is still more aspiration than reality.

THE AMERICAN DREAM

More than any other country in the world, America has conflated its political, economic, and social ideals. Nancy Snow, an expert on public diplomacy, characterizes it as marriage of salesmanship and statesmanship. She writes:

> The United States has a one-hundred-year history of marrying commerce with politics and tapping public relations to "brand" America abroad. President Woodrow Wilson told the International Congress of Salesmanship to "go out and sell goods that will make the world more comfortable and more happy, and convert them to the principles of America." That was in 1916.[20]

One of Wilson's successors, President Calvin Coolidge, summed things up in his taciturn way by saying that "the chief business of the American people is business."[21] For its part, American business understood its role. For decades, the IBM building on Madison Avenue in New York City bore a plaque that read: WORLD PEACE THROUGH WORLD TRADE.[22]

Thinkers since de Tocqueville have noted how these essentially mercantile ideals helped shape the American character. Writer John Burton Brimer joked that only an American would attempt to mix fun, prayer, and profit: "America is a place where Jewish merchants sell Zen love beads to agnostics for Christmas,"[23] he wrote. Brian Lamb, the founder of the C-SPAN cable network, has probably interviewed more politicians, historians, and authors than anyone else on television. He has said:

> There are some things that are unusual about the American character that, more than anything, come from the way the country was founded. The free enterprise system where somebody who really wants to get ahead in life . . . can excel, and they don't have to ask permission of anybody in government, or—for that matter—anybody [at all]. . . . The American character more than anything else, I think, comes from this ambition.[24]

But the American Dream has also been criticized by some people who consider it, at best, a cynical illusion created to entertain and distract the lower classes or, at worse, a materialistic nightmare. Philosophers decry the materialism of the American Dream. Economists compute its improbability. Ethicists worry that it gives the rich an excuse to ignore the poor. And at least one European economic research group debunks the whole idea. Jo Blanden, of the Centre for Economic Performance in London, told the BBC that based on her team's statistical analysis, "If you are born into poverty in the U.S., you are actually more likely to remain in poverty than in other countries in Europe, the Nordic countries, even Canada, which you would think would not be that different."[25] And the United Nations Human Development Index, which measures a country's "livability" as a composite of life expectancy, education, and income per person, ranked the United States only tenth in 2005, after Norway, Iceland, Australia, Luxemburg, Canada, Sweden, Switzerland, Ireland, and Belgium.[26]

Foreign governments have also noted the close ties between the U.S. government and American businesses. But Jeffrey Garten, former dean of the school of management at Yale University and undersecretary of commerce for international trade from 1993 to 1995, is unapologetic about "Foreign Policy Inc." He says that throughout most of American history, as in other countries, commercial interests have played a central role in foreign policy, and vice versa. "At one time," he says, "protecting the interests of a company like United Fruit was synonymous with policy toward Latin America."[27] If anything, he believes the collaboration should be even closer. "The connection between American business and foreign policy is poorly thought out and mismanaged, on both sides," he says. "It is, however, vital to the national interest."[28]

In theory, few would disagree. The big difference may lie in America's relative success. As already noted, of the top-100 international brands, sixty-four are American-owned. The five top brands in the 2006 study conducted by the Interbrand consultancy are U.S.-based. They range from Coke and Microsoft (in first and second positions, respectively) to industrial giants IBM, GE, and Intel (in third, fourth, and fifth places). From the perspective of a global customer, the only thing those companies have in common is their "American personality." More significantly, American companies dominate three of the world's most valuable business sectors: entertainment, financial services, and information technologies. That all three play such important roles in the quality of people's lives may account for some of the resentment so many people feel toward America. But it may also represent a point of leverage.

"Give me a lever long enough and a fulcrum on which to place it," Archimedes said, "and I shall move the world." For America, the natural quest to improve the quality of one's life may be that fulcrum. And a partnership between the government and businesses of the United States could be a lever of sufficient length to move the world.

CHAPTER 21

A LEVER TO MOVE THE WORLD

"The single biggest gift that America has shared with the impoverished billions on our planet is hope. America has taught the people of the world that one's fate is not determined at birth."[1]
—Kishore Mahbubani, diplomat and author of *Beyond the Age of Innocence: Rebuilding Trust Between America and the World*

MUCH OF WHAT IS LEFT OF THE UNITED STATES INFORMATION Agency—arguably the country's most cost-effective weapon during the Cold War—is housed in two nondescript government office buildings just across the National Mall from the Smithsonian's world-class collection of historical artifacts. From one of the buildings, erected just before World War II and adorned with art deco touches in its lobby, the Voice of America beams radio and television programs to the rest of the world. From the other much newer building, State Department staffers churn out government information in seven languages and manage cultural and exchange programs.

The nearby museums are an apt setting for communication programs that haven't changed much since the 1950s, except in superficial ways. Government bureaucrats had dismantled the USIA so precipitously, they obliterated the part that was most relevant to the new challenges facing the country—its worldwide network of operatives schooled in the techniques of reading and influencing public opinion—and kept the Washington, D.C.-based broadcasting, information, and exchange services, though at much lower levels than during the Cold War.

Despite its name, the USIA was never, at its heart, a passive purveyor of "information."[2] It certainly performed that role, and admirably, in an era when a good part of the world lived in an information vacuum, deprived of unbiased news about current events. But the USIA was more than a government agency with antennas. It was a global network of foreign service officers who were sufficiently independent from their local ambassadorial clients to give them candid counsel. USIA officers multiplied their effectiveness by recruiting local employees capable of telling America's story in the local language and with sensitivity to local concerns. Their responsibilities went far beyond distributing news releases or implementing headquarters-driven programs. The USIA was specifically charged with ensuring "that our government adequately understands foreign public opinion and culture for policymaking purposes. . . ."[3]

However, when the USIA was "reorganized" in 1998, its various functions were dispersed into different drawers of the U.S. State Department bureaucracy and its charter to contribute to the formulation of foreign policy fell between the cracks.[4]

The theory was to infuse the career foreign service with new skills of public diplomacy, but the reorganization effectively destroyed the capability, as the State Department's old-line bureaucracy reacted as if a troublesome virus had invaded its bloodstream.

"Ironically, both the CIA and the U.S. Foreign Service made the same mistake in the 1990s," according to Helena K. Finn, a Tel Aviv–based senior American diplomat. Just as the intelligence community relied far too heavily on electronically acquired data and too little on what they call "HUMINT" (human intelligence gathered by real, live people), the State Department replaced most of its overseas public diplomacy officers with technology. "As a result," Finn says, "local foreign-newspaper editors critical of U.S. policy no longer get visits from a press attaché, let alone invitations to visit the United States, but instead receive mass-produced e-mail messages assembled thousands of miles away."[5]

RECOMMENDATIONS FOR IMPROVEMENT

The autoimmune reaction did not go unnoticed. By the end of 2005, the State Department had identified twenty-nine different studies designed to restore its capabilities in public diplomacy since the USIA was abolished in 1999.[6] The most striking thing about these reports was that, even though they came from organizations as disparate as the General Accounting Office, the Defense Science Board, the United States Advisory Commission on Public Diplomacy, and the Council on Foreign Relations, they had a unanimous fix on the importance of the issue. They all agreed that current levels of anti-Americanism reflected more than a temporary drop in esteem. They unanimously believed that the stakes involved were more critical than losing a popularity contest. And they did not think the solution lay in glossy ad campaigns, but called for a far more strategic approach.

They even had many of the same recommendations: dramatically increase the budget for public diplomacy, reorganize how it's currently being done, define an overall strategy, and increase the private sector's involvement. The first three recommendations are pretty standard stuff for any quasigovernmental study. Throwing money at a problem is practically a reflex action inside the Beltway, but it clearly makes sense in this case. Even though the State Department's budget for information programs and U.S. international broadcasting has been significantly increased in recent years, it is still only about one-quarter of one percent of the military budget and still less than in the days before the 9/11 attacks. Furthermore, reorganizing the structure of public diplomacy would be obvious to anyone who tried to understand the crazy quilt of overlapping responsibilities in this area that extend from the White House to the Department of State, the U.S. Agency for International Development, and the Pentagon. Defining an overall strategy is equally obvious, if only because of its glaring absence in the mishmash of agencies that think they are responsible for public diplomacy.

Even the notion of involving the private sector seemed to be gathering momentum at the end of 2006. Keith Reinhard, of course, had been trying to drum up interest within the private sector for five years, with varying degrees of success. But if Reinhard's fellow CEOs are reluctant, think-tanks and the foreign affairs establishment seem to be relatively enthusiastic about engaging business people in the public diplomacy effort. Nearly half the studies recommended that businesses be tapped for their expertise. The Council on Foreign Relations even suggested creating a private organization similar to the Corporation for Public Broadcasting as a vehicle for harnessing the private sector's involvement. It's not an entirely unprecedented notion. The Carnegie Endowment for International Peace was originally founded in 1910 on the principle that "government, although representing the will of the people in a mechanical sense, could not possibly give expression to a nation's soul. Only the voluntary, spontaneous activity of the people themselves—as expressed in their art, literature, science, education, and religion—could adequately provide a complete cultural portrait."[7] And the Edward R. Murrow Center's definition of public diplomacy includes "the interaction of private groups and interests in one country with those of another."[8]

CORPORATE DIPLOMACY

Precedent aside, one might be forgiven for asking why business should get involved in the first place. Five reasons suggest themselves. First, as discussed, America's global companies are part of the problem. They have a reputation for practicing a brand of selfish capitalism that the rest of the world deems unseemly at best and inhuman at worst.

Second, if anti-Americanism is allowed to fester, American businesses will eventually pay the price. The United States may command unmatched military power, but anti-Americanism hobbles U.S. efforts to expand global markets and assist American business abroad. Trying to hide a company's American roots is fraught with its own dangers and probably impossible.

Third, unless U.S. businesses get involved, they risk suffering a backlash from the government's own efforts. Tightened immigration laws have already made it more difficult for U.S. businesses to hire foreign-born technical talent, even if the talent was acquired in American universities. Some of the best talent is going to competitors in Asia and Europe.

Fourth, although they're often hammered for focusing on short-term financial results, American businesses are actually more skilled and experienced in making long-term investments, particularly in new markets. Politicians come and go with every election cycle, taking their programs with them. Business can give what will be a generation-long undertaking more continuity than any elected officials can.

Fifth, and perhaps most important, American global companies are in a better position than government to help solve the problem. They have more people in the trenches around the world; they have, for the moment, greater credibility; and politics being what it is, they have greater flexibility. U.S. businesses have enormous power to counter negative sentiments toward their home country—and toward themselves. A week after the Asian tsunami in December 2004, a Global Market Insite poll of 20,000 consumers worldwide found 59 percent so pleased with the relief efforts of American corporations that their impressions of those companies' brands had improved.[9]

Environmentalist Bill Shireman, who has developed a specialty in resolving conflicts between large corporations and what he calls "eco-militants," acknowledges that "the world is demanding a lot of the modern corporation." On the other hand, when a company captures market share, it also captures mind share that can lead to support if a company behaves responsibly. "When the host population perceives a corporation as a good citizen," he says, "it produces collateral benefits for the home country."[10]

From their position on the frontlines of American global influence, corporate executives can help educate U.S. political leaders about global trends and developments that may not wend their way through the government reporting apparatus. Corporate leaders should be more willing to expend their political capital in Washington, advocating a strong role for public diplomacy in the formulation, as well as the explanation, of government actions. And they should commit their businesses to play a significant role in public diplomacy.

This is not a temporary need stemming from the war in Iraq or the war on terror. It reflects a permanent shift in how governments relate to each other. Charles de Gaulle's observation that great powers "have no friends, only interests" is still true. But in a world of instant communications and growing democratization, a government's interests are determined to a greater extent than ever by taking the temperature of public opinion. Helping to inform political leadership's foreign policy choices is not simply a matter of social consciousness or even of patriotism; it is a necessary part of doing business in the twenty-first century.

One needs to be clear, however, on business's role in public diplomacy. It is *not* to insert commercial considerations into the formulation of foreign policy. The nation's elected leaders need to consider a far broader array of interests, and America's security interests trump any commercial considerations. Nor should American businesses be expected to serve as the country's marketing arm. Besides the obvious and inherent conflicts, there has been a serious mismatch between marketing's capabilities and the expectations of some public officials.

Selling Brand America is not as straightforward as selling Uncle Ben's rice. For one thing, if advertising gives someone a craving for Uncle Ben's, she can trot down to the supermarket and buy a box without consulting anyone else. She can make and consume it in the privacy of her home. And if she doesn't like the rice for some reason, she can always switch to another brand, because there are many on the store shelf. Buying into Brand America, on the other hand, is a much more complex act with significant communal implications.

The roots of anti-Americanism are deep, tightly twisted together, and anchored in ideas and emotions that will take generations to dislodge.

INFORMATION AND ENGAGEMENT

Public diplomacy involves two kinds of activities: information and engagement. Information is one-way and task-oriented—for example, communicating a policy, helping people understand it, correcting misinformation, debating opponents, and in some cases, discrediting them. But public diplomacy is not like a political campaign, where negative ads can leave an opponent curled by the side of the road in a fetal position. And while a sufficiently strong and determined message *meister* can impose some measure of message discipline, no one can control its meaning. Twenty-four-hour satellite television, talk radio, podcasts, e-mail, blogs, instant messaging, and chat rooms interpret events and "official statements" in real time. Every message has pragmatic, as well as semantic, meaning. There will be as much chatter about *why* a message is issued as what it literally says. All the cleverest spin doctor can do is run to catch up.

There is nothing wrong with vigorous advocacy. It's an essential element of public diplomacy, but we should be aware of its limitations: It seldom changes minds, usually invites greater scrutiny, and often mobilizes opponents more forcefully than allies. It is essentially one-way communication, closed-ended by design. It isn't considered successful until the recipient stops asking questions and accepts delivery of the message.

Politicians—perhaps influenced by the searing experience of their own election campaigns—are in love with "messaging" and the tools of information dissemination. Many ascribe almost magical powers to them.

The solution to anti-Americanism is not a matter of better information. Lots of information is loose in the world; people are bombarded by it. Even in the most restrictive Muslim countries, people have easy access to television broadcasts from America and around the globe. During the Iraq War, falafel vendors in Syria reportedly switched between CNN, Al Jazeera, and Fox News for the latest reports from the battle zone. As former ambassador Joseph Nye has pointed out, the challenge today is not the dissemination of information, it is the winning of attention. And that, in turn, requires a keen understanding of what Nye calls "the cultural filters that affect how others hear U.S. messages."[11]

At times, it will be clear that those filters are so thick, so caked with prior disappointment, that the government would be better served communicating through others, such as nongovernmental organizations (NGOs) and other third parties with greater credibility. In fact, American businesses should insist that, as part of its engagement strategy, the United States should make it a high priority to protect members of the so-called "civil society" (i.e., NGOs, nonprofits, labor unions, business associations, etc.) from crackdowns, especially by governments that are American allies. Such actions would say more about U.S. support for democratic institutions than any number of news releases or speeches. And supporting local press freedoms would do far more good than adding another television station.

The most powerful tools of public diplomacy have been tools of engagement—a two-way conversation that is open-ended by design. For example, educational and cultural exchanges build mutual trust and understanding over time. They take longer, but their effect is deeper. The fast media of radio and television may grant a temporary unilateral advantage in a controversy, but these effects are fleeting and easily displaced. Long-term problems demand long-term solutions.

ENGAGEMENT

The United States needs to engage directly with the people of other countries on a deeply personal level. A one-size-fits-all strategy won't work. The Islamic world, for example, which seems so monolithic to

Americans, is actually very diverse, spreading across Eastern Europe, the Balkans, the Middle East, most of Asia (including parts of Russia and China), most of sub-Saharan Africa, parts of Latin and Central America, and of course, the United States and Western Europe. Muslims, in fact, are the majority in fifty-two nations and speak more than sixty languages. They share the same religious beliefs, but they have different histories, standards of living, cultures, and attitudes toward the United States. No single ad campaign or broadcast is going to be meaningful to all those people. The Voice of America and its offshoots already speak to them in their own languages with little apparent effect. But if America is to help Islam enter the modern world, which is the only long-term solution to radical Islamic terrorism, it must engage with its adherents at a deeper level.

America has a long history of such engagements, though they have received relatively little funding—and even less attention—in recent years. Since World War II, the U.S. government has sponsored exchange programs that have enabled more than 700,000 men and women from the United States and other countries to observe each other's political, economic, and cultural institutions. U.N. Secretary General Kofi Annan, U.K. Prime Minister Tony Blair, Afghan President Hamid Karzai, Egyptian President Anwar Sadat, German Chancellor Helmut Schmidt, Lady Margaret Thatcher, and many other leaders in public affairs and business participated in these exchanges when they were young students.

American cultural centers in many countries served as local front doors to America. They stocked American magazines and books, showed American films, maintained files on all manner of Americana, mounted exhibitions, and scheduled lectures by visiting American celebrities. Today, most of those centers have been shuttered. Though *Amerika Haus* in Berlin has never been officially closed, its entrance is locked and it's surrounded by a chain link fence. A rusted sign directs all visitors to the American embassy, where you had better have an appointment if you want to get as far as the metal detectors. In Paris, the same fate befell *Le Centre Culturel Américain* (The American Cultural Center), a striking concrete and glass structure designed by Frank Gehry & Associates on the edge of Parc de Bercy, a hip new area filled with restaurants and shops. Abandoned for nearly a decade, the French government eventually took over the privately owned building and, since September 2005, it has housed *La Cinémathèque Française* (The French Cinematic Society).

AMERICAN CORNERS

Most of the larger cultural centers and libraries run by the USIA were closed when the agency was disbanded in 1999. And given heightened security concerns at all U.S. installations overseas, the State Department is not inclined to reopen any large facilities outside embassy walls. But resourceful embassy staffs have scratched together enough money to open 257 "American Corners" across Eastern Europe, the Middle East, Africa, and Asia. Most of the American Corners are literally that—simply a desk, a couple of computers with Internet access, and shelves of books tucked into a corner of donated space in a university library. The American Corner at the newly accredited American University of Kuwait, for example, is on the second floor of the school's library. It has around 200 books on American subjects ranging from *Film Posters of the 1980s* to law and history tomes. A few comfortable chairs define a reading area and the sole staff member, a bilingual university employee, was trained by embassy staff to help visitors find answers to their questions about the United States.

The first American Corner was opened in Russia in October 2000, and the idea spread rapidly to embassies around the world, especially after Undersecretary Charlotte Beers discovered and championed it. The concept is relatively inexpensive. Some embassies even enlist corporate and individual donations to defray the cost of buying books and equipment; the host institution—usually a public library, school, or local chamber of commerce office—provides the space and the staff. American Corners have hosted speakers, workshops, American film series, and English classes in convenient and relatively secure facilities.

CULTURE VULTURES

At the height of the Cold War, the United States government sponsored world tours for many prominent American performers and artists such as jazz great Dizzy Gillespie and choreographer Martha Graham. From 1963 up to his death in 1974, for example, Duke Ellington was practically an adjunct employee of the State Department, traveling to the Soviet Union, Africa (three times), South America, and Asia (multiple trips). When Ellington demanded that the public clamoring outside the concert hall in Moscow be allowed in, he spoke more loudly about American concepts of equality than any political speech might have. But as electronic media brought more of these performances into people's homes and American popular culture became globally ubiquitous, there seemed to be less reason for government sponsorship of such "cultural ambassadors." (The discovery in the late 1960s that many of the cultural programs were being secretly funded by the Central Intelligence Agency may have also dimmed their allure.)

That view may prove as short-sighted as the decision to disband the USIA itself. As Cynthia Schneider, former ambassador to the Netherlands, has observed, "Cultural diplomacy in all its variety provides a critical, maybe even the best, tool to communicate the intangibles that make America great: individual freedoms; justice and opportunity for all; diversity and tolerance."[12] Well-considered cultural events can celebrate what two nations have in common, as well as highlight cherished American values. Ambassador Schneider, for example, made a lasting impression on the Dutch when she invited local officials and their spouses to join her at a late-afternoon matinee of the film *Saving Private Ryan,* followed by dinner and discussion. She says:

> Viewing the movie together sparked a discussion that was unforgettable in its honesty. Moved by the film's unflinching portrayal of war, Dutch and Americans, husbands and wives shared opinions on the meaning of the military today, on whether they wanted their children to join, on the nature of authority in the military, and on other topics.[13]

The close relations forged through that experience enabled Schneider to cut through endless red tape in her dealings with officials in The Hague.

It might be argued that the world has plenty of access to American culture—arguably too *much* access. For some, American culture is like a giant tsunami washing away everything in its path. But because that wave consists primarily of mass-market, popular entertainment, the world tends to equate America with violence and pornography and knows relatively little else about America's real culture. So there's a special need to expose the world to America's more serious, but not necessarily solemn, arts and culture, with special attention to works that would appeal to Muslim audiences, especially the young. In fact, the government—or some enlightened corporate sponsors—would be smart to underwrite the translation of great American novels and plays into languages such as Arabic and Chinese. No more than 10,000 foreign books have been translated into Arabic in the past thousand years—about the same number translated into Spanish annually.[14]

Reading *Death of a Salesman* or *Our Town* would not give Arab or Chinese youth a sanitized view of America, but it would give them a firsthand demonstration of the country's values, hopes, and dreams. "When the United States is criticized for its arrogance, self-criticism might be one of our most effective weapons," writes Ambassador Schneider. "American arts and culture abound in thoughtful analyses of myriad aspects of our society."[15] She goes on to suggest stocking embassy libraries with films such as *Glory* or *Gettysburg* that reveal aspects of American history and values. Or *My Big Fat Greek Wedding* to illustrate American diversity. Or *Field of Dreams* and *Annie* to demonstrate America's boundless optimism.

And corporate sponsors would also be smart to partner with the State Department's Bureau of Educational and Cultural Affairs, which sends such artists as Yo-Yo Ma, Denyce Graves, Wynton Marsalis, and Frank McCourt as "cultural ambassadors" to youth audiences around the world. Partnerships with American businesses, as well as schools, foundations, and local governments, have accounted for more than a third of its $500 million annual budget in recent years.

LANGUAGE TRAINING

But if someone were to conduct a cost-benefit analysis of all the programs the United States could undertake in the international arena, one would stand out both for its simplicity and long-term return: language training. "A substantial increase in funding for English-language training abroad may be the most valuable marginal dollar that could be spent for public diplomacy,"[16] according to a State Department Advisory Committee on International Economic Policy. A working knowledge of English would give young people around the world a "portal to globalization" that would greatly increase America's chances to be heard.

Similarly, America has no hope of understanding or reaching the people of other countries if it must always do it through interpreters. At the end of 2005, there were an estimated 279 Arabic speakers in the U.S. Foreign Service, only about fifty-seven of whom were fluent and only five who were capable of representing the United States on Al Jazeera's Arabic television service. The situation is probably similar in other non-Western languages.

America's public diplomacy will not be fully capable until it is staffed by a core of foreign service officers who can speak the languages of the countries they are assigned to. The beauty of speaking another person's language is not so much that you can be heard, but that you can listen and understand, which can inform your actions. And that is the clearest language of all.

SHARING BRAND VALUES

In an ideal world, both the government's information and engagement strategies would support the same overall message and communicate the same core brand values. Brand values are more than advertising or packaging. They are the "essence" of a product, what it means to consumers at a deeply emotional level. Corporations make heavy investments in communicating those values, not only through their formal communications, but through every interaction with consumers in a virtuous circle of values, actions, presence, involvement, dialogue, relationship, and experience. Successful companies "live their brands" and do whatever is necessary to protect them.

Many corporate executives feel their control of brand values is constantly under attack and they are just one misstep away from the graveyard of fallen brands. But, by comparison with government, they have near total command of their brand's meaning. The United States cannot control its image simply because so many independent actors influence it, from Hollywood to Wall Street to Guantánamo Bay, Bill Gates to Madonna, Wal-Mart to Enron. America's image emerges from this potent mix of contradictory influences, as well as from its own actions.

Brand America's strength depends on its physical and psychic presence in a country. "A country that is exposed to only Hollywood violent movies and video games is likely to have a distorted image of the USA," observed N. D. Batra, a professor of communications, writing in *The Statesman* of India. "But add to it a McDonald's, university campus, cultural centre, and a garment factory; you see the image of the USA in that country begins to change."[17] Unfortunately, America's image changes even more rapidly when stories of political corruption, corporate malfeasance, and the human cost of U.S.-led wars are added to the mix.

But if America does not control all the forces influencing its brand image, it has more alternatives than trying to outshout its opponents or giving up in frustration. As in any successful political or marketing campaign, if the messages and actions the United States *does* control are grounded in consistent brand values, over time "living the brand" will win out. Of course, that requires a level of strategic agreement and concerted action few countries can muster except in times of war. America had such a moment in the days immediately after the attacks of September 11, but it dissolved in the acrimony leading up to the war in Iraq. "Although the U.S. has massive promotional power and influence," notes brand expert Wally Olins, "it has never attempted to project a clear coordinated idea of itself, either domestically or externally."[18]

And that's why most prescriptions for fixing what ails Brand America peter off in generalities and pleasantries. It's one thing to say McDonald's stands for "food, family, and fun," and entirely another to speak so definitively about a country as multifaceted and complex as America. Furthermore, rebuilding Brand America is a generational proposition, far beyond the tenure of most public officials. For all these reasons, the search for Brand America needs to be the product of a rigorous debate between key players in the public and private sectors.

CHAPTER 22

WAGING PEACE

"I view my job as waging peace."[1]
—Karen Hughes, undersecretary of state for public diplomacy and public affairs

KAREN HUGHES LOST THE LAST VESTIGES OF ANONYMITY WHEN she became undersecretary of state for public diplomacy and public affairs in September 2005.

"I was with my husband and son on an elevator—deep and crowded," she has told friends. "Finally, two elderly ladies got on— one looked at me, looked away, looked again, elbowed her friend, and said in a loud stage whisper: 'Condi Rice is on this elevator.'"

Nearly six feet tall in flats, with thick silvery hair and bright blue eyes, Hughes could hardly be mistaken for the first African American woman to be secretary of state. But it's not hard to understand why Hughes attracts attention—she has one of the toughest jobs in Washington, the moral equivalent of the hard combat being directed from the Pentagon. She calls her job "waging peace," by which she means that the war on terrorism will not be won by force of arms alone, but in the battle for people's minds and hearts.

That battle is more than metaphorical. America has always stood for something more than a particular place, nation, or state. From the very beginning, America was presented to the world as an ideal. The Declaration of Independence not only put King George on notice, it was a message to the whole world that something new was afoot in the affairs of man. For nearly two and a half centuries, America's core ideal—the prospect of limitless possibilities—attracted people of all classes, religions, and ethnicities to its shores and nourished the hopes of those left behind.

Those hopes are still meaningful to Japanese salarymen riding the bullet train home, to call center operators in Bangalore beginning an overnight shift, to Peruvian farmhands coaxing potatoes out of the rocky Andean soil, and to the sanitation people who spray down the streets of Paris before dawn every morning. People around the world want to improve their lot in life, they want their children to have an easier life than they did.

THE UPWARDLY MOBILE

Research shows that the upwardly mobile segment of nearly every society has the most favorable impression of the United States. They consider it a nation that stands for personal opportunity based on the mutually regulating values of individual liberty and respect for others. The other values that many people associate with America—for example, individual initiative, self-expression, innovation, ambition, entrepreneurship, freedom of speech, and competition—could be seen as either the means or the result of giving people the opportunity to improve their lives.

The upwardly mobile are not only the likeliest to admire America; they are also most likely to persuade others if given the opportunity. In addition to this global constituency, America has a receptive audience among the so-called "secularists" of the Muslim world—business people, scientists, educators, public officials, musicians, artists, poets, writers, journalists, actors, and their audiences and admirers. These are powerful constituencies who, like the upwardly mobile, are receptive to values of personal opportunity, individual liberty, and respect for others. The French foreign minister who tagged America a "hyperpower" admits that he based his assessment at least in part on America's ability "to inspire the dreams and desires of others."[2]

That's not a bad place to start in defining Brand America. But it won't happen by news release or presidential directive. Government policies and programs must demonstrate those brand values. For example, the U.S. Agency for International Development empowers other countries to increase opportunities for their citizens within the framework of their own political and social systems. Dozens of domestic programs—from federal Pell educational grants to Small Business Administration loans to equal opportunity statutes—represent government action to spread opportunity. The key is that people in the United States and abroad need to experience Brand America rather than just read about it. And every group needs to be addressed differently because they all have different perceptions of America and different expectations.

That's why the United States has to do a better job of gathering real-time intelligence on the state of public opinion in other countries, not only regarding their attitudes toward the United States, but in terms of their personal fears, hopes, and aspirations. Such research would help the State Department better understand not only where the United States is disliked most, but what the trends are, where the next hot spots are likely to be, and most important, what elements within even the most negative countries can be counted on for support. The United States needs an independent center to conduct public opinion research and to share its analysis with all government agencies with responsibility for public diplomacy and the formulation of foreign policy. Expert opinions collected by the Government Accountability Office suggest the federal government should spend $30 million to $50 million on such research.[3] An increase of that scale should be accompanied by the amendment or repeal of the Smith-Mundt Act, which currently restricts the dissemination of such information.

BRAND AMERICA

America's brand is not a slogan or an advertising campaign. It is a cogent, succinct statement of what America should mean to those of us who live in the United States and to people around the world. It should strike a responsive chord with those who call themselves Americans and those America would influence. Advertising, if it is ever launched, would be designed to reinforce the concrete actions taken by the public and private sectors to demonstrate America's brand values, not to communicate the values themselves. In many ways, many of those concrete actions are already under way, though in such a scattered and incoherent fashion that the initiatives often cancel each other out.

For example, the president's 2007 budget includes $9.3 billion for development and humanitarian assistance administered by the U.S. Agency for International Development. As a concrete expression of America's commitment to personal opportunity based on liberty and respect for others, it represents a strategic branding opportunity. But recent USAID efforts to gain publicity for overseas programs, while commendable, have been uncoordinated and are not aligned with a more comprehensive public diplomacy strategy. Secretary of State Condoleezza Rice has taken steps to correct this by giving the administrator of the USAID a "second hat" as director of foreign assistance within the State Department itself. But much more needs to be done to make foreign aid an effective tool of public diplomacy.

FAULT LINES

One of the most far-reaching conclusions reached by the 9/11 Commission is that "in the post-9/11 world, threats are defined more by the fault lines within societies than by the territorial boundaries between them."[4] For the first time in recent history, those fault lines are not primarily between the rich and poor or the educated and the illiterate. Islamist terrorists, for example, find willing recruits among well-educated Arab youth because few Muslim democracies give them alternative models for the future. The role of corporate and public diplomacy is to provide those alternatives. Corporations do so not only through the exercise of social responsibility, but by supporting civil society, providing jobs, promoting entrepreneurship, and contributing to the development of vibrant local economies. The U.S. government does so not only through its rhetoric, but by targeting its influence and its aid to the development of free and open societies.

For example, many people believe Muslim religious schools, or madrasahs, are training grounds for terrorists. In reality, more known Islamic terrorists have attended Western universities than madrasahs, but even allowing that some Muslim religious schools are run by radical Islamists, most of them are the equivalent of strict Catholic schools of the 1950s. For many young Muslim youth, they may be the only path to literacy. For the poor, they are social service agencies. And for U.S. policymakers, according to British diplomat Alexander Evans, "the vast majority of madrasahs present an opportunity, not a threat."[5] A policy of engagement with the madrasahs of the Muslim world represents a chance to ensure that tomorrow's Muslim leaders don't see the West as an enemy.

The American government and business community should also remember that there is a large and growing community of Muslims outside the Middle East, not only in Asia and Africa, but in Europe. European Muslims, in particular, are an increasingly alienated diaspora that have yet to be assimilated by their new communities. Young Muslim men, in particular, are two or three times as likely to be unemployed as other young people, making them prime prospects for radicalization. To date, European authorities have been unsuccessful in integrating their Muslim communities. The United States cannot afford hopeful watching. It must engage moderate forces within the Muslim community in a generational battle for mutual understanding. Countering Islamic terrorism will only succeed if it is built on empowering nonviolent moderates, isolating the terrorists. America's strongest ally in that effort could be the Islamic community in the United States; in fact, groups such as the Islamic Society of North America have organized internships and scholarships for Muslim imams, teachers, and students. American businesses should support such programs.

But neither American businesses nor the government should limit their efforts to the Muslim world, simply because that's where the current crisis is. They should make targeted investments in the next fronts of the anti-Americanism struggle. American companies doing business in Africa could contribute to the development of a strong middle class in sub-Saharan countries by investing in higher education there. Not counting South Africa, sub-Saharan Africa has one-tenth of the world's population but only a dozen small, high-quality business schools and they can't supply a fraction of the skilled staff that local businesses, governments, or nongovernmental organizations (NGOs) need. Four of the largest U.S. foundations—Ford, Rockefeller, MacArthur, and Carnegie—have started the Partnership for Higher Education in Africa. The World Bank founded the Global Business School Network to help develop African management schools. And twenty-two of the schools themselves have formed an association to draw potential donors' attention to the importance of management education in Africa's development.

THE ROLE OF BUSINESS

Corporations cannot afford to be simply followers or observers in the process of rebuilding Brand America. Doing business globally in the twenty-first century requires skills in corporate diplomacy equal to those in finance and marketing. Global leaders sink roots wherever they do business, sharing their customers' cares and their dreams. In addition to following the best practices of successful global brands, corporate leaders need to find ways to create better understanding between the business communities of different countries, perhaps through employee exchange programs with foreign customers and suppliers, U.S. internships for promising foreign students, or more active participation in overseas business associations and chambers of commerce.

But the most significant contribution that U.S.-based corporations can make to rebuilding Brand America is to become the domestic constituency for America's public diplomacy. Given that the future of their companies depends on its success, they should be a demanding, as well as supportive, constituency.

Just as America's most successful corporations have learned that public relations is more about what a company *does* than what it says, public diplomacy is not a substitute for good policy or for constructive engagement with the global community. Corporate leaders need to convince America's political leaders that talking about freedom, democracy, and opportunity is not nearly as credible or powerful as taking concrete actions to make those values a reality for people around the world. Public diplomacy is only effective when it complements a country's policies and actions.

Even then, America will be fighting an uphill battle to reverse the cumulative impact of the Iraq War, controversy about the detention of enemy combatants, graphic photos of prisoner abuse at Abu Ghraib, debates about the use of torture, and stories of innocent citizens of other countries being whisked off the street by the CIA in a policy of "rendition"—all of which reinforce the belief that the United States considers itself above generally expected standards of behavior. Changing perceptions of American exceptionalism may take a series of dramatic gestures, such as joining the Kyoto Protocol on global warming or ratifying the treaties banning land mines and creating an International Criminal Court. Something equally unexpected is necessary for America to reclaim what foreign policy expert Julia Sweig perceptively noted it has lost: "the intangible resource [the United States] had cultivated in the twentieth century—the benefit of the doubt."[6] Once lost, trust is exceedingly difficult to restore.

ACTION PLAN

As a practical matter, such a grand gesture may have to await a change in administration. Meanwhile, Corporate America should ensure that America's public diplomacy capabilities are realigned and reinvigorated. There have been so many reports on what needs to be done (and so many of the recommendations are so consistent) that the government knows what to do. It simply needs the prodding to do it and some helpful blocking and tackling when the inevitable special interests come onto the field. Existing business organizations, such as Business for Diplomatic Action, the Business Roundtable, and the Business Council, should use their lobbying muscle to support ten key reforms:

1. Amend U.S. visa policies and immigration procedures to make America more welcoming to foreign students, workers, and visitors.

2. Expand educational and cultural exchanges in countries where perceptions of America are most poor.

3. Increase language training, both in English as a second language abroad and in key foreign languages within the United States.

4. Expand the innovative American Corners concept overseas.

5. Field more extensive public opinion research in other countries and improve real-time analysis.

6. Repeal or amend the Smith-Mundt Act to allow the sharing of information acquired abroad across government agencies.

7. Reorganize all government-sponsored international broadcasting to ensure it is part of the public diplomacy effort.

8. Recruit, train, and deploy more experts in public diplomacy and more commercial officers attuned to the needs of American business.

9. Create a foreign service officer "reserve corps" of academics and business people with specialized expertise who could accept short-term assignments abroad.

10. Develop a single comprehensive strategy to drive all America's relations with foreign publics.

This last recommendation is so sweeping it deserves some elaboration. At one level, public diplomacy is just one arrow in a bulging quiver the United States can use to influence other countries, including foreign aid, trade negotiations, government-to-government diplomacy, and—in exigent circumstances—military action. But on a more meaningful level, public diplomacy cuts across all the other instruments of statecraft because it provides the strategic logic that ties them to the nation's interests and values. That strategic logic is what marketers would call America's "Brand Strategy." It is more than a "message theme" or a simple alignment of goals and methods. It is a defining, coherent statement of what America means within the context of its values and the day's overarching issues, from nuclear proliferation and terrorism to famine and genocide.

The implementation of such a brand strategy should likewise cut across organizational stovepipes. Whoever is entrusted with responsibility for America's public diplomacy needs more than the coordinating power of an air traffic controller. He or she should have the authority to assign tasks and compel outcomes across the government bureaucracy. For that reason, corporate leaders should insist that America's public diplomacy be led by a person with sufficient credibility to counsel the president of the United States and command the respect of his most trusted advisers.

Someone, in Edward R. Murrow's words, who would be in on the "take-offs" of public policy decisions, not just the "crash landings."[7] Unless America's public diplomacy is in the hands of such a person, it will forever be on the sidelines of foreign policy formulation rather than in the huddles where the plays are called. Without strong leadership, the piece parts of public diplomacy will never be brought together under a single strategy that can be modulated to the specific needs of different global audiences, not only in words but in actions.

The issue is not simply to ensure that someone is thinking of how to "sell" policy while it is being formulated, but someone who can weigh in from the very beginning to ensure that U.S. policies take into account the values and interests of others, not just Americans.

KAREN HUGHES

In some quarters, Karen Hughes was a controversial choice to assume such a position. Foggy Bottom regulars worried that she lacked international experience and the hard-to-define quality of "gravitas" that diplomats value so highly. Hughes's staunchest supporters had to concede as much. She started her career as a local television reporter in Texas, moved into George Bush's orbit as campaign spokesperson when he ran for governor of the state, and followed him to Washington as a communications counselor when he was elected president. She likes to describe herself as a "working mom." And, in fact, she took leave of the White House to return to Texas so her only son could complete high school there, returning only when he left for college.

The Washington Post characterized the job that drew her back to Washington as "the least noticed, least respected, and most important job in the State Department."[8] Some people worried that she still had the instincts of a political operative, reflexively protective of her candidate's reputation above all else. In fact, some assumed she had been put in her position to protect Bush's legacy more than to restore America's reputation. They assumed she would follow the familiar playbook of political campaign operatives by focusing everyone on a positive message rather than dealing with the long-term implications of anti-Americanism.

A memo she sent to chiefs of mission, deputy chiefs of mission, and public affairs officers at U.S. embassies around the world in early 2006 found its way into the gossipy blogs that have sprouted around Washington. It outlined what she called "Karen's Rules" on dealing with the media and seemed to confirm her critics' worse fears.

Karen's Rule No. 1: "Think advocacy. I want all of you to think of yourselves as advocates for America's story each day. My Echo Chamber messages are meant to provide you clear talking points in a conversational format on the 'hot' issues of the day."[9]

Time would demonstrate that the memo was only part of a multifaceted effort to improve America's public diplomacy. Letting it define Hughes's approach to the job was as unfair as characterizing Charlotte Beers as an "ad gal."

WAGING PEACE

Hughes's lack of passport stamps and bylines in *Foreign Affairs* appears to be outweighed by her closeness to the country's brand manager in chief. During President Bush's first term, people inside the Beltway claimed that when he spoke in public, Karen Hughes's lips moved. She wrote his autobiography. She hired and fired his spokespeople. She shaped his words and message. One senior member of the White House staff was even moved to say: "She knows how he talks, but also how he thinks. It's like they're one person. She can literally manufacture him. The only one who can do it. Over time, people have understood that if you have an idea, a proposal, Karen better like it or it won't have a chance in any event."[10]

Few other people could have convinced the president of the United States to invite half a dozen CEOs to drop by the Oval Office so that he could personally invite them to accompany Hughes on a survey of the earthquake devastation in Pakistan in 2005. She did, and she followed that up with similar invitations to have corporate executives accompany her on a tour of the far less publicized mud slides in Guatemala. Both trips not only demonstrated the softer, caring side of U.S. businesses to skeptical foreign publics, but moved the companies themselves into closer partnership with the government's aid efforts. Following visits to the disaster sites, major corporations such as Pfizer, Citigroup, Xerox, GE, UPS, PepsiCo, John Deere, American Electric Power, and Asset Management Advisors have raised more than $100 million to help victims of Pakistan's earthquake and the flooding in Central America.

Hughes has also demonstrated a refreshing openness to the opinions of others. She even seems open to one of the more controversial recommendations made to improve public diplomacy—creating a private foundation to strengthen the U.S. State Department's partnership with the private sector. She has a working team looking at the idea and has even begun brainstorming projects from "producing quality television programming" to "translating great works of literature."[11]

Meanwhile, Hughes has managed to sidestep the hurdles that entangled her predecessors and even has some Beltway cynics reconsidering their initial assessment. She's putting money behind programs with proven track records and the greatest leverage for altering long-term perceptions of America. For example, in a difficult budget environment, she increased funding for exchanges and language training by $48 million in 2007, on top of a $70 million increase in 2006. She's unleashed people in the field, scrapping rules requiring preclearance from Washington before an ambassador or foreign service officer could do media interviews. As a result, U.S. representatives made 148 appearances on Arab and regional media in the first two months of 2006 alone, many of them addressing their audience in Arabic.

She's won a place for public diplomacy at the policy-setting table. Hughes and members of her senior staff now attend the secretary of state's senior policy meetings. Perhaps even more significantly, she put new deputy assistant secretaries for public diplomacy in each of the six regional bureaus[12] where a lot of policy originates. They report both to the regional assistant secretary and to her, actually knitting together policy and public diplomacy.

She is engaging business and civic leaders. For example, she brought the leading American university presidents together in Washington for the first time and convinced them to work with the Commerce Department to better market American higher education to students around the world. She sponsored a program to bring women business leaders from around the world to America to work with women at Fortune 500 companies. She encouraged the Aspen Institute to bring international journalists to the United States for work-study programs.

Hughes has accomplished a lot in a relatively short time despite the skepticism—and even cynicism—expressed by some. She also seems to be focused on the right problems. In her own words, "we must offer people throughout the world a positive vision of hope that is rooted in America's belief in freedom, justice, opportunity, and respect for all."[13] Assuming she stays in office until President Bush completes his second term, Corporate America may have less than a year to ensure that the progress she has made is institutionalized and that her successor builds on the foundation she has set. It's not time to be wasted.

CODA

THE LAST THREE FEET

"It has always seemed to me the real art in this business is not so much moving information five or ten thousand miles. That is an electronic problem. The real art is to move it the last three feet in face-to-face conversation."[1]

—Edward R. Murrow

BY THE BEGINNING OF 2006, KEITH REINHARD HAD PROMOTED Business for Diplomatic Action by appearing on everything from the BBC to *The Daily Show with Jon Stewart* on the Comedy Central cable network. It had taken him ten years to break into advertising and now, at age 71, it looked as if it would take him at least that long to get the right people to do something about America's declining reputation around the world.

The average American was still oblivious to the issue, but American business leaders were beginning to pay more attention. Executives from Microsoft, ExxonMobil, and Weyerhaeuser joined McDonald's on the board of Business for Diplomatic Action. Other major companies were considering membership. And a trip Reinhard took to Dubai had drummed up interest in an internship program for young Arab business students in American companies. The program would start small, focusing on well-vetted individuals who admittedly might have won positions on their own; even so, the path to engaging Arab youth "in the street" was getting clearer. Reinhard's vision of "outrecruiting bin Laden" might not be a pipedream, after all.

Following a media analysis of newspaper editorials published across Europe, Reinhard decided to focus his group's efforts on Germany, where anti-Americanism is just as pronounced as in France, but the local business community seems to be more interested in healing the breach. Of twenty-seven editorials analyzed in German newspapers, only two were positive. At first, Reinhard said that's simply in the nature of editorials. "No one writes about planes that land safely," he said. "Of course, they're going to focus on problems." But then his team showed him an equal number of German newspaper editorials about China. They were uniformly positive. At the beginning of 2006, Business for Diplomatic Action was designing its first pilot project directed at a foreign audience by building stronger relationships with U.S.-based German reporters. Reinhard's short-term goal was to get them to write feature stories about America that go behind the headlines of the day.

Reinhard was even cautiously talking about advertising, but not ads directed at foreign audiences to convince them we're nice people, he was always quick to say. What he had in mind was advertising that would sensitize Americans themselves to how the country—and they—are perceived around the world. Simon Anholt, the acknowledged master of place branding and a member of Business for Diplomatic Action's advisory council, has an interesting twist on the intersection of branding and public diplomacy. "The term 'public diplomacy' is closer in meaning to nation branding," he wrote, "if the word 'public' is applied to the messenger as well as the audience."[2]

In other words, efforts to counter anti-Americanism need to involve the American public before they can rise above the level of promotion and rebuttal. Just as companies have to "live their brand" to be credible and relevant, the people of the United States need to understand and reflect Brand America—the combination of liberty and respect for others—in all their dealings with the people of the world.

The toughest part isn't teaching Americans to be nicer—often that's as simple as showing them how they're perceived. Once they know that they're considered "loud," for example, most people quiet down, though they might grumble about it. Reinhard's group had already developed highly successful travel guides for college students and business travelers that were making a difference in Americans' behavior abroad, despite snickers from some quarters that they reflected the Emily Post brand of public diplomacy. Business for Diplomatic Action had even been asked to develop an intensive one-day training program for business people new to the global marketplace.

The bigger problem is agreeing on the core message that everyone is supposed to reflect. Every ad agency has a different process for developing this message or brand concept. Reinhard calls his a "foundation process." It starts with an in-depth analysis of everything known about the brand and its users. Then all that research and analysis is turned over to a group of knowledgeable people with a stake in the outcome, and they're locked away to hash over it for a couple of days with some specially trained facilitators.

What usually comes out of the process is what's known as a "positioning concept," a highly specific distillation of how you want people to think and feel about your brand compared to its alternatives. Often, a positioning concept can be expressed as the right combination of three Ps: a point of view, a promise, and a personality.

Jack Trout, who probably did more than anyone to popularize the notion of positioning, says that America's current positioning is terrible. "America had one idea attached to its brand," he wrote. "We presented ourselves as the world's first superpower. And that was the world's worst branding idea."[3] Reinhard thought America could do better, and in late 2005, he and the Travel Industry Association of America gathered a high-powered group of people together to develop a positioning strategy for "Destination USA," which would be a subset of the larger idea of Brand America.

He turned the positioning idea over to a group of advertising students at Virginia Commonwealth University and charged them with developing a Destination USA ad campaign under the direction of Rick Boyko, one of the ad industry's top creative directors. Lacking a client who can speak for Brand America as a whole, Reinhard has settled for the travel industry, which has been hit most dramatically by the rise in anti-Americanism. In fact, one of his new goals is to get foreign tourism back to pre-9/11 levels. "Do you know the United States is one of the only countries in the world without a minister of tourism?" he asks.

That was the principal issue he brought to his first one-on-one meeting with Karen Hughes, the undersecretary of state for public diplomacy. She was already aware of the economic impact of the decline in U.S. tourism, but she wasn't prepared for the image impact resulting from the inconsiderate way foreign visitors are treated when entering the United States. "Perceptions of American arrogance are simply confirmed and exacerbated by our visa and entry policies," Reinhard told her. When one of Hughes's staffers countered that the situation was getting better, she cut him off, saying "I know we're getting better, but it's still an issue."

Reinhard's pitch was not for more advertising, even though Australia spends more than twelve times as much as the United States to promote itself as a tourist destination. He didn't want to add sizzle to the pan, he wanted to fix the steak. He reasoned it would actually be counterproductive to persuade foreign visitors to come to the United States and then treat them like suspects in a terrorist ring when they got here. It seemed to him that the "three feet" between millions of visitors to the United States and the glass booth of an immigration officer might be the easiest—and most productive—space to bridge.

"A Dutch men's magazine recently ran an article listing fifteen things that are surprisingly complicated," he told Hughes. "Number one on the list is semipornographic, but number six is 'getting into the United States.' "

New rules implemented after the September 11 attacks require almost all nonimmigrant visa applicants to undergo face-to-face interviews, which of course are only held in U.S. embassies or consular offices. The wait for an interview can take from three to five months. People in Russia or Brazil often have to travel six hours just to stand in line for a visa at the U.S. embassy. An orchestra in Manchester, England, would have had to fly all 100 musicians and staff members to the U.S. embassy in London for personal interviews at a cost of $80,000. Instead, they canceled their U.S. tour. Since the fall of 2005, French tourists have had to stand in long lines outside the U.S. embassy and pay more than $100 to get visas because they didn't have passports embedded with electronic chips. In early 2006, British newspapers warned travelers that, because of new U.S. entry rules, they would have to tell the airlines where they would be staying their first night in the country before they could get a boarding pass. And they should expect longer lines at ticket counters as a result.

But in many ways, the worst part of the experience is at America's borders, where jet-lagged visitors are greeted by gun-toting security guards, sniffed by dogs, shuffled into long lines, and cross-examined by someone at a computer terminal who barely looks up except to warily check that the picture on the passport matches the weary face in front of him. "Why can't the government tap the private sector to give the guys in the immigration booths some training in human relations?" Reinhard asked. "And why can't the customs office hire someone to make the country's front parlor more inviting and friendlier?"

A NOTE ABOUT THE ENDNOTES

MOST WRITERS ARE AMBIVALENT ABOUT NOTES. THOSE LITTLE superscript numbers interrupt whatever rhetorical flow a writer can get going. They strike some people as a little pretentious and show-offy, and few readers pay much attention to them. On the other hand, a book such as this was informed by hundreds of sources, and the interested reader deserves to know which ones were the most influential. Some writers stand on the shoulders of giants. I make no such claim. Rather, I have hitchhiked on the backs of such original thinkers as de Tocqueville in the nineteenth century, Walter Lippmann in the twentieth, and Fareed Zakaria and Joseph Nye in the twenty-first. I've credited such sources in the text itself and cited the names of other people and organizations that provided the most insightful contributions. These endnotes expand on those references and also direct interested readers to specific bibliographic information. I've also tried to provide Web addresses for source material whenever possible. But, as most readers know, Internet links can be unreliable and out of date, so I've also indicated when I last accessed the site myself.

Just a few days after his meeting with Hughes, Secretary of State Condoleezza Rice and Secretary of Homeland Security Michael Chertoff jointly announced that Washington-Dulles and Houston international airports would become "model" ports of entry under a pilot U.S. program to present a warmer welcome to foreign visitors who face tighter security following the attacks of September 11, 2001. Reinhard doesn't take the credit—the Travel Industry Association had been hammering on this very issue for years—but Hughes's demeanor in the meeting, and the fact she asked for a follow-up, told him he had struck a nerve.

The model ports of entry program will provide customized video messages, "friendly greeters" to assist travelers entering the United States, and might even include a more welcoming redesign of the immigrations areas. Under the slogan "Secure Borders, Open Doors," Rice and Chertoff said they will create a single, governmentwide resolution process to provide "one-stop shopping" for travelers with complaints about transportation, customs, or State Department screening. Reinhard wasn't even discouraged when he learned the Departments of State and Homeland Security would each assign twenty-two people to the project's steering committee.

"It's a start," Reinhard says.

NOTES

Introduction

1. Ivan Krastev, "The Anti-American Century?" *Journal of Democracy* (April 2004). See www.journalofdemocracy.org/articles/toc/tocapr04.html (last accessed on July 14, 2006).
2. Global Market Insite's 2004 survey of people in twenty countries found that 35 percent say "U.S. foreign policy is the most important factor in formulating their image of America."
3. Nicolas Albanese et al., *Streetwise Italian Dictionary/Thesaurus* (New York: McGraw Hill, 2005).
4. Julianne Malveaux, "The African American Bridge," *USA Today* (January 3, 2003).
5. Kishore Mahbubani, *Beyond the Age of Innocence: Rebuilding Trust Between America and the World* (New York: Perseus, 2005), p. 39.
6. Department of Defense, "Active Duty Military Personnel Strengths by Regional Area and by Country" (309A), June 30, 2005.
7. According to the Federation of American Scientists; see www.fas.org/main/home.jsp.
8. Bernard Chazelle, "Anti-Americanism: A Clinical Study," Princeton University, 2004. See www.cs.princeton.edu/~chazelle/politics/antiam.html (last accessed on July 13, 2006).
9. Francis Fukuyama, *America at the Crossroads* (New Haven, CT: Yale University Press, 2006), p. 103.
10. Tony Judt, *Postwar: A History of Europe Since 1945* (New York: Penguin Press, 2005), p. 353.
11. Political scientist Samuel Huntington coined the phrase "clash of civilizations" in a seminal *Foreign Affairs* magazine article, notable not only for its insight but its predictive accuracy. Written in the summer of 1993, following the collapse of the Soviet Union, Huntington forecast that the cultural gulf between Western Christianity and Islam would be the fault line of conflict in the future. See Samuel Huntington, "The Clash of Civilizations?" *Foreign Affairs* (Summer 1993).
12. Lee Harris, "The Intellectual Origins of America Bashing," *Policy Review* No. 116 (December 2002/January 2003).
13. Joseph S. Nye, Jr. "Bush Can Reverse America's Declining Popularity," *Newsday* (December 22, 2004).
14. "A Major Change of Public Opinion in the Muslim World," a poll commissioned by Terror Free Tomorrow and conducted by the Indonesian Survey Institute February 1–6, 2005. The poll included 1,200 respondents nationwide and had a margin of error of 2.9 percent. See www.terrorfreetomorrow.org/articlenav.php?id = 56 (last accessed on March 15, 2006).

15. Mojo refers to a type of magic charm. The word originated in Africa and entered the English language in the late-nineteenth century or early-twentieth century through use by African Americans. It reflects the belief, common in many cultures, that some people have the ability to influence others to their own advantage, by casting spells.

16. Walter Russell Mean, "Why Do They Hate Us? Two Books Take Aim at Anti-Americanism," *Foreign Affairs* (March–April 2003).

17. Woodrow Wilson first used the term "public diplomacy" in an address to Congress on February 11, 1918, but Edmund Gullion gave it its current meaning. In 1965, Gullion used the term to describe the charter of a new center established at Tufts University to house the papers of Edward R. Murrow, one of the foremost journalists of the twentieth century and director of the United States Information Agency (USIA) under President John F. Kennedy. The USIA embraced both the term and its implicit responsibilities. For other definitions of public diplomacy, see the website of the University of Southern California's Center on Public Diplomacy: www.uscpublicdiplomacy.org/index.php/about/whatis_pd. For a review of the phrase's etymology, see " 'Public Diplomacy' Before Gullion" at www.uscpublicdiplomacy.com/pdfs/gullion.pdf.

Chapter 1

1. Keith Reinhard's testimony before the House Subcommittee on National Security, Emerging Threats, and International Relations, Washington, D.C., August 23, 2004.

2. Author interviews, March 9, 2005, and February 13, 2006.

3. "Selling the Flag," *The Economist* (February 26, 2004).

4. Transcript of Presidential News Conference, October 11, 2001. Available at www.whitehouse.gov/news/releases/2001/10/20011011-7.html (last accessed on March 21, 2006).

5. The original line, which appeared in Robert Burns's poem "To a Louse: On Seeing One on a Lady's Bonnet at Church" (1786), was: "O wad some Power the giftie gie us / To see oursels as ithers see us!"

Chapter 2

1. Richard Holbrooke, "Get the Message Out," *The Washington Post* (October 28, 2001).

2. Congressman Henry Hyde's remarks were delivered at a meeting of the House International Relations Committee, which he chaired, on October 10, 2001.

3. *The Report of the Defense Science Board Task Force on Strategic Communication,* Office of the Undersecretary of Defense for Acquisition, Technology, and Logistics, Washington, D.C., September 2004, p. 24.

4. From the transcript of an informal meeting with the news media while Secretary Rumsfeld was en route to Chile on November 18, 2002. Available at http://www.defenselink.mil/transcripts/2002/t11212002_t1118sd2.html (last accessed on July 13, 2006).

5. David Hoffman, "Beyond Public Diplomacy," *Foreign Affairs* (March–April 2002).

6. Jeff Gerth, "Military's Information War Is Vast and Often Secretive," *The New York Times* (December 11, 2005).

7. Edward R. Murrow addressed these widely quoted words to a congressional committee in May 1963, when he was director of the United States Information Agency.

8. EntertainmentStudios.com interview with Charlotte Beers. See: www.enter tainmentstudios.com/everywoman/index.asp?ID = 1493 (last accessed on July 16, 2006).

9. Secretary of State Colin Powell's remarks were delivered at the NetDiplomacy 2001 Conference, Washington, D.C., September 6, 2001.

10. Alexandra Starr, "Charlotte Beers' Toughest Sell," *BusinessWeek* (December 17, 2001).

11. Frank Rich, "Journal: How to Lose a War," *The New York Times* (October 27, 2001).

12. Comments are from a National Public Radio interview with Charlotte Beers by Bob Garfield, "On the Media," March 26, 2004. A full transcript is available at www.onthemedia.org/transcripts/transcripts_032604_selling.html (last accessed on July 14, 2006).

13. Charlotte Beers, undersecretary for public diplomacy and public affairs, during testimony before the House International Relations Committee, Washington, D.C., October 10, 2001.

14. See www.tate.gov/secretary/former/powell/remarks/2002/8038.htm (last accessed on July 14, 2006).

15. The research from which Beers drew this insight was the 2002 "Valuescope" survey conducted by Roper ASW Worldwide in thirty-five countries. Beers reviewed highlights of the study in a speech at the National Press Club on December 18, 2002.

16. NPR interview with Charlotte Beers by Bob Garfield, "On the Media," March 26, 2004.

17. Alice Kendrick and Jami Fullerton, *Advertising's War on Terrorism* (Spokane, Wash.: Marquette Books, 2006), pp. 167–194. Kendrick and Fullerton showed the U.S. Department of State videos to 152 students in London, 38 in Cairo, and 328 in Singapore between July 2003 and September 2005. Results were based on the difference in attitudes between pre- and postviewing

18. Jane Perlez, "Muslim-as-Apple-Pie Videos Are Greeted with Skepticism," *The New York Times* (October 30, 2002).

19. Robert Satloff, "Battling for the Hearts and Minds in the Middle East: A Critique of U.S. Public Diplomacy, Post-September 11," speech delivered at the Washington Institute for Near East Policy, September 17, 2002.

20. As'ad AbuKhalil is quoted by Michelle Goldberg in "To know America is to love America? Advertising maven Charlotte Beers is trying to sell the U.S. to the Muslim world, but nobody's buying it," *Salon* (December 19, 2002).

21. Sheldon Rampton and John Stauber, *Weapons of Mass Deception: The Uses of Propaganda in Bush's War in Iraq* (New York: Tarcher, 2003), p. 27.

22. David Frum and Richard Perle, *An End to Evil: How to Win the War on Terror* (New York: Random House, 2003), p. 148

23. Steven Weisman, "Powell Aide Quits Position Promoting U.S.," *The New York Times* (March 4, 2003).

Chapter 3

1. The opening quote actually comes from the 1951 Disney movie based on Lewis Carroll's books *Alice's Adventures in Wonderland* and *Through the Looking Glass*.

2. Bob Garfield interview with Charlotte Beers on NPR's "On the Media," March 26, 2004.
3. Edward Djerejian was interviewed by Peter Peterson at the Council on Foreign Relations on October 7, 2003. A full transcript is at www.cfr.org/publication .html?id = 6417 (last accessed on January 31, 2006).
4. U.S. Advisory Commission on Public Diplomacy, "Building America's Public Diplomacy Through a Reformed Structure and Additional Resources," U.S. Department of State, 2002, p. 10.
5. Radio Sawa (which means "coming together") originates in Washington, D.C., and is broadcast over a combination of frequencies from stations in the Middle East. Although Egypt, Saudi Arabia, Syria, Lebanon, and most of North Africa still refuse to let the network use their radio frequencies, its programming spills in from friendlier countries such as Abu Dhabi, Morocco, and Jordan. For example, Radio Sawa reaches most of Egypt, Lebanon, and Syria from a high-powered AM transmitter in Cyprus.
6. *The Report of the Defense Science Board Task Force on Strategic Communication,* Office of the Undersecretary of Defense for Acquisition, Technology, and Logistics, Washington, D.C., September 2004, pp. 41–42.
7. John Esposito, "Political Islam: Beyond the Green Menace," *Current History* (January 1994). See www.uga.edu/islam/espo.html (last accessed on July 14, 2006).
8. See "Report of the Defense Science Board Task Force on Strategic Communication," Office of the Undersecretary of Defense for Acquisition, Technology, and Logistics, Washington, D.C., September 2004, pp. 33–41.
9. Gordon Robison, "The Rest of Arab Television," USC Center on Public Diplomacy, June 2005.
10. Martha Bayles, "Goodwill Hunting," *The Wilson Quarterly* (Summer 2005).
11. Quote is taken from the transcript of the Daily Press Briefing with Philip T. Reeker, deputy spokesman, State Department, Washington, D.C., October 16, 2001.
12. Charles Wolf and Brian Rosen, "Public Diplomacy: How to Think About and Improve It," Rand Corporation, 2004.
13. Edward Djerejian interviewed by Peter Peterson at the Council on Foreign Relations on October 7, 2003.
14. Fred Kaplan, "Karen Hughes Sells America," *Slate* (March 15, 2005).
15. Beers was quoted in *Advertising's War on Terrorism,* written by Jami Fullerton and Alice Kendrick (Spokane, Wash.: Marquette Books, 2006), p. 123.
16. Ibid, p. 125.
17. Ibid, p. 124.

Chapter 4

1. John Zogby, interviewed by Elizabeth Wasserman for the June 2004 issue of *Inc.* magazine.
2. Fouad Ajami, "How to Win the Battle of Ideas in the Middle East," remarks delivered at the Washington Institute for Near East Policy on November 10, 2004.
3. As quoted by Larissa Macfarquhar in "The Pollster," *The New Yorker* (October 10, 2004).
4. Ibid.
5. The Zogby poll first received wide publicity in an article by Michael Pollan,

"An Animal's Place," *The New York Times (Sunday)Magazine* (November 10, 2002).

6. Chris Mooney, "John Zogby's Creative Polls," *The American Prospect* (February 1, 2003).

7. As quoted by Michael Barone in "The Man Behind the Numbers," *U.S. News and World Report* (February 16, 2004).

8. Mooney, "John Zogby's Creative Polls."

9. From the "Militant Islam Monitor" weblog on October 25, 2004. See www .militantislammonitor.org/article/id/304 (last accessed on July 14, 2006).

10. Morton Klein, president of the Zionist Organization of America, was quoted in a news release the group issued on December 4, 2002.

11. Scott Shepherd, "Mom's Advice Helps Zogby Brothers in D.C. Scene," *Austin American-Statesman* (June 30, 2002).

12. Both Information International surveys were based on approximately 600 interviews conducted in Greater Beirut, Lebanon.

13. "The 2002 Gallup Poll of the Islamic World" was conducted in January and February 2002. Researchers conducted hour-long, in-person interviews in Saudi Arabia, Iran, Pakistan, Indonesia, Turkey, Lebanon, Kuwait, Jordan, and Morocco.

14. Shibley Telhami, "A View from the Arab World," survey findings published by The Brookings Institution, March 13, 2003.

15. Interestingly, Republican political strategist Kevin Phillips also believes the Iraq War was undertaken to enable the United States to control the country's vast oil reserves and ultimately lower oil prices. He articulated his theory in *American Theocracy* (New York: Viking, 2006).

16. Quoted by Afshin Molavi, "Anti-U.S. Sentiment in Arab World Soars to New Heights," Al Jazeera English Service, March 25, 2003.

17. John Zogby, "Why Do They Hate Us?" *Rochester Democrat and Chronicle* (July 11, 2003), and *The Link*, Vol. 36, Issue 4, published by Americans for Middle East Understanding, October–November 2003.

18. Zogby, "Why Do They Hate Us?"

19. As quoted by Maha Al-Azar in her story "Poll Shows Negative Views of U.S.," *(Lebanon) Daily Star* (March 20, 2003).

20. See, for example, an excellent study by Giacomo Chiozza, who was then a graduate student at New York University, "Love and Hate: Anti-Americanism in the Islamic World," November 7, 2004.

21. Testimony of Andrew Kohut, president of the Pew Research Center, before the Senate Foreign Relations Committee, Subcommittee on Oversight and Investigations, November 10, 2005.

22. Ibid.

23. Ibid.

24. See, for example, Francis Fukuyama, *America at the Crossroads* (New Haven, CT: Yale University Press, 2006) or Kevin Phillips, *American Theocracy* (New York: Viking, 2006).

Chapter 5

1. Quoted by Jeffrey Goldberg, "Behind Mubarak," *The New Yorker* (October 8, 2001).

2. Bruce Bawer, "Hating America," *The Hudson Review* (Spring 2004).

3. Ibid.

4. Ibid.

5. Ibid.

6. "Global Opinion: The Spread of Anti-Americanism," the Pew Research Center, March 2004.

7. Ibid.

8. Pew Global Attitudes Project, "America's Image Slips, but Allies Share U.S. Concerns Over Iran, Hamas," June 13, 2006. The survey was fielded from March 31 to May 14, 2006, in seventeen countries.

9. "Global Opinion: The Spread of Anti-Americanism." The full data are as follows: 61 percent of the British, 69 percent of Germans, and 73 percent of Russians believed the United States failed to take other countries' interests into account. Fifty-eight percent of the French, 51 percent of Russians, 60 percent of Germans, 65 percent of Moroccans, 64 percent of Turks, 63 percent of Moroccans, 71 percent of Jordanians, and 54 percent of Pakistanis thought America's real motive in invading Iraq was "to control Mideast oil."

10. "Global Opinion: The Spread of Anti-Americanism." In Western Europe, 69 percent of French, 70 percent of Germans, 58 percent of Italians, and 53 percent of Britons believe United States policies increase the poverty gap. In Latin America, 74 percent of Bolivians, 67 percent of Argentineans, and 60 percent of Brazilians express the same sentiment. And in Asia, there is the same finding from 69 percent of Japanese and 67 percent of South Koreans.

11. "Global Opinion: The Spread of Anti-Americanism." Fifty-eight percent of non-Americans believe "U.S. policy caused the 9/11 attacks." Seventy percent believe it's "good for the U.S. to feel vulnerable" following the attacks.

12. Garry Wills, "Jimmy Carter and the Culture of Death," *The New York Review of Books* 53, No 2 (February 9, 2006).

13. The newspapers involved were *La Presse* of Canada, *Le Monde* of France, *The Guardian* of Britain, *El Pais* of Spain, *Asahi Shimbun* of Japan, *JoongAng Ilbo* of South Korea, *The Sydney Morning Herald* and *Melbourne Age* of Australia, *Reforma* of Mexico, *Haaretz* of Israel, and the *Moscow News* of Russia. The surveys were conducted from September through early October 2004. Results were posted on each newspaper's website.

14. From a news release issued by Harris Interactive on April 2, 2004, "A Comparison of American, Canadian, and European Perceptions of the United States." The company surveyed 1,010 adults in the United States and 1,017 adults in Canada between March 9 and March 16, 2004, and 10,265 adults in England, Spain, France, Germany, and Italy between February 27 and March 4, 2004. For the complete release, including methodology, see www.harrisinteractive .com/news/allnewsbydate.asp?NewsID = 786 (last accessed on October 4, 2006).

15. Peter Ford, "Is America 'the Good Guy'?" *Christian Science Monitor,* September 11, 2002.

16. Pew Global Attitudes Project, "America's Image Slips, but Allies Share U.S. Concerns Over Iran, Hamas," June 13, 2006.

17. Pew Global Attitudes Project, "U.S. Image Up Slightly, but Still Negative," June 23, 2005. The survey was fielded in April and May of 2005 in sixteen countries.

18. Richard Kuisel, *French Opinion and the Deteriorating Image of the United States* (Georgetown University manuscript, 2004) quoted by Bernard Chazelle in *Anti-Americanism: A Clinical Study* (Princeton University, 2004).

19. Research International news release, "Being American," April 11, 2004.

20. "L'Empire s'empire," *Libération*, November 3, 2004.

21. Adam Gopnik, "The Anti-Anti-Americans," *The New Yorker* (September 1, 2005).
22. London *Daily Mirror*, November 4, 2004, front page.
23. YouGov *Daily Telegraph* survey, July 7, 2006.
24. "U.S. Image Up Slightly, but Still Negative."
25. Audrey Woods, "U.S. Is Arrogant," *Philadelphia Inquirer*, June 19, 2003.
26. "U.S. Image Up Slightly, but Still Negative."
27. Findings are from a 2003 Eurobarometer survey conducted by the European Union.
28. Ivan Cook, "Australians Speak 2005: Public Opinion and Foreign Policy," The Lowy Institute for International Policy. See www.lowyinstitute.org/publica tion.asp?pid = 236 (last accessed on July 17, 2006).
29. The Transatlantic Trends survey of American and European public opinion was fielded in June 2005. Polling was conducted in the United States and ten European countries: France, Germany, Italy, the Netherlands, Poland, Portugal, Slovakia, Spain, Turkey, and the United Kingdom. The survey is a project of the German Marshall Fund of the United States and the Compagnia di San Paolo, with additional support from the Fundação Luso-Americana and Fundación BBVA.
30. Pew Global Attitudes Project, "America's Image Slips, but Allies Share U.S. Concerns Over Iran, Hamas," (June 13, 2006).
31. "Methode Wild-West," *Stern*, October 20, 2004.
32. The Edelman Trust Barometer, January 2006.
33. The Global Market Insite (GMI) World Poll surveyed 8,000 consumers in eight countries online in December 2004.
34. Research International, "Being American," April 11, 2004.
35. Zbigniew Brzezinski, *The Choice: Global Domination or Global Leadership* (New York: Basic Books, 2004), p. 162.

Chapter 6

1. Fouad Ajami was interviewed on *The NewsHour with Jim Lehrer* on PBS on May 5, 2004.
2. James Thurber, "Lippmann Scares Me This Morning," *The New Yorker,* April 20, 1935.
3. Walter Lippmann, *Public Opinion* (New York: Macmillan Company, 1922, reprinted by Penguin, 1946), p. 20.
4. Ibid, p. 154.
5. Robert Toscano is quoted by Eric Alterman in "USA Oui! Bush Non!" *The Nation* (February 10, 2003).
6. Paul Hollander, *Understanding Anti-Americanism* (Chicago: Ivan R. Dee, 2004), p. 9.
7. Ibid, p. 8.
8. Ibid, p. 38.
9. See Cornelius de Pauw, *Recherches Philosophiques sur les Américains,* first published in Berlin, 1768–1769. Alexander Hamilton summarized the argument, with some disbelief, in the *Federalist Papers*: "Men admired as profound philosophers have, in direct terms, attributed to [Europe's] inhabitants a physical superiority and have gravely asserted that all animals, and with them the human species, degenerate in America—that even dogs cease to bark after having breathed awhile in our atmosphere."

10. James W. Ceaser, *Reconstructing America* (New Haven, CT: Yale University Press, 1997).

11. Tony Judt, *Postwar: A History of Europe Since 1945* (New York: Penguin Press, 2005), p. 353.

12. Paul Berman, "France's Failures, Hatreds, and Signs of a New Look at America," *The New Republic* (November 28, 2005).

13. Emmanuel Todd, *After the Empire: The Breakdown of the American Order* (New York: Columbia University Press, 2003), p. 20 (originally published as *Après l'Empire* [Paris: Gallimard, 2002]).

14. They are: *Pourquoi le monde déteste-t-il l'Amérique? (Why Does the World Detest America?)* by Ziauddin Sardar and Merryl Wyn Davies (Paris: Fayard, 2003); *Le Livre noir des États-Unis (The Black Book of the United States)* by Peter Scowen (Paris: Mango, 2003); and *Dangereuse Amérique: Chronique d'une guerre annoncée (Dangerous America: Chronicle of a War)* by Noël Mamère and Patrick Farbiaz (Paris: Ramsay, 2003).

15. Hebe de Bonafini is quoted by Michael Radu, "A Matter of Identity: The Anti-Americanism of Latin American Intellectuals," in Paul Hollander's *Understanding Anti-Americanism* (Chicago: Ivan R. Dee, 2004), pp. 155–156.

16. In an e-mail newsletter quoted by *The New York Times,* September 22, 2001.

17. Jean-François Revel, *Anti-Americanism* (San Francisco: Encounter Books, 2003), p. 62.

18. Ibid, p. 61.

19. Ibid, p. 170.

20. Quoted by Michael Radu, "A Matter of Identity: The Anti-Americanism of Latin American Intellectuals," in Hollander, *Understanding Anti-Americanism,* p. 147.

21. Barry Rubin, "The Real Roots of Arab Anti-Americanism," *Foreign Affairs* (November–December 2002).

22. *Wag the Dog* was a film by Barry Levinson about political consultants who fabricate a war to distract the public from a president's personal missteps. The technique has also been called a "weapon of mass distraction" by numerous writers, including Christopher Hitchens in the November 1999 issue of *Vanity Fair* and Dan Plesch in the September 29, 2002, issue of *The Observer.* Jean-François Revel was reportedly the first to attach the phrase to anti-Americanism, although I haven't been able to pin down the exact source.

23. Fareed Zakaria, "Hating America," *Foreign Policy* (September–October 2004).

24. Fernand Braudel, *Civilization and Capitalism, 15th–18th Century,* 3 vols. (New York: HarperCollins, 1985).

25. Fareed Zakaria, "The Politics of Rage: Why Do They Hate Us?" *Newsweek* (October 15, 2001).

26. Abdurrahman Wahid, "Right Islam vs. Wrong Islam," *The Wall Street Journal* (December 30, 2005).

27. Pew Global Attitudes Project, "U.S. Image Up Slightly, but Still Negative," June 23, 2005.

28. Samuel Huntington, "The Clash of Civilizations," *Foreign Affairs* (Summer 1993).

Chapter 7

1. Osama Siblani was quoted by William Douglas in "U.S. Turns to Madison Avenue for PR War," *Newsday* (October 23, 2001).

2. Jon Stewart of *The Daily Show* was quoted calling Zakaria "an intellectual heartthrob" by Joy Press in "The Interpreter," *The Village Voice* (August 16, 2005).

3. Michael Massing, "Press Watch," *The Nation* (October 18, 2001).

4. Oliver Zöllner, ed., *Beyond Borders: Research for International Broadcasting 2003*, Vol. 2 (Bonn, Germany: The Conference of International Broadcasters' Audience Research Services, 2004).

5. Fareed Zakaria, "The Politics of Rage: Why Do They Hate Us?" *Newsweek* (October 15, 2001).

6. Thomas Friedman, "Empty Pockets, Angry Minds," *The New York Times* (February 22, 2006).

7. Based on a February 2006 presentation by the World Bank's chief economist for the region. See: http://siteresources.worldbank.org/INTMENA/Resources/2006GenderRoundtable.pdf (last accessed on March 7, 2006).

8. Zakaria, "The Politics of Rage: Why Do They Hate Us?"

9. "Transformation Not Restoration," Statement of Dissent to the Public Diplomacy Council's report *A Call for Action on Public Diplomacy*, January 2005.

10. Oliver Zöllner, ed., *Beyond Borders: Research for International Broadcasting* (Bonn, Germany: CIBAR, 2004).

11. Fareed Zakaria, *The Future of Freedom* (New York: W. W. Norton & Company, 2004), p. 152.

12. Sarah Baxter, "Rumsfeld's Al-Jazeera Outburst," *The (London) Sunday Times* (November 27, 2005).

13. Ibid.

14. Mohammed El-Nawawy, coauthor of *Al-Jazeera: How the Free Arab News Network Scooped the World and Changed the Middle East*, in a speech to the Carnegie Council on Ethics and International Affairs, April 15, 2002.

15. Mohammed El-Nawawy and Adel Iskandar, *Al-Jazeera: How the Free Arab News Network Scooped the World and Changed the Middle East* (Boulder, CO: Westview Press, 2003), p. 27.

16. "Arab Media," *The Economist* (September 2, 2002).

17. Walter Lippmann, *Public Opinion* (New York: Macmillan Company, 1922, reprinted by Penguin, 1946), Chapter Six.

18. Lippmann, *Public Opinion,* p. 267.

19. *Changing Minds, Winning Peace,* Report of the House Advisory Group on Public Diplomacy for the Arab and Muslim World, Edward P. Djerejian, chairman, October 1, 2003, p. 21.

20. Stephen E. Siwek, "Engines of Growth," The U.S. Intellectual Property Industries, November 7, 2005. See weblog.ipcentral.info/archives/2005/11/ip_as_the_engin_1.html (last accessed on July 14, 2006).

21. Some films, such as *The Lord of the Rings* trilogy, were coproductions with U.S. companies.

22. Dave McNary, "O'seas B.O. Goes for a Little Dip," *Variety* (January 3, 2006). Worldwide sales do not include locally produced films in India or China.

23. Thomas Huckin and James Coady, "Incidental Vocabulary Acquisition in a Second Language: A Review," *Studies in Second Language Acquisition* 21 (1999), pp. 181–193.

24. Madeline A. Dalton et al., "Effect of Viewing Smoking in Movies on Adolescent Smoking Imitation: A Cohort Study," *Lancet* 361, No. 9273 (June 2003).

25. James D. Sargent et al., "Exposure to Movie Smoking: Its Relation to Smoking Initiation Among U.S. Adolescents," *Pediatrics* 116, No. 5 (November 7,

2005), pp. 1183–1191. In the news release issued by Dartmouth Medical School when the study was published, Dr. Sargent noted that the impact of movies "outweighs whether peers or parents smoke or whether the child is involved in other activities, like sports."

26. Melvin DeFleur, Ph.D., and Margaret DeFleur, Ph.D., *Learning to Hate Americans* (Spokane, WA: Marquette Books, 2003), p. 72.
27. Ibid.
28. C. Samuel Craig, William H. Greene, and Susan P. Douglas, "Found in Translation," *SternBusiness* (Fall/Winter 2005).
29. DeFleur, *Learning to Hate Americans*, p. 14.
30. Ibid.

Chapter 8

1. Takeo Fujisawa is quoted by Paul Holmes in "The Many Faces of Global Capitalism," *The Holmes Report* (December 7, 1992). See: http://holmesreport .com/holmestemp/story.cfm?edit_id = 1061&typeid = 2 (last accessed on March 7, 2006).
2. Keith Reinhard as quoted in "The Corporate Citizen," published by the U.S. Chamber of Commerce, August–September, 2004.
3. Keith Reinhard, testimony before the House Subcommittee on National Security, Emerging Threats, and International Relations, Washington, D.C., August 23, 2004.
4. *WSJ* is quoted by James Fallows, "How the World Works," *The Atlantic Monthly* (December 1993).
5. "Views of a Changing World, 2003," Pew Research Center for the People and the Press, June 3, 2003.
6. Woodrow Wilson, *The New Freedom: A Call for the Emancipation of the Generous Energies of a People* (New York: Doubleday and Page, 1913).
7. *Dodge v. Ford Motor Co.*, Michigan Supreme Court, 170 N.W. 668 (1919).
8. Jeremy Rifkin, "Capitalism's Future on Trial," *The Guardian* (June 22, 2005).
9. Katinka Barysch, "Liberal versus Social Europe," in Centre for European Reform *Bulletin* (August–September 2005). See www.cer.org.uk/articles/43_ barysch.html (last accessed on July 14, 2006).
10. Charles Hampden-Turner and Alfons Trompenaars, *The Seven Cultures of Capitalism: Value Systems for Creating Wealth in the United States, Japan, Germany, France, Britain, Sweden, and the Netherlands* (New York: Doubleday, 1993).
11. Robert Kagan, "Power and Weakness," *Policy Review*, No. 113 (June 2002); available online at www.policyreview.org (last accessed on July 13, 2006).
12. Quoted by Noah Stoffman in "The Life and Times of Thomas L. Friedman," *Varsity Review* (December 1997).
13. 2003 Eurobarometer survey.
14. Clark S. Judge, "Hegemony of the Heart," *Policy Review*, No. 110 (December 2001–January 2002).
15. Aaron Bernstein, "Too Much Corporate Power?" *BusinessWeek* (September 11, 2000).
16. Karlyn Bowman, "Taking Stock of Business: Public Opinion After the Corporate Scandals," American Enterprise Institute, November 2003.
17. Claudia H. Deutsch, "Take Your Best Shot: New Survey Shows Business Has a PR Problem," *The New York Times* (December 9, 2005).

18. Harris Interactive, "What Do Europeans Like and Dislike About the United States?" March 24, 2004 (last accessed on January 8, 2005, at www.harris interactive.com/news/allnewsbydate.asp?NewsID = 780).
19. Keith Reinhard as quoted in "The Corporate Citizen," August–September 2004.
20. Raymond Williams in *Loyalties* (London: Chatto and Windus, 1985), Part 3, Chapter 2.
21. John Quelch was quoted in an April 21, 2003, interview for *Working Knowledge*, published by the Harvard Business School.
22. Stoffman, "The Life and Times of Thomas L. Friedman."
23. Quoted by Michael Novak, *Universal Hunger for Liberty: Why the Clash of Civilizations Is Not Inevitable* (New York: Basic Books, 2004), p. 226.
24. Todd Gitlin, "Anti-Anti-Americanism," *Dissent* (Summer 2003).

Chapter 9

1. From the Landor Associates website: www.landor.com/index.cfm?do = cNews .news&storyid = 184 (last accessed on March 7, 2006).
2. "All About Branding," www.allaboutbranding.com/index.lasso?article = 22 (last accessed on March 7, 2006).
3. Thomas Oliver, *The Real Coke, the Real Story* (New York: Random House, 1986), p. 43.
4. David Greising, *I'd Like to Buy the World a Coke: The Life and Leadership of Roberto Goizueta* (New York: John Wiley & Sons, 1997), p. 133.
5. Donald Calne, *Within Reason: Rationality and Human Behavior* (New York: Pantheon, 1999), p. 236.
6. Sybill Ackerman, "BP Is Deserving of Censure, but Not a Vendetta," *Financial Times,* August 31, 2006.
7. S. M. McClure et al., "Neural Correlates of Behavioral Preference for Culturally Familiar Drinks," *Neuron* 44 (October 14, 2004), pp. 379–387.
8. Peter van Ham, "The Rise of the Brand State," *Foreign Affairs* (September–October, 2001).
9. From a December 3, 2003, interview with Frank Lutz on PBS Television's *Frontline: The Persuaders;* available at www.pbs.org/wgbh/pages/frontline/ shows/persuaders/interviews/luntz.html (last accessed on January 10, 2005).

Chapter 10

1. Jean Baudrillard, *America* (London: Verso, 1989), p. 34.
2. Naomi Klein, "America Is Not a Hamburger," *The Guardian* (March 14, 2002).
3. Benjamin Barber is quoted by David Barboza in "When Golden Arches Are Too Red, White, and Blue," *The New York Times* (October 14, 2001).
4. Simon Anholt and Jeremy Hildreth, *Brand America: The Mother of All Brands* (London: Cyan Communications, 2005).
5. Ibid., p. 21.
6. Wally Olins, *On Brand* (London: Thames & Hudson, 2003), p. 151.
7. Peterson made his remarks at a meeting of the Council on Foreign Relations on October 7, 2003. A full transcript is available at www.cfr.org/publication .html?id = 6417.

8. Daniel Yankelovich, "The Tipping Points," *Foreign Affairs* (May–June 2006).

9. *The Report of the Defense Science Board Task Force on Strategic Communication,* Office of the Undersecretary of Defense for Acquisition, Technology, and Logistics, Washington, D.C., September 2004.

10. Commonly known as the Smith-Mundt Act, the United States Information and Educational Exchanges Act of 1948, as amended, 22 U.S.C. 1431, prohibits the dissemination of informational materials produced for overseas use in the United States or to U.S. citizens or residents. It has been interpreted to include research data. The act, which was reportedly passed to prevent government "propaganda" from reaching the American people, is seriously outdated in an age of easy access to information through the Internet.

11. Greg Sargent, "Intelligencer: Bush Threatens U.N. Over Clinton Speech," *New York* (December 9, 2005).

12. Joseph S. Nye, "Bush Could Do with Decent PR Help," *Bangkok Post* (January 21, 2005).

13. Poll results from the June 2005 Global Attitudes Survey conducted by the Pew Research Center.

14. Robert Kagan, "Power and Weakness," *Policy Review*, No. 113 (June 2002); available online at www.policyreview.org.

15. Kishore Mahbubani, *Beyond the Age of Innocence: Rebuilding Trust Between America and the World* (New York: Perseus, 2005), p. 166.

16. The Columbia University study was quoted by Alkman Granitsas in "America Is Tuning Out the World," *YaleGlobal* (November 24, 2005).

17. Project for Excellence in Journalism Reported by Howard Kurtz, "Brad Pitt Journalism," *The Washington Post* (March 16, 1998).

18. Claude Moisy, "Myths of the Global Information Village," *Foreign Policy* (Summer 1997).

19. Conference Board of Canada, "The Potential Impact of a Western Hemisphere Travel Initiative Passport Requirement for Canada's Tourism Industry," Canadian Tourism Commission, July 29, 2005.

20. National Geographic Society, "Survey Reveals Geographic Illiteracy," November 20, 2002. See http://news.nationalgeographic.com/news/2002/11/1120_021120_GeoRoperSurvey.html (last accessed on October 4, 2006).

21. Pew Global Attitudes Project, released July 14, 2005. See http://pewglobal.org/reports/display.php?ReportID = 801 (last accessed on July 16, 2006).

Chapter 11

1. Claudia Deutsch, "U.S.: Poll Shows Americans Distrust Corporations," *The New York Times* (December 10, 2005).

2. Ibid.

3. Peggy Noonan, "A Time of Lore," *The Wall Street Journal Online*, July 26, 2002. See: www.opinionjournal.com/columnists/pnoonan/?id = 110002038/ (last accessed on February 3, 2006).

4. The Justice Department's list of "Significant Criminal Cases and Charging Documents" is available at www.usdoj.gov/dag/cftf/cases.htm (last accessed on February 4, 2006).

5. Harrison was on a panel entitled "Global Business—Saviour or Scapegoat?" January 28, 2006. See: www.weforum.org/site/knowledgenavigator.nsf/Content/_S15369?open&topic_ideq200115000&theme_id = 200 (last accessed on February 4, 2006).

6. Author interview, December 1, 2005.
7. Mark Gimein, "You Bought, They Sold," *Fortune* (September 2, 2002).
8. "The Boss' Pay," *The Wall Street Journal* (April 10, 2006). Total direct compensation consists of cash, stock, gains from the exercise of stock options, and the value of restricted shares at the time of grant.
9. Lawrence Mishel, "CEO-to-Worker Imbalance Grows," Economic Policy Institute (June 21, 2006). See www.epinet.org/content.cfm/webfeatures_snapshots_20060621 (last accessed on July 15, 2006). The Economic Policy Institute based its analysis on the same Mercer Management data used by the *Wall Street Journal.* In contrast, The Business Roundtable commissioned a study that valued options on the day they were granted, rather than when exercised, among other differences. It put the CEO to worker compensation ratio at 187 to 1. ("Research on CEO Compensation" by Frederick Cook is available at www.businessroundtable.org.) Towers Perrin used a similar method for valuing options but discounted them by 3 percent a year over their expected term. Towers Perrin also compared CEO compensation to the pay of manufacturing employees rather than that of all workers. On that basis, in 2005–2006, the ratio ranged from a high of 63 to 1 in Mexico to a low of 11 to 1 in Japan. The ratio in the United States was 39 to 1. See www.towersperrin.com/towersperrin/r/wwtr05_eng.htm (last accessed on July 14, 2006).
10. Lawrence Mishel, Jared Bernstein, and Sylvia Allegretto, *The State of Working America, 2004–2005* (Ithaca, NY: Cornell University Press, 2005).
11. Jesse Eisinger, "No Excessive Pay, We're British," *The Wall Street Journal* (February 8, 2006).
12. Bloomberg Financial Markets.
13. Emily Thornton et al., "Fat Merger Payouts for CEOs," *BusinessWeek* (December 12, 2005).
14. Ibid.
15. Watson Wyatt Worldwide survey, as reported in *BusinessWeek* (February 13, 2006), p. 16.
16. "S&P 500 CEO Total Direct Compensation Increases 7.5% in 2004 Based on Equilar Study," Equilar news release, June 10, 2005. See: http://equilar.com/press_20050610.html (last accessed on March 21, 2006). Equilar's study showed that the value of options granted in 2005 declined. A study by H. Najat Seyhun of the University of Michigan, however, found that the average number of options granted in 2005 grew 24 percent, suggesting that the companies' methods of valuing them were more conservative. See Mark Hulbert, "No Rain on the Stock Option Parade," *The New York Times* (July 16, 2006).
17. Alice LaPlante, "Excessive Executive Pay Makes Headlines, But So What?" Stanford Graduate School of Business, February 2006.
18. Buffet was quoted by Floyd Norris, "Which Bosses Really Care if Shares Rise?" *The New York Times* (June 2, 2006).
19. "Executive Alert: NIRI Issues 2006 Survey Results on Earnings Guidance Practices," news release issued by National Investor Relations Institute, April 6, 2006.
20. "Separation of CEO and Chairman Role Increases, According to Russell Reynolds Research," Russell Reynolds news release, February 1, 2006.
21. *Spencer Stuart 2005 Board Index,* November 2005, p. 4.
22. Claudia Deutsch, "Behind Big Dollars, Worrisome Boards," *The New York Times* (April 9, 2006).
23. John Bogle, "What Went Wrong in Corporate America," remarks at the Com-

munity Forum Distinguished Speaker Series, Bryn Mawr Presbyterian Church, Bryn Mawr, PA, February 24, 2003.

24. See, for example, Charles Handy, "What's a Company For?" *The Harvard Business Review* (December 2002).

Chapter 12

1. Quoted by Naomi Klein, "America Is Not a Hamburger," *The Guardian* (March 14, 2002), and many others.
2. "Wars and Boycotts, Both Fade Away," *Business Week Online* (April 8, 2003). See http://www.businessweek.com/bwdaily/dnflash/apr2003/nf2003048_2414_db053.htm (last accessed on July 7, 2006).
3. Leo Burnett survey, April 2004. Global Market Insite (GMI) Insite survey, December 2004.
4. Eric Kirschbaum, "EU: Boycott of American Goods Over Iraq War Gains Momentum," Reuters (March 25, 2003).
5. "Report on Corporate and Foreign Policy," prepared for Business for Diplomatic Action by Zogby International, Fall 2005.
6. Ibid, p. 6.
7. Author interview, February 11, 2005.
8. Author interview, March 4, 2005.
9. "Spot the Difference," *The Economist* (December 20, 2005).
10. "American Multinationals," *The Economist* (December 14, 2005).
11. Tony Judt, *Postwar: A History of Europe Since 1945* (New York: Penguin Press, 2005), p. 221.
12. Janet Guyon, "Brand America," *Fortune* (October 27, 2003).
13. Douglas B. Holt, John A. Quelch, and Earl A. Taylor, "How Global Brands Compete," *Harvard Business Review* (September 2004).
14. Peter J. Katzenstein and Robert O. Keohane, "Varieties of Anti-Americanism: A Framework of Analysis," in Peter J. Katzenstein and Robert O. Keohane, eds., *Anti-Americanism in World Politics*, pp. 28–37 (Ithica: Cornell University Press, 2007).
15. "American Multinationals," *The Economist* (December 14, 2005).
16. Author interview, March 10, 2005.
17. Federal Reserve, "H-10 Foreign Exchange Historical Rates for Euro Area." See: http://federalreserve.gov/releases/H10/Hist/ (last accessed on July 17, 2006).
18. U.S. Department of Commerce, Office of Travel and Tourism Industries, "International Arrivals to U.S.—Historical Visitation, 1998–2005."
19. Business leader quoted in "Report on Corporate and Foreign Policy," prepared for Business for Diplomatic Action by Zogby International, Fall 2005, p. 22.
20. U.S. Department of Commerce, Office of Travel and Tourism Industries, "International Arrivals to U.S.—Historical Visitation, 1998–2005."
21. Anholt Nations Brands Index, June 2005. The NBI interviews a thousand consumers in each of eighteen countries, measuring each country's "brand image" across six dimensions: exports, governance, investment, culture, people, and tourism. The tourism category measures "aspiration to visit" rather than direct "experience" of a visit.
22. United Nations World Tourism Organization, *Tourism Highlights* (June 2005).
23. Tom Chesshyre, "Don't Mention the War," *The (London) Times* (March 11, 2006).

24. Peter York was quoted in Peter van Ham's "The Rise of the Brand State," *Foreign Affairs* (September–October, 2001).
25. John Quelch, quoted in an April 21, 2003, interview for *Working Knowledge,* published by the Harvard Business School.
26. Douglas B. Holt, John A. Quelch, and Earl L. Taylor, "How Global Brands Compete," *Harvard Business Review* (September 2004).
27. Peter Gumbel, "Branding America," *Time* (March 2005), p. A14.
28. "Wars and Boycotts, Both Fade Away," *BusinessWeek Online* (April 8, 2003).
29. "Anti-American Sentiments and Their Long-Term Impact on International Corporations," Weber Shandwick report, July 2003.
30. Jack Leslie was speaking to the French American Chamber of Commerce in Paris on May 20, 2003, and was quoted by Kevin McCauley in the June 2003 issue of *Jack O'Dwyer's Newsletter.*
31. Ian Davis and Elizabeth Stephenson, "Ten Trends to Watch in 2006," *The McKinsey Quarterly* (January 2006). See: www.mckinseyquarterly.com/article_page.aspx?ar=1734&L2=18&L3=30 (last accessed on July 16, 2006) (member registration required for viewing).
32. Author interview, March 14, 2005.
33. GE 2004 Annual Report, "Letter to Stakeholders."
34. This assessment is from S&P equity market strategist Alec Young, who was quoted by Daniel Gross in "Invest Globally, Stagnate Locally," *The New York Times* (April 2, 2006).
35. Joseph Nye, *Soft Power* (New York: PublicAffairs, 2004), p. 18.
36. Mark E. Manyin, "South Korean Politics and Rising Anti-Americanism," report for Congress, May 6, 2003.
37. Richard Haass, *The Opportunity: America's Moment to Alter History's Course* (New York: PublicAffairs, 2005), p. 202.
38. Tamás Dávid-Barrett spoke at a panel debate titled "Does Anti-Americanism Matter to American Foreign Policy?" Washington, D.C., November 3, 2005, cosponsored by the Carnegie Endowment for International Peace and the Central European University.
39. Haass, *The Opportunity: America's Moment to Alter History's Course,* p. 203.
40. Nye, *Soft Power,* p. 130.
41. "America Has Image Woes, Not Its Brands," *BusinessWeek Online* (August 4, 2003).

Chapter 13

1. "The Powell Lesson," *The Wall Street Journal* (November, 16, 2004).
2. Anthony O'Reilly is quoted in "Can Sustainability Sell?" published by the McCann-Erickson advertising agency, 2002. See: www.uneptie.org/PC/sustain/reports/advertising/can-sustainability-sell%20.pdf (last accessed on July 16, 2006).
3. Tunku Varadarajan, "French Kiss," *The Wall Street Journal* (January 21, 2006).
4. Others may have alternative definitions for "public philosopher." Mine is based in large measure on Walter Lippmann's definition. See his *Essays in the Public Philosophy* (Boston: Little, Brown, 1955).
5. Lévy was interviewed by David Brooks at the New York Public Library on

April 6, 2005. The interview appeared on the *Atlantic Monthly*'s website on April 22 as "America in Foreign Eyes." Available to subscribers only.

6. "BHL, Unbuttoned," *Vanity Fair* (January 2006).

7. Lévy made these comments at a 2003 event, "Mind the Gap," organized by the PEN American Center

8. Bernard-Henri Lévy, "Anti-Americanism in the Old Europe," *New Perspectives Quarterly*, Spring 2003, p. 117.

9. Lévy's comments at "Mind the Gap," PEN American Center.

10. Michael Ignatieff, "Who Are Americans to Think That Freedom Is Theirs to Spread?" *The New York Times (Sunday) Magazine* (June 26, 2005).

11. Giddens told the story in the fifth of a series of lectures under the title "Runaway World" given in London, Washington, New Delhi, and Hong Kong in 1999.

12. A 2005 survey by the Gallup organization found that Muslim women do not think they are conditioned to accept second-class status, nor do they view themselves as oppressed. Although a strong majority believe they should have the rights to vote and work outside the home, they do not see such issues as a priority. See Helena Andrews, "Muslim Women Don't See Themselves as Oppressed," *The New York Times* (June 8, 2006).

13. Fawaz Gerges, "Democracy in the Middle East: Disentangling Myth from Reality," The Institute for Social Policy and Understanding, Policy Brief #10, March 2005.

14. YouGov *Daily Telegraph* survey, July 7, 2006.

15. Michael Novak, *Universal Hunger for Liberty: Why the Clash of Civilizations Is Not Inevitable* (New York: Basic Books, 2004), p. 15.

16. See Abdurrahman Wahid, "Right Islam vs. Wrong Islam: Muslims and Non-Muslims Must Unite to Defeat the Wahhabi Ideology," *The Wall Street Journal* (December 30, 2005).

17. Ahmed H. al-Rahim, "Book Review: *Universal Hunger for Liberty*," *Journal of Democracy* (January 2006), pp. 166–167.

18. Ibid, p. 204.

19. Fareed Zakaria, "The Politics of Rage: Why Do They Hate Us?" *Newsweek* (October 15, 2001).

20. Ibid.

21. Mark Tessler, "Do Islamic Orientations Influence Attitudes Toward Democracy in the Arab World? Evidence from Egypt, Jordan, Morocco, and Algeria," The World Values Survey, www.worldvaluessurvey.org/Upload/5_TessIslam Dem_2.pdf (last accessed on March 15, 2006).

22. Pew Global Attitudes Survey, July 14, 2005. See: http://pewglobal.org/reports/display.php?ReportID=248 (last accessed on March 12, 2006).

23. "Islam and Democracy: Survey Shows What Iraqis Want," University of Michigan Institute for Social Research, January 15, 2006. See www.umich.edu/news/index.html?Releases/2006/Jan06/r011706 (last accessed on March 15, 2006).

24. Vali Nasr, "The Rise of Muslim Democracy," *Journal of Democracy* (April 2005).

25. F. Gregory Gause III, "Can Democracy Stop Terrorism?" *Foreign Affairs* (September–October, 2005).

26. Ibid.

27. Jack Trout, "Extreme Makeover," *Forbes* (August 22, 2005).

Chapter 14

1. John Mackey, "Putting Customers Ahead of Investors," *Reason,* October 2005.
2. Ronald Inglehart and Christian Welzel, *Modernization, Cultural Change, and Democracy: The Human Development Sequence* (New York and Cambridge: Cambridge University Press, 2005).
3. Ronald Inglehart, "Globalization and Post-Modern Values," *The Washington Quarterly* (Winter 2000).
4. Ronald Inglehart and Hans-Dieter Klingemann, "Genes, Culture, Democracy, and Happiness," Ed Diener and E. M. Suh, eds., *Subjective Well-Being Across Cultures* (Cambridge, MA: MIT Press, 2000).
5. Ron Inglehart, "Culture and Democracy," in Lawrence E. Harrington and Samuel Huntington, eds., *Culture Matters: How Values Shape Human Progress* (New York: Basic Books, 2000), p. 96.
6. Anthony Shadid, *Legacy of the Prophet* (Boulder, CO: Westview Press, 2001), p. 294.
7. Data are from "Freedom in the World 2006," a report from Freedom House, an independent nongovernmental organization that believes freedom is possible only when governments are elected in a popular vote; the rule of law prevails; and freedoms of expression, association, belief, and respect for the rights of minorities and women are guaranteed. See www.freedomhouse.org/uploads/pdf/Charts2006.pdf (last accessed on March 15, 2006).
8. According to Fareed Zakaria's *The Future of Freedom* (New York: W. W. Norton & Company, 2004), in four elections between 1930 and 1933, the National Socialist (Nazi) party in Germany won more legislative seats than any other. For example, in 1933, the Nazis won 288 seats compared to the Social Democrats' 120 seats, the Communists' 81 seats, and the Center (Catholic) party's 73 seats.
9. Zakaria, *The Future of Freedom,* p. 45.
10. Fareed Zakaria, "How to Wage the Peace," *Newsweek* (April 21, 2003).
11. Ibid.
12. At the end of 2005, Freedom House ranked eighty-nine countries with nearly 3 billion people as "free," fifty-eight countries with 1.2 billion people as "partly free," and forty-five countries with 2.3 billion people as "not free."
13. The GlobeScan survey was conducted between June and August 2005 and released on January 11, 2006. See www.worldpublicopinion.org/pipa/articles/home_related/154.php?nid = &id = & p nt = 154&lb = btgl (last accessed on February 14, 2006). In addition to showing a strong consensus in favor of the free-market system, the survey also showed strong preference for greater regulation of large companies.
14. Seymour Martin Lipset, "Some Social Requisites of Democracy: Economic Development and Political Legitimacy," *American Political Science Review* (March 1959).
15. Shibley Telhami, "A View from the Arab World: A Survey in Five Countries," The Brookings Institution, March 13, 2003.
16. Nicolas Papadopoulos of Carleton University in Ottawa counted 766 major papers by 789 authors on country-of-origin effect between the 1950s and 2001.
17. Peter Foster, "I'll Change India to Bharat, Says Hindi Party Chief," *(London) Daily Telegraph* (April 13, 2004).
18. Audhesh K. Paswan and Dheeraj Sharma, "Brand-Country of Origin Knowl-

edge and Image: Investigation in an Emerging Franchise Market," *Journal of Product and Brand Management* 13, No. 3 (March 2004), pp. 144–155.

19. "23 Nation Poll: Who Will Lead the World?" See http://www.worldpublic opinion.org / pipa / articles / views_on_countriesregions_bt / 114.php?nid = &id = &pnt = 114&lb = btvoc (last accessed on July 8, 2006).

20. Anne Applebaum, "Who Are the Pro-Americans?" *The Washington Post* (June 29, 2005).

21. Ian Davis and Elizabeth Stephenson, "Ten Trends to Watch in 2006," *McKinsey Quarterly* (January 2006).

22. Diana Farrell et al., "The Value of China's Emerging Middle Class," *McKinsey Quarterly*, 2006 special edition. See www.mckinseyquarterly.com/article_page .aspx?ar = 1798&L2 = 7&L3 = 10 (last accessed on July 15, 2006) (member registration required for viewing).

23. William McEwen et al., "Inside the Mind of the Chinese Consumer," *Harvard Business Review* (March 2006).

24. Branko Milanovic and Shlomo Yitzhaki, "Decomposing World Income Distribution: Does the World Have a Middle Class?" *Review of Income and Wealth* 48, No. 2 (June 2002).

25. Zakaria, *The Future of Freedom,* p. 151.

Chapter 15

1. Author interview, March 29, 2005.

2. Interviewed by William J. Holstein in "Armchair MBA: The Multinational as Cultural Chameleon," *The New York Times* (April 10, 2005).

3. Theodore Levitt, "Yes, Throw Money at Problems," *The New York Times* (April 28, 1978).

4. Theodore Levitt, "The Globalization of Markets," *Harvard Business Review* (May–June 1983).

5. Ibid.

6. Ibid.

7. Tom Freston was quoted in Simon Anholt's *Brand New Justice* (Oxford: Butterworth-Heinemann, 2003).

8. Rawi Abdelal, and Richard S. Tedlow, "Theodore Levitt's 'The Globalization of Markets': An Evaluation After Two Decades" (February 2003), Harvard NOM Working Paper No. 03-20; Harvard Business School Working Paper No. 03-082.

9. Levitt, "The Globalization of Markets."

10. McDonald's plays to local palates, too. In France, you can have your McDonald's cheeseburger made with Roquefort. In Germany, the menu includes beer as well as McCroissants. In Turkey, customers order double kofte burgers (made with meat patties, onions, and Turkish spices) and wash them down with a chilled yogurt drink. McSpaghetti is popular in the Philippines; McLaks (grilled salmon sandwiches) in Norway; McHuevo (poached egg hamburgers) in Uruguay; and Samurai Pork Burgers with sweet sauce in Thailand. It's espresso and cold pasta in Italy, teriyaki burgers in Japan, and vegetarian burgers in the Netherlands. In Saudi Arabia, single men eat separately from women and children. The McDonald's in Bahrain features the McArabia—two patties of grilled kofta dressed with tahina sauce, lettuce, tomatoes, and onions, all wrapped in pita bread. In Indonesia, diners can choose a burger and fries or a "Rice Package," combining fried chicken, scrambled eggs, and rice. Instead

of ketchup, dispensers pump out the ubiquitous Indonesian chili sauce called "sambal." In China, the Big Mac is still two all-beef patties on a sesame seed bun, but it's known as a "ju-wu-ba," which means "Great Imperial Warlord."

11. Cassell Bryan-Low, Andrew Morse, and Miho Inada, "Vodafone's Global Ambitions Got Hung Up in Japan," *The Wall Street Journal* (March 18, 2006).

12. Mike Eskew is quoted by Gail Dutton in "Grassroots Diplomacy," *Across the Board* (May–June 2005).

13. For more on the Thai culture and character, see www.ThaiWebsites.com.

14. Yongshik Bong, "Yongmi: Pragmatic Anti-Americanism in South Korea," *Brown Journal of World Affairs* (Winter–Spring 2004).

15. David Lague, "Selling in China? Which One Is It?" *International Herald Tribune* (January 16, 2006).

16. Dexter Roberts, Michael Arndt, and Pete Engardio, "Why U.S. Companies Love China," *BusinessWeek* (September 13, 2005).

17. Charles Decker, *Winning with the P&G 99* (New York: Pocket Books, 1998), p. 133.

18. Ibid., p. 143.

19. Laurent Philippe as quoted in Jacques Penhirin, "Understanding the Chinese Consumer," *McKinsey Quarterly* (September 2004).

20. Robin D. Rusch, "MTV Networks Internationally," BrandChannel.com (July 26, 2004). See www.brandchannel.com/features_effect.asp?pf_id=221 (last accessed on July 8, 2006).

21. Johny K. Johansson, *In Your Face: How American Marketing Excess Fuels Anti-Americanism* (Upper Saddle River, NJ: Prentice Hall, 2004), p. 112.

22. Roland Robertson, "Comments on the Global Triad and Glocalization," in *Globalization and Indigenous Culture,* from the Institute for Japanese Culture and Classics, Kokugakuin University, Tokyo, 1997.

Chapter 16

1. Rene Dubos coined the phrase in 1972 at a United Nations Environmental Conference he helped organize when he became frustrated by the difficulty of organizing global initiatives to protect the environment.

2. Aizu coined the phrase while trying to prevent the Japanese government from building housing for the U.S. military in Ikego Forest outside Tokyo. The project was stopped when Japanese legislators received letters and phone calls from the United States within hours of Aizu's posting for support on the Internet.

3. Author interview, March 10, 2005.

4. Richard Pells, "American Culture Goes Global, or Does It?" *The Chronicle of Higher Education* (April 12, 2002).

5. Philippe Legrain, "Cultural Globalization Is Not Americanization," *The Chronicle of Higher Education* (May 9, 2003).

6. See Tyler Cowen, *Creative Destruction: How Globalization Is Changing the World's Cultures* (Princeton, NJ: Princeton University Press, 2002).

7. Claude Lévi-Strauss, *Structural Anthropology* (Chicago: University of Chicago Press, 1976), p. 328.

8. Frank Lechner and John Boli, eds., *The Globalization Reader* (Oxford: Blackwell, 2003), p. 125.

9. Author interview, March 4, 2005.

10. Quoted by David Barboza, "When Golden Arches Are Too Red, White and Blue," *The New York Times* (October 14, 2001).

11. Geoffrey Fowler and Merissa Mark, "Disney and the Great Wall," *The Wall Street Journal* (February 9, 2006).
12. Gary Knell spoke at a meeting of the Corporate Communications Institute of Fairleigh Dickinson University on April 29, 2004.
13. Orit Gadiesh, "Risk-Proofing Your Brand," *European Business Forum*, Issue 18 (July 2004). See www.ebfonline.com/main_feat/trends/trends.asp?id=496 (last accessed on January 20, 2006).
14. Author interview, March 17, 2005.
15. News release issued by U.S. Representative Chris Smith (R-NJ) on January 25, 2006.
16. David Kirkpatrick, "Google Founder Defends China Portal," *Fortune* (January 25, 2006, posted online). See: http://money.cnn.com/2006/01/25/news/international/davos_fortune (last accessed on February 7, 2006).

Chapter 17

1. Kofi Annan, "Message on the International Day for the Eradication of Poverty," October 17, 2000.
2. Milton Friedman, *Capitalism and Freedom* (Chicago: University of Chicago Press, 1962), p. 133.
3. Allgood was quoted by Sarah Ellison and Eric Bellman, "Success Without Profits," *The Wall Street Journal Classroom Edition* (May 2005).
4. Quoted by Theresa Howard, "Starbucks Takes up Cause of Safe Drinking Water," *USA Today* (August 3, 2005).
5. Moyiga Noluree, "Winds of Change," *New Internationalist* (December 2004).
6. Ibid.
7. Milton Friedman, "The Social Responsibility of Business Is to Increase Its Profits," *The New York Times (Sunday) Magazine* (September 13, 1970).
8. Douglas B. Holt, John A. Quelch, and Earl L. Taylor, "How Global Brands Compete," *Harvard Business Review* (September 2004).
9. Ibid.
10. From the 1999 Millennium Poll, conducted by Environics, the Prince of Wales International Business Leaders Forum, and The Conference Board.
11. Thomas Friedman, *The World Is Flat* (New York: Farrar, Straus and Giroux, 2005), p. 297.
12. Charles (Chuck) Prince was interviewed at the World Economic Forum, January 2006.
13. David Cogman and Jeremy M. Oppenheim, "Controversy Incorporated," *McKinsey Quarterly*, Issue 4 (2002).
14. Arthur W. Page, *The Bell Telephone System* (New York: Harper & Brothers, 1941), p. 154.
15. "Rethinking the Social Responsibility of Business," *Reason* (October 2005).
16. "Communication from the Commission Concerning Corporate Social Responsibility: A Business Contribution to Sustainable Development" (July 2002). See http://www.csr.ee/orb.aw/class=file/action=preview/id=447/csr2002_en.pdf (last accessed on July 8, 2006).
17. James Allen and James Root, "The New Brand Tax," *The Wall Street Journal* (September 7, 2004).
18. Author interview, March 14, 2005.
19. Claudio Vignali, "McDonald's: Think Global, Act Local," *British Food Journal* (March 2001), pp. 91–111.

20. Sean Silverstone, "The Geography of Corporate Giving," Harvard Business School *Working Knowledge* (November 21, 2005).
21. See Bob Langert's blog at http://csr.blogs.mcdonalds.com/ (last accessed on January 28, 2006).
22. In 2001, Unilever sold its Gorton's of Gloucester brand to Nippon Suisan (USA), Inc., a subsidiary of Nippon Suisan Kaisha, Ltd. of Japan.
23. Unmesh Kher, "Getting Smart at Being Good," *Time* (December 12, 2005).
24. Edelman Trust Barometer, January 2006. "A person like yourself" experienced a significant jump in credibility in the U.S. (from 22 percent in 2003 to 56 percent in 2006) and in Europe (from 33 percent to 53 percent in the same period).
25. Author interview, March 14, 2005.
26. Bruce Bawer, "Hating America," *The Hudson Review* (Spring 2004).

Chapter 18

1. Deepak Lal, "NGOs and International Civil Society," *Business Standard* (October 3, 2003).
2. Jessica Mathews, "Power Shift," *Foreign Affairs* (January–February 1997).
3. Remarks by Ken P. Cohen, vice president, Public Affairs, Exxon Mobil Corporation, at the Gitelson Symposium, Columbia University, January 26, 2001.
4. This comment has most frequently been attributed to a member of the environmental group Greenpeace, but the sentiment is broadly shared among many NGOs.
5. Randall Hayes was quoted in "The 21st Century NGO: In the Market for Change," *SustainAbility Report* (2003), p. 30.
6. Peter Drucker, *The New Realities* (New York: Harper and Row, 1989).
7. Aarskog syndrome is a congenital disease marked by multiple limb and genital abnormalities.
8. Zoonotic bacterial diseases are those diseases that are shared by man and animal, such as bubonic plague.
9. Edelman Trust Barometer, January 2006.
10. Michael Bond, "The Backlash Against NGOs," *Prospect* (April 2000).
11. Sebastian Mallaby, *The World's Banker* (New York: Penguin Press, 2005).
12. Mathews, "Power Shift."
13. Jake Batsell, "Starbucks Turned a Shot into a Grande," *Seattle Times* (November 2, 2001).
14. Carol Hymowitz, "Big Companies Become Targets Unless They Guard Their Images," *The Wall Street Journal* (December 16, 2005).
15. Batsell, "Starbucks Turned a Shot into a Grande."
16. From the report of the panel on "Strategic Alliances Between Business and NGOs" at the 2004 World Economic Forum.
17. From Douglas Hurd's remarks at a seminar sponsored by Edelman Public Relations, "NGOs and the Corporate Sector," London, December 7, 2000.
18. Author interview, March 14, 2005.
19. Melchett was speaking at a seminar on "NGOs and the Corporate Sector," sponsored by Edelman Public Relations, New York City, December 2, 2000.
20. Ian Davis, "What Is the Business of Business?" *McKinsey Quarterly*, Issue 3 (2005).
21. Drucker, *The New Realities*, p. 91.

22. Stuart L. Hart and C. K. Prahalad, "Strategies for the Bottom of the Pyramid: Creating Sustainable Development," *Strategy + Business* (First Quarter 2002).
23. Claude Smadja, "Business in a Hostile Environment: Confronting Global Volatility," speech delivered at a meeting of the Asia Society in Hong Kong on July 25, 2003.
24. Author interview, March 17, 2006.
25. "KPMG International Survey of Corporate Responsibility Reporting 2005," June 2005.
26. KDPaine & Partners. See www.measuresofsuccess.com/News + and + Press + Releases/Press + Releases/407.aspx.
27. Unilever's social and environmental reports are available online at http://unilever.com/ourvalues/environmentandsociety/.
28. See Howard Rheingold, *Smart Mobs* (New York: Perseus Books, 2002).
29. See McDonald's corporate responsibility blog at http://csr.blogs.mcdonalds.com/default.asp (last accessed on February 14, 2006).

Chapter 19

1. President George W. Bush was speaking in the Czech Republic, November 21, 2004.
2. Robert Kagan, "Power and Weakness," *Policy Review* (June–July 2002).
3. Up until Super Bowl XL in 2006, only four other Super Bowls had spreads of more than twenty-nine points: Super Bowl XXIV, San Francisco over Denver (55–10); Super Bowl XX, Chicago over New England (46–10); XXVII, Dallas over Buffalo (52–17); and XXII, Washington over Denver (42–10).
4. "Brand USA," *Foreign Policy* (November–December 2001), p. 19.
5. Barry Fulton et al., "A Dissent: Transformation, Not Restoration," Public Diplomacy Council, George Washington University, December 21, 2004.
6. Emma Lazarus, "The New Colossus," 1883. Written to help raise money for the construction of the Statue of Liberty's pedestal, the poem is now inscribed over the statue's main entrance.
7. Quoted by Theresa Howard, "Ad Campaign Tells Women to Celebrate Who They Are," *USA Today* (July 8, 2005).
8. See www.campaignforrealbeauty.com (last accessed on February 13, 2006).
9. Steven Weisman, "Saudi Women Have Message for U.S. Envoy," *The New York Times* (September 28, 2005).
10. Douglas B. Holt, John A. Quelch, and Earl L. Taylor, "How Global Brands Compete," *Harvard Business Review* (September 2004).
11. Author interview, March 21, 2005.
12. Janet Guyon, "Vive le Big Mac," *Fortune* (October 27, 2003).
13. Howard Schultz, *Pour Your Heart into It* (New York: Hyperion, 1999), pp. 11–12.
14. Murphy was quoted by Gerry Khermouch in "America Has Image Woes, Not Its Brands," *BusinessWeek* (August 4, 2003).
15. Laurence Vincent, *Legendary Brands: Unleashing the Power of Storytelling to Create a Winning Market Strategy* (Chicago: Kaplan, 2002).

Chapter 20

1. Henry James, letter (1872), in biographical note to *Letters of Henry James*, Vol. 1 (1920), Percy Lubbock, ed., cited in *Bartlett's Familiar Quotations*, 16th ed. (Boston, MA: Little, Brown and Company, 1992), p. 548.

2. G. K. Chesterton, *On Lying in Bed and Other Essays* (Calgary, Alberta, Canada: Bayeux Arts, 2000), p. 390.
3. Quoted by Gail Dutton, "Is 'Brand America' Going to Be an Endangered Species in World Markets?" *World Trade* (March 1, 2005).
4. Ibid.
5. Quoted by "America Has Image Woes, Not Its Brands," *BusinessWeek* (August 4, 2003).
6. Ayn Rand, *The Ayn Rand Letter* (Second Renaissance Inc., 1979), p. 109; quoted in Harry Binswanger, ed., *The Ayn Rand Lexicon* (New York: New American Library, 1986), p. 13.
7. V. S. Naipaul, "Our Universal Civilization," *The New York Times* (November 5, 1990).
8. Simon Anholt and Jeremy Hildreth, *Brand America: The Mother of All Brands* (London: Cyan Communications, 2005), p. 82.
9. Michael Bond, "The Pursuit of Happiness," *New Scientist* (October 4, 2003).
10. Alan C. Robles, "Happiness Viewpoint: It Doesn't Take Much," *Time International* (February 20, 2005).
11. Edward William Bok, *The Americanization of Edward Bok* (Oxford: Osprey Classics, 2003), p. 301.
12. Ibid.
13. The Ralph Waldo Emerson quotation, among others, is available at the Quote Garden. See www.quotegarden.com/patriotic-usa.html (last accessed on March 21, 2006).
14. The truth is Roosevelt did not use the "my fellow immigrants" opening line, but he did take care to emphasize ". . . that all of us, and you and I especially, are descended from immigrants and revolutionists." President Franklin D. Roosevelt, remarks before the Daughters of the American Revolution, Washington, D.C., April 21, 1938, in *The Public Papers and Addresses of Franklin D. Roosevelt* (New York: Random House, 1938), p. 259.
15. U.S. Census Bureau, Population Division, "2005 American Community Survey," August 2006. See www.census.gov/acs/www/index.html (last accessed on August 16, 2006).
16. Migration Policy Institute, www.migrationinformation.org/index.cfm.
17. Counting people who were born in U.S. territories and people born to U.S. citizens living in other countries who later moved to the United States, the total foreign-born population approaches 40 million people.
18. Julian L. Simon, "Immigration: The Demographic and Economic Facts," The Cato Institute, December 11, 1995.
19. James Truslow Adams, *The Epic of America* (Boston: Little, Brown, 1930), pp. 214–215.
20. Nancy Snow, *Information War: American Propaganda, Free Speech, and Opinion Control Since 9/11* (New York: Seven Stories Press, 2003), p. 25.
21. Calvin Coolidge, speech to the American Society of Newspaper Editors, Washington, D.C., January 17, 1925. Some believe this line, often taken out of context, can give a false impression of the president's views on the purpose of business. The next few lines of his speech are: "Of course, the accumulation of wealth cannot be justified as the chief end of existence. But we are compelled to recognize it as a means to well-nigh every desirable achievement. So long as wealth is made the means and not the end, we need not greatly fear it . . ."
22. Kevin Maney, *The Maverick and His Machine: Thomas Watson, Sr. and the Making of IBM* (New York: John Wiley & Sons, 2003), p. 219.

23. From ThinkExist.com. See www.en.thinkexist.com/quotation/america_is_a_ place_where_jewish_merchants_sell/210021.html.
24. Brian Lamb spoke on CNN, July 2, 2004.
25. Humphrey Hawksley, "Stark Reality of the American Dream," broadcast by the BBC on August 18, 2005. The original study was by Jo Blanden, Paul Gregg, and Stephen Machin, "Intergenerational Mobility in Europe and North America," Centre for Economic Performance, April 2005.
26. *Human Development Report 2005.* See http://hdr.undp.org/reports/global/ 2005/.
27. Jeffrey E. Garten, "Business and Foreign Policy," *Foreign Affairs* (May–June 1997).
28. Ibid.

Chapter 21

1. Kishore Mahbubani, *Beyond the Age of Innocence: Rebuilding Trust Between America and the World* (New York: Perseus Books, 2005), p. 1.
2. For a concise look at public diplomacy as practiced by the United States Information Agency, see Wilson Dizard, "Remembering USIA," *Foreign Service Journal* (July–August 2003).
3. From "Reorganization Plan No. 2," described in a March 13, 1977, memo from President Jimmy Carter to USIA Director John Reinhardt.
4. For more background on the reorganization, see "Reorganization Plan and Report (revised March 1999) Submitted Pursuant to Section 1601 of the Foreign Affairs Reform and Restructuring Act of 1998, as Contained in Public Law 105–277."
5. Helena K. Finn, "The Case for Cultural Diplomacy," *Foreign Affairs* (November–December 2003).
6. See, for example, the Congressional Research Service's report "Public Diplomacy: A Review of Past Recommendations," September 2, 2005.
7. Frank Ninkovich, *The Diplomacy of Ideas* (Cambridge University Press, 1981), p. 13.
8. This definition is from one of the Edward R. Murrow Center's earliest brochures, as reported on its website at http://fletcher.tufts.edu/murrow/public-diplomacy.html.
9. The Global Market Insite (GMI) poll was released on February 2, 2005. The results are available online at www.gmi-mr.com/gmipoll/press_room_wppk_ pr_02022005.phtml (last accessed on January 28, 2006).
10. From Bill Shireman's keynote address at the Owens Corning Executive Summit in Tampa, Florida, quoted in the *New Statesman* of India on November 22, 2005.
11. Joseph Nye, *Soft Power* (New York: PublicAffairs, 2004), p. 125.
12. Cynthia Schneider, *Diplomacy That Works: Best Practices in Cultural Diplomacy,* Center for Arts and Culture, 2003, p. 2. See www.culturalpolicy.org/ pdf/schneider.pdf (last accessed on July 15, 2006).
13. Ibid., p. 12.
14. United Nations Development Program, *Arab Human Development Report 2003,* New York, October 2003.
15. Cynthia Schneider, "There's an Art to Telling the World About America," *The Washington Post* (August 25, 2002).

16. Report of the Subcommittee on Public-Private Partnerships and Public Diplomacy, June 4, 2003.
17. N. D. Batra, "Changing USA's Image," *The Statesman* (September 14, 2005).
18. Wally Olins, *On Brand* (London: Thames & Hudson, 2003), p. 150.

Chapter 22

1. Karen Hughes, undersecretary for public diplomacy and public affairs, statement before the House International Relations Committee, remarks at the opening of the Third Annual U.S.–Islamic World Forum, Doha, Qatar, February 18, 2006.
2. Hubert Védrine with Dominique Moïsi, *France in an Age of Globalization* (Washington, D.C.: Brookings Institution Press, 2001), p. 3.
3. U.S. Government Accountability Office, "U.S. Public Diplomacy," p. 24, and U.S. Advisory Commission on Public Diplomacy, "Building America's Public Diplomacy," p. 22. See www.state.gov/documents/organization/13622.pdf (last accessed on July 15, 2006).
4. *The 9/11 Commission Report* (Washington, D.C.: U.S. Government Printing Office, 2004), p. 361.
5. Alexander Evans, "Understand Madrasahs: How Threatening Are They?" *Foreign Affairs* (January–February 2006).
6. Julia Sweig, *Friendly Fire* (New York: Public Affairs, 2006), p. 172.
7. Leo Bogart, *Cool Words, Cold War* (Washington, D.C.: American University Press, 1995), p. xvii.
8. Anne Applebaum, "Think Again, Karen Hughes," *The Washington Post* (July 27, 2005), A21.
9. Hughes's memo was quoted by David Corn's blog on January 17, 2006. See www.thenation.com/blogs/capitalgames (last accessed on January 28, 2006).
10. White House Communications Director Dan Bartlett was quoted by Ron Suskind, "Mrs. Hughes Takes Her Leave," *Esquire* (July 2002).
11. Karen Hughes, undersecretary for public diplomacy and public affairs, statement before the House International Relations Committee, Washington, D.C., November 10, 2005.
12. The six geographic bureaus, which are led by assistant secretaries of state and report to the undersecretary for political affairs, are Africa, East Asia and the Pacific, Europe and Eurasia, the Near East, South and Central Asia, and the Western Hemisphere. A seventh bureau manages relationships with international organizations.
13. Karen Hughes, remarks delivered at the Shell Distinguished Lecture Series at the Baker Institute for Public Policy, March 29, 2006.

Coda

1. Edward R. Murrow is quoted by Hans N. Tuch in *Communicating with the World* (New York: St. Martin's Press, 1990), p. 26.
2. Simon Anholt and Jeremy Hildreth, *Brand America: The Mother of All Brands* (London: Cyan Communications, 2005), p. 52.
3. Jack Trout, "Extreme Makeover," *Forbes* (August 22, 2005).

ACKNOWLEDGMENTS

ACCORDING TO MY WIFE, GINNY, I SHOULD ACKNOWLEDGE THE contribution of the La-Z-Boy company, which manufactured the chair in which I wrote most of this book. In addition to warning me that I should sit on both sides of the chair, my wife also read various versions of the manuscript, pushing for clarity and conciseness. Any failings on that score were entirely mine, as the condition of my now listing recliner attests.

Other friends were also generous with their time as this manuscript took shape, and it profited from their comments. Marilyn Laurie, who was my boss at AT&T for nearly two decades, easily resumed her natural role of cheerleader, guide, and sounding board. Vic Pelson, another former AT&T senior executive, gave me the benefit of his broad and deep experience navigating global markets. Bill Clossey, who led AT&T's international public affairs for several years, helped sharpen the book's argument and kept me from getting lost in the statistics. Michael Goodman, the director of the Corporate Communications Institute at Fairleigh Dickinson University, shared his own extensive research on anti-Americanism and was one of the first to urge me to tackle the subject. David Goodman, a young expat living in Paris, kept me in touch with the local media in what many people consider ground zero for anti-Americanism. Steve Kowitt made a number of thoughtful suggestions that improved the book's structure. Marcel Martin allowed me to tap his years of experience as a United Nations official and provided many helpful suggestions. And Bill Culley not only shared his experiences with the United States Information Agency and the Voice of America, but took my photo for the book jacket.

Among the many business people I interviewed in the course of my research, I particularly want to single out the following for generously sharing their time and experience: Eric Almquist of Mercer Management's Boston office, George Carpenter of P&G, Jack Daly of McDonald's, Bernard Demeure of Mercer Management's Paris office, Robert Duboff of Hawk Consulting, Richard Edelman of Edelman Public Relations, Cari Eggspuehler of Business for Diplomatic Action, Phil Kotler of the Kellogg School of Management at Northwestern University, Bill Margaritis of FedEx, Tim Ranzetta of Equilar, and Keith Reinhard of Business for Diplomatic Action. I'd also like to thank the many other executives who shared their experiences with me but prefer not to be singled out for various reasons.

Ed Reilly and Hank Kennedy of the American Management Association were early champions of this project. I will always appreciate their confidence in me. My editor at AMACOM, Ellen Kadin, kept faith in the project even when mine was flagging. I would never have completed this book were it not for her enthusiasm. And, on that score, now that this is my second book for this publisher, I know enough to express deep appreciation to the AMACOM editorial, production, sales, and marketing staffs.

Finally, I would like to acknowledge that parts of this book appeared originally in the *Journal of Business Strategy*.

INDEX